Theory of Happiness

Theory of Happiness

Unlocking a happy life through the wisdom of Stoicism

Ben van de Beld

Epictetus

Next Group Pty. Limited

Copyright © 2023 by Ben van de Beld

All rights reserved. No part of this publication may be reproduced, distributed, or transmitted in any form or by any means, including photocopying, recording, or other electronic or mechanical methods, without the prior written permission of the publisher, except in the case of brief quotations embodied in critical reviews and certain other non-commercial uses permitted by copyright law.

Book Title: Theory of Happiness
Author: Ben van de Beld
Print ISBN: 978-0-6457902-0-7
eBook ISBN: 978-0-6457902-1-4

Published by Next Group Pty. Limited, Australia
Cover Design by Ben van de Beld

First Edition: July 2023
This edition published globally in 2023

Disclaimer:

The views and interpretations presented in this book belong to the author and are intended to stimulate thought and foster philosophical discussion, not to provide definitive answers. They do not necessarily reflect the opinions of the publisher or any affiliated entities. All information is provided 'as is', without any implied or explicit warranty. The author and publisher bear no responsibility for any actions or consequences resulting from the ideas in this book and assume no responsibility for errors, omissions, or contrasting interpretations of the subject matter. Every effort has been made to ensure the correct citation and acknowledgment of intellectual property; any unintentional oversights will be corrected in subsequent editions. Readers are advised to seek professional advice for a deeper understanding of the subjects discussed. The moral rights of the author have been asserted.

To the Usual Suspects

To Epictetus, who may have never fathomed his ancient words would one day weave into a book about happiness. Your wisdom, distilled through time, has found its way into modern musings. Your Enchiridion still enchants, perplexes, and provokes. Here's to you, old friend, may your philosophy continue to shine like the North Star in our intellectual sky.

And to my Inner Procrastinator, that charming devil, forever whispering, "Let's do it tomorrow". You've been with me through thick and thin, always ready with a tempting diversion just when the writing seemed hardest. This book, finished in spite of—and perhaps, because of—you, is the testament of our dance, a pirouette of chaos and creation. Here's to tomorrow; I couldn't have done it without you.

CONTENTS

TO THE USUAL SUSPECTS v
GETTING OUR PHILOSOPHICAL BEARINGS xi
EPICTETUS, FROM SLAVERY TO STOIC SAGE xv

1 | Mastering Life's Remote Control — 1

2 | Navigating Desires and Distastes — 9

3 | Reality, Relics, and Relationships — 17

4 | Tranquillity Amidst Life's Ripples — 25

5 | The Art of Perspective — 33

6 | Pixels, Zen, and Surfboards — 40

7 | Prioritising Amidst Distractions — 48

8 | Life's Quirky Dance — 57

9 | Laughter in Adversity — 64

CONTENTS

10 | Unveiling Your Superpowers 71

11 | Borrowed Not Lost 78

12 | Embracing Life's Chaos 86

13 | Serenity in Life's Circus 93

14 | Letting Go For Happiness 100

15 | Feasting with Wisdom 109

16 | Harmonising Empathy 116

17 | Navigating Life's Grand Theatre 123

18 | Balancing Chaos 130

19 | Dancing with Invincibility 138

20 | Reframe, Pacify, Pause, Soothe 146

21 | Befriending the Monsters Within 154

22 | Facing Uncertainty 162

23 | Impress Yourself 170

24 | Being a Nobody 178

CONTENTS

25 | The Social Spotlight 186

26 | Calm Amidst the Chaos 194

27 | Life's Labyrinth 203

28 | Your Mental Kingdom 211

29 | Choice and Commitment 219

30 | The Relationship Tango 229

31 | The Universal Rhythm 237

32 | The Voyage of Wisdom 246

33 | Sailing the Social Seas 256

34 | Savouring Self-Control 266

35 | Wearing Authenticity 274

36 | Choices and Connections 282

37 | Being True to Oneself 289

38 | The Mind's Lego Maze 297

39 | Shallow Splendour 305

CONTENTS

40 | Inner Awesomeness 312

41 | Brains vs Brawn 319

42 | Criticism into Comedy 327

43 | The Serene Suitcase 335

44 | Interweaving Self-Worth 344

45 | Beyond Quick Judgments 352

46 | Epictetus at the Dinner Table 360

47 | Balancing Thrift and Discretion 368

48 | From Spectator to Philosopher 375

49 | Living Philosophy 385

50 | Your Inner Socrates 394

51 | The Philosophy Game 404

REFLECTING AFTER THE MIND MARATHON 415

GETTING OUR
PHILOSOPHICAL BEARINGS

Fasten your mental seatbelts, for we are about to embark on an enthralling journey that traverses through the annals of time! Our expedition won't be limited to the architectural splendour of the Roman Empire, noted for its towering ivory structures and grand marble pillars. On the contrary, we will be immersing ourselves in the kaleidoscopic whirlpool of human thought and experience, our only equipment being our keen intellect, this book, and a compact ancient philosophical tome filled with wisdom and insights that one would usually garner from expensive therapeutic sessions.

Our guide on this cerebral odyssey is none other than Epictetus. He was a straightforward and unwavering philosopher, whose extraordinary trajectory from slavery to becoming one of the most respected thinkers of his epoch continues to inspire us today. Through his life and teachings, he demonstrated that our responses to life's happenings, rather than the events themselves, are the essential drivers that sculpt our existence.

Our final stop on this expedition lies within the modest but potent pages of the "Enchiridion of Epictetus". This compact volume is a treasure trove of deep-seated principles and insights that could make even the philosophical treatises of Plato seem like simple night-time tales. However, a word of caution for our readers: this book holds such transformative power that it could bear a warning sign reading, "Caution: May lead to sudden paradigm shifts and explosive bursts of wisdom".

To help navigate this transformative journey, each chapter in this book starts with original extracts from Epictetus' Enchiridion, highlighting the teachings under exploration. Armed with these timeless nuggets of wisdom, we shall undertake an examination of Epictetus' philosophy through a contemporary lens. My objective is to render these profound concepts both digestible and relatable, ensuring they deeply resonate with you.

Our voyage doesn't conclude here. Each chapter is punctuated with exercises that go beyond mere homework, designed to fortify your understanding of Epictetus' wisdom while offering an interactive, enjoyable learning experience. Ranging from creative visualisation to comic strip designing, these activities break away from traditional learning modalities and stimulate your philosophical journey. Each assignment offers a unique chance to delve into Epictetus' doctrines, scrutinise them from diverse angles, and seamlessly integrate them into your everyday life. These engaging exercises inspire self-reflection and revision, making your philosophical journey not only insightful but equally pleasurable.

Whether you're a philosophical connoisseur, an intrigued novice, or someone who's simply been enticed by the compelling title of this book (I don't blame you—it is indeed captivating), prepare yourself for a deep dive into Epictetus' wisdom. Strap in, dear readers. The exhilarating exploration of Epictetus's Enchiridion is set to commence. Remember the timeless wisdom of our beloved philosopher, "It's not what happens to you, but how you react to it that truly matters". Now, without further ado, let's set sail on this philosophical voyage and stir the sea of wisdom!

Ben van de Beld
Australia, 20 July 2023

EPICTETUS, FROM SLAVERY TO STOIC SAGE

Let's dive into the compelling life story of Epictetus. Picture yourself around 50 A.D., the backdrop for the beginning of Epictetus' life, a beginning devoid of privilege. Born a slave, Epictetus was initially tasked with domestic chores while in service to one of Emperor Nero's associates in Rome. Despite these humble beginnings, he had an unquenchable thirst for knowledge, attending lectures delivered by the prominent Stoic philosopher Musonius Rufus. Recognising Epictetus' exceptional intellectual prowess, Rufus became his mentor, nurturing him to become an influential disseminator of Stoic wisdom.

Teaching philosophy was by no means a smooth journey for Epictetus. He didn't confine himself to traditional philosophical circles; rather, he ventured out into the streets, squares, and bustling markets, sharing his insights in less conventional venues. Over time, his teachings gained recognition, but they also met resistance. Emperor Domitian notably took issue with the growing influence of philosophers. Between 89 and 92 A.D.,

Epictetus and other philosophers were banished from Rome—an event that might have discouraged less resilient individuals.

Epictetus was a living embodiment of the Stoic virtue of resilience. Unperturbed by the banishment, he set sail for Nicopolis, in Epirus, where he founded his philosophy school. His teachings quickly garnered wide attention, attracting students from as far away as Athens and Rome. Nicopolis soon became a prominent centre of philosophy, outshining many renowned institutions of the time.

One of Epictetus' most distinguished students was Flavius Arrian, who would later serve as consul under Emperor Hadrian. Captivated by Epictetus' informal discussions, Arrian set out to transcribe them, thereby preserving the teachings for posterity. We owe a debt of gratitude to Arrian for safeguarding these invaluable discourses.

Epictetus remained true to the essence of Stoic philosophy, focusing on morality and living in harmony with nature. His central tenet was the distinction between what we can control—our thoughts and actions—and what we cannot—such as our reputation, health, and wealth. His "Enchiridion" serves as a succinct guide to Stoic principles, covering topics from social decorum to cognitive reframing, including also sexual asceticism. It has become a timeless reference, a sort of precursor to the "Stoicism for Dummies" series!

The Enchiridion has had a profound impact on thinkers, philosophers, and those seeking spiritual alternatives over the centuries. It's been translated into numerous languages, gaining worldwide recognition and significantly influencing modern philosophy. This humble book has played a remarkable role in shaping thought and practice well into the modern era.

In essence, the Enchiridion serves as a testament to Epictetus' intellectual brilliance and perseverance. Despite beginning life as a slave, he rose to become one of the most influential philosophers in history, exemplifying that with the right mindset, one can transcend even the most challenging circumstances. Whether you're delving into philosophy or merely seeking guidance in life's complex journey, the Enchiridion is a pocket-sized manual of happiness, freedom, and tranquillity. Consider it a nourishing philosophical feast, sustaining both the mind and the spirit.

1

Mastering Life's Remote Control

There are things which are within our power, and there are things which are beyond our power. Within our power are opinion, aim, desire, aversion, and, in one-word, whatever affairs are our own. Beyond our power are body, property, reputation, office, and, in one word, whatever are not properly our own affairs.

Now the things within our power are by nature free, unrestricted, unhindered; but those beyond our power are weak, dependent, restricted, alien. Remember, then, that if you attribute freedom to things by nature dependent and take what belongs to others for your own, you will be hindered, you will lament, you will be disturbed, you will find fault both with gods and men. But if you take for your own only that which is your own and view what belongs to others just as it really is, then no one will ever compel you, no one will restrict you; you will find fault with no one, you will accuse no one, you will do nothing against your will; no one will hurt you, you will not have an enemy, nor will you suffer any harm.

Aiming, therefore, at such great things, remember that you must not allow yourself any inclination, however slight, toward the attainment of the others; but that you must entirely quit some of them, and for the present postpone the rest. But if you would have these, and possess power and wealth likewise, you may miss the latter in seeking the former; and you will certainly fail of that by which alone happiness and freedom are procured.

Seek at once, therefore, to be able to say to every unpleasing semblance, "You are but a semblance and by no means the real thing." And then examine it by those rules which you have; and first and chiefly by this: whether it concerns the things which are within our own power or those which are not; and if it concerns anything beyond our power, be prepared to say that it is nothing to you.

Step into the captivating realm of philosophy, interpreted through the teachings of Epictetus—an emblem of Stoicism and a revered sage. Our intellectual expedition seeks to untangle the intricate concept of happiness.

Visualise life as a vast landscape, demarcated by two types of terrain—those we can manipulate (the controllable) and those that elude our grasp (the uncontrollable). This dichotomy is at the heart of Epictetus's philosophy, a route we'll navigate during our exploration.

The controllable terrain, akin to a TV remote, bestows upon us power over our perspectives, desires, and preferences. It is comparable to a skilled footballer who has mastery over the game—you can guide your actions and choices within this sphere. Deciding to enjoy a piece of chocolate cake or embarking on a new hobby are examples of elements entirely within your conscious control.

In contrast, the uncontrollable terrain signifies life's unpredictable elements, much like the ever-changing weather. This sphere encompasses factors that lie beyond your immediate control: your height, your financial status, your reputation, even the trajectory of your career. They operate on their own rhythm, as unpredictable and elusive as leaves caught in a gust of wind.

For the controllable aspects of life, envision yourself as a stallion galloping freely across open fields. This image embodies a sense of empowerment and control—you're free to choose your direction, speed, and path. These choices, hinged on your individual decisions and actions, are entirely within your sphere of control.

However, the uncontrollable elements of life are like leaves subject to a gust of wind, tossed, and turned by forces beyond their control. This image reflects the uncertainty and unpredictability of life's aspects we cannot influence, such as the actions of others, the economic climate, or unforeseen events. Attempting to command these variables can feel as fruitless as trying to control the wind itself. Instead, focusing on how we adapt and respond to these uncontrollable circumstances proves more beneficial.

Epictetus imparts a crucial lesson here. Convincing ourselves that we can control life's uncontrollable aspects leads to frustration and blame. Instead, Epictetus encourages us to channel our energies towards the controllable aspects, learning to flow with the unpredictability of life's 'weather'.

Adopting this perspective, we attain a state of tranquillity, akin to a sailor smoothly navigating a ship amidst a stormy sea, unfazed by the erratic waves around him. This serenity mirrors what we can achieve when we cease wrestling against the uncontrollable and concentrate instead on what lies within our sphere of control.

Epictetus's wisdom advises us to focus less on life's unpredictable 'weather' and more on mastering our 'remote control'—our attitudes, reactions, and perspectives. This 'remote control' offers transformative potential. It enables us to alter our approach when adversity strikes, regulate the volume of our internal dialogue, press pause for reflection and self-care, and press play to continue on our journey of personal growth.

In the grand theatre of life, it's easy to become obsessed with controlling the uncontrollable. It's akin to a puppeteer attempting to manipulate illusory strings. Epictetus counsels us to concentrate on handling our own 'strings'—those genuinely under our control.

The essence of Epictetus's philosophy suggests that the road to happiness isn't paved with riches or accolades but lies in the powerful act of relinquishing control over the uncontrollable.

By directing our attention towards areas we can influence—our reactions, attitudes, and beliefs—we not only regain peace but also draw closer to the elusive concept of happiness.

Epictetus's wisdom lies in understanding this dichotomy and learning to navigate life's unpredictable 'weather' with our 'remote control' firmly in hand. Happiness, then, isn't about forecasting the weather but learning to weather the storm.

As we traverse the path set out by Epictetus, we realise that some things in life are within our control and others are not. Accepting this philosophy doesn't imply ignoring life's challenges or adopting a defeatist attitude. Instead, it enables us to focus our energies where we can make a significant impact, fostering a healthier and more balanced approach to life.

We now pivot from thought to deed. We've relished Epictetus' ideas, and now it's time to put them to the test in real-life situations. The following exercises will be your guide, connecting you from historical wisdom to contemporary living. Ready to make this journey? Let's transition from the abstract to the tangible and give life to our *Theory of Happiness*.

Our first exercise is dubbed "Journal Journey". For a week, categorise your daily experiences into two sections: *Remote Control* (elements you can control) and *Weather Forecast* (elements you can't). Chronicle these adventures in a journal specifically reserved for this purpose. Personalise it with a whimsical illustration of a remote and a cloud to signify the essence of this exercise. In the quiet moments of your evening, perhaps over a cup of herbal tea, reflect on the day's entries and their implications.

The next activity is "Aloha Acceptance". During instances when life presents you with something beyond your control, envisage yourself as a relaxed Hawaiian retiree, extending a warm "Aloha, I accept you as you are" to the situation. This mental exercise fosters acceptance of circumstances as they transpire, discouraging futile attempts to control them.

Then, we have "Disco Ball Dismissal". When you find yourself preoccupied with uncontrollable issues, remind yourself: "You're as relevant to me as a chocolate teapot!" This amusing phrase serves as a prompt to release the uncontrollable, just as you would abandon the vain effort of teaching a parrot to play poker.

Lastly, engage in "Illusion Busting". Routinely inspect your stressors. Determine whether they lie within your control or are merely illusory. Whenever you identify an illusion, let out a hearty laugh and declare, "You're as plausible as a penguin playing ping pong!"

As we wrap up these exercises, remember that each step taken today brings you closer to a life guided by wisdom, not just in thought but also in action. Epictetus' philosophy isn't merely an intellectual exercise but a practical toolkit for everyday living. It's not enough to simply comprehend these principles; real transformation occurs when we integrate them into our lives. Use these exercises as a foundation, a starting point. Continue to engage with them, tweak them, and make them your own. With consistent practice, you will not just understand Epictetus' philosophy, but you will live it, and it's in this living wisdom that true personal growth and contentment lie.

Before we conclude, let's revisit Epictetus' teachings. He fervently advises us to release our vain attempts to control life's uncontrollable elements. Life's unpredictable shifts—its metaphorical weather—are beyond our influence. Any effort to command it is as fruitless and ridiculous as demanding the wind to change its direction.

Instead, Epictetus directs our focus to the areas within our control—our life's 'remote control'. This metaphorical remote symbolises our attitudes, responses, and choices. We can navigate these elements as comfortably as switching TV channels, savouring the exhilarating freedom that comes with shaping our aspirations, our character, and ultimately, our destiny.

With this newfound understanding and freedom, we experience tranquillity akin to a serene lake on a calm morning —unruffled by the outer world's disarray. This tranquillity permeates our existence, radiating a sense of contentment and liberation. It feels as if we've transformed into a bird, gracefully soaring above life's tumultuous landscape, unperturbed by the turbulence below, and revelling in the vast, boundless sky—a true embodiment of serene freedom.

This philosophy is not a call to surrender to life's challenges or a practice of defeat in the face of uncontrollable events.

Instead, it empowers us to direct our energies where they can make a tangible difference, encouraging a healthier and more balanced approach to life.

In conclusion, let's strive to not merely comprehend Epictetus' wisdom, but also to internalise and live it. True happiness is not found in controlling every facet of our journey; it's in traversing this path with wisdom, grace, and a sense of humour. We may not command the wind, but we can certainly adjust our sails.

Sail on, fellow voyagers, knowing that life's storms do not control you. You are the master of your ship, steering your life towards the horizons you choose. The task isn't merely weathering the storm but learning to dance in the rain. So, here's to a journey steeped in peace, laughter, and understanding as you master the art of sailing the vast sea of life, the Epictetus way.

2

Navigating Desires and Distastes

Remember that desire demands the attainment of that of which you are desirous; and aversion demands the avoidance of that to which you are averse; that he who fails of the object of his desires is disappointed; and he who incurs the object of his aversion is wretched. If, then, you shun only those undesirable things which you can control, you will never incur anything which you shun; but if you shun sickness, or death, or poverty, you will run the risk of wretchedness. Remove [the habit of] aversion, then, from all things that are not within our power, and apply it to things undesirable which are within our power. But for the present, altogether restrain desire; for if you desire any of the things not within our own power, you must necessarily be disappointed; and you are not yet secure of those which are within our power, and so are legitimate objects of desire. Where it is practically necessary for you to pursue or avoid anything, do even this with discretion and gentleness and moderation.

As we delve deeper into the teachings of Epictetus, we encounter the intricate dance of desire and aversion. These two forces, powerful and often opposing, not only shape our lives, but also influence our decisions, mould our experiences, and create the prismatic lens through which we view the world. In this chapter, we embark on a journey into the often-tumultuous territory of these emotions. Using Epictetus's wisdom as our compass, we aim to unearth strategies that will allow us to navigate this complex emotional landscape, fostering a life of greater fulfillment, balance, and joy.

The tendrils of desire and aversion extend into every corner of our daily lives, colouring our interactions and experiences. Consider the demanding task of adhering to a strict celery juice cleanse, only to be confronted by the tantalising temptation of a sumptuous triple-chocolate sundae. The desire ignited by this layered temptation tests your resolve, feeling as though the universe itself is conspiring against your firm commitment. Such moments encapsulate the essence of desire — a deep, resonant longing that can often lead us off the path we've set for ourselves.

On the other end of the spectrum, we encounter aversion, our hardwired drive to avoid discomfort or displeasure. Imagine the momentary shock of mistaking a bitter, potent espresso shot for a sweet and soothing hot chocolate. Or the unexpected, startling pain from stepping barefoot on a stray drawing pin. Such experiences serve as vivid illustrations of our innate inclination to sidestep unpleasant sensations and experiences.

Epictetus's teachings illuminate the pervasive impact of desire and aversion on our everyday experiences. Who among us hasn't felt the sting of disappointment when something we eagerly desire remains out of our reach — like arriving at a much-anticipated pizza party, only to find an empty box? Such instances evoke a poignant sense of loss, fuelling our longing for the comprehensive, satisfying experiences we'd so vividly envisioned in our minds.

Similarly, life has a knack for presenting us with situations we would much rather avoid. Like the moment when we eagerly uncap a chilled soda, anticipating its exhilarating fizz and refreshing taste, only to find it flat, dull, and devoid of its characteristic sparkle. These moments serve as reality checks, upending our expectations and leaving us pining for the enjoyable experiences we believed were within our reach.

In his profound wisdom, Epictetus advises that we limit our aversions to those things we can control — such as avoiding overcooked broccoli or cringe-inducing dad jokes. In this way, we can protect ourselves from undue stress and disappointment. However, he cautions that attempting to dodge life's inevitable aspects — like the unyielding passage of time or the unpredictable swings of the stock market — is akin to setting ourselves up for swift disappointment. Such attempts are as futile as trying to outrun our own shadow, an exercise in fruitless exertion.

Regarding our desires, Epictetus offers sage advice: exercise control and restraint. A constant yearning for the unattainable leads to persistent disappointment. Even within the sphere of controllable desires, we must remain vigilant, acknowledging their inherently capricious nature. Desires can be as unpredictable as a cat, purring contentedly in your lap one moment and the next, baring its claws in unexpected defiance.

As we journey through life, we continually encounter opportunities and challenges, forks in the road where we must decide between pursuit or avoidance. In such moments, Epictetus encourages us to emulate the spirit of a ninja — balanced, precise, and composed. This approach allows us to deftly navigate life's twists and turns, evading the swings of fortune and extreme reactions that can throw us off balance.

By deepening our understanding of the delicate interplay between desire and aversion, we're able to judiciously apply Epictetus's teachings to our own lives. As we do so, we experience a profound transformation. We become philosophical ninjas, equipped with the wisdom to embrace what we can control, and the grace to accept what lies beyond our influence. Like an adept tightrope walker, we learn to savour life's highs and lows, maintaining a precarious balance, never losing our footing even amidst the swirling winds of change.

Once again, we're at that exciting juncture where ideas spark action. We've savoured the philosophical feast Epictetus provides. Now, we digest it, turning theory into lived experience. The exercises to come are our bridges from ancient wisdom to modern reality. Shall we cross this threshold? Let's bring Epictetus' wisdom from the pages into our daily lives, enriching our own *Theory of Happiness*.

Our first exercise, which we'll call the "Desire/Aversion Diary", prompts us to become more conscious of our daily impulses. To begin, procure a journal and, over the course of a week, document your cravings and evasions. Make a note of each instance and identify whether they stem from factors within your control or those beyond your grasp. As you delve into this introspective practice, patterns will begin to emerge, standing out as clearly as a hippo attempting to blend into a herd of delicate gazelles. This exercise allows you to track your reactions, gain insights into your tendencies, and eventually help to modulate your desires and aversions in line with Epictetus's teachings.

Next, let's dive into the playful practice of "Ninja Moves". The aim here is to cultivate awareness of our habitual responses. Each time you catch yourself lusting after the unattainable or shying away from something within your power, adopt a 'ninja pose'. This could be anything from a subtle gesture, like a sly eyebrow wiggle, to a more conspicuous one—like a swift sidestep. Let this serve as a jovial, physical reminder to uphold your philosophical equilibrium amidst the ebb and flow of desire and aversion.

Finally, we extend an intriguing invitation for you to engage in a day of "Stoic Cosplay". Imagine waking with the dawn, and with your first conscious breath, kindling the wisdom of Epictetus within your mind. As you venture through your day, engage with every desire and confrontation as if through the eyes of Epictetus. Ask yourself, "How would the great Stoic philosopher handle this?" Embrace each moment as a learning experience, where every misstep is not a setback but an opportunity for growth and understanding. As you proceed, subtle shifts will begin to take shape in your perceptions and reactions. These shifts may blend into your life as seamlessly as a chameleon disappearing into a leafy backdrop, but their profound impact will resonate deeply within you.

As we conclude these exercises, bear in mind that each stride we take embodies the teachings of Epictetus not just in theory but also in practice. These principles are more than ideas; they're the blueprint for an enlightened life. Their power lies not just in knowing them but in living them. Treat these exercises as the seed. Water it, nurture it, and watch it bloom. As you cultivate this practice, you'll find that philosophy isn't merely studied, it's lived.

In conclusion, Epictetus urges us to exercise greater discernment in managing our desires and aversions, offering us practical wisdom to navigate life's manifold challenges. He stresses that desire should not be an indiscriminate chase after all that shines, but a thoughtful pursuit of virtues that genuinely enrich our lives. He guides us to desire sagely, coveting not just external achievements or accolades, but also internal qualities like wisdom, integrity, and patience.

Similarly, Epictetus encourages us to approach aversions with caution. This approach transcends merely avoiding external discomforts or hardships; it also includes distancing ourselves from internal negativity, such as ignorance, deceit, and impatience.

Epictetus's teachings serve as a compass, guiding us through life's labyrinth of complexities. By instructing us to nurture desires that truly feed our soul and to avert influences that could harm our spirit, Epictetus aims to help us harmonise our external circumstances with our internal tranquillity.

As we internalise and apply these teachings, we transform into philosophical ninjas — masters of maintaining balance amidst life's undulating rhythms. We hone our ability to gracefully navigate the peaks and valleys life presents, wielding the wisdom of discernment like a trusted weapon. We learn to approach moments of success with humility, and periods of difficulty with an eye for growth and understanding.

More importantly, as these philosophical ninjas, we learn to find joy in our journey through existence. We embrace not just the destination, but the journey itself, savouring the lessons learned, the strength developed, and the resilience acquired along the way.

In essence, Epictetus's teachings guide us towards a more conscious, intentional life. We are encouraged to live fully, appreciating every high and low, and finding a sense of contentment in our passage through existence. This chapter serves as a potent reminder of this deep philosophical perspective, encouraging us towards a path marked by wisdom, resilience, and inner peace.

3

Reality, Relics, and Relationships

With regard to whatever objects either delight the mind or contribute to use or are tenderly beloved, remind yourself of what nature they are, beginning with the merest trifles: if you have a favourite cup, that it is but a cup of which you are fond of—for thus, if it is broken, you can bear it; if you embrace your child or your wife, that you embrace a mortal—and thus, if either of them dies, you can bear it.

Epictetus gifts us an invaluable perspective that serves as a catalyst for self-reflection, prodding us to reassess our personal attachments. He encourages us to undertake a meticulous examination of the various objects and relationships that occupy significant positions within our hearts and minds. This change in perspective - an understanding and acceptance of the impermanent nature of physical goods and human relationships - can transform our interaction with the world around us. It guides us towards a path of equilibrium, facilitating the construction of a more fulfilling and content life.

To exemplify this, let us embark on this introspective journey with something that may appear inconsequential at first glance, yet holds a unique place in our everyday routine – your cherished coffee mug. Maybe, it bears an amusing inscription, 'World's Okayest Philosopher', bringing a wry smile to your face every morning. Epictetus, in his stoic wisdom, entreats us to probe deeper beyond the object's superficial charm, reminding us that it's merely a receptacle for our morning beverage. Although this particular item might carry sentimental value for you, it is not an enchanted goblet, overflowing with infinite joy and happiness. Certainly, a perfectly steeped pot of English breakfast tea might evoke fleeting moments of euphoria, but these feelings are transient. Hence, if this beloved mug were to inadvertently slip from your grasp, shattering into countless fragments, refrain from succumbing to the impulse to hold a sombre memorial service or to mourn its destruction as if it were the very elixir of life itself. Instead, allow this incident to serve as an opportunity to ruminate on the temporary nature of all material objects. Acknowledge the fact that stowed away in your kitchen cupboard are numerous replacement mugs, all eager and ready to serve their purpose in your morning ritual. This awakening will enable you to divest the broken mug of any excessive significance it may have previously held, allowing you to appreciate its inherent simplicity instead — an unpretentious vessel that contributed to the comfort and routine of your daily life.

Continuing this exploration into the realm of human connections, consider those intimate moments when you share a warm embrace with your child or partner. It is crucial to remember that you are holding another individual, an irreplaceable entity teeming with their own thoughts, dreams, and emotions. However, as difficult as it may be, we must come face-to-face with a reality we often keep at arm's length — like all living creatures, humans are transient entities, present in our lives for a limited duration. Embracing this stark truth does not necessitate treating our loved ones like passing guests or obsessing over the cyclical nature of life and death. Instead, it deepens our sense of appreciation for their existence. Recognising the impermanence of our relationships helps us cultivate a heightened sense of gratitude, encouraging us to relish shared moments and devote our energies towards nurturing deep, meaningful connections. This acute awareness inspires us to prioritise love, empathy, and mutual understanding in all our interactions, enabling us to make the most of the invaluable time we have with our loved ones.

The next time you detect yourself succumbing to excessive attachment towards a material object or individual, recall Epictetus's wise counsel. Shun the propensity to blow minor incidents out of proportion, metamorphosing them into significant dramas, or to perceive the breakage of objects as personal calamities. Instead, consider, metaphorically, the act of applying philosophical 'Handle with Care' labels onto your environment. Just as such a label on a package signal that its contents are fragile and should be treated with extra caution, applying these metaphorical labels to your environment means treating your relationships, possessions, and experiences with a greater degree of mindfulness and respect. For example, when applied to material possessions, this label might remind you to appreciate an object for what it is, understand its impermanence, and not attach too much emotional significance to it. In terms of relationships, the label could serve as a reminder to appreciate your loved ones for who they are, understand the transient nature of life, and cherish the time you spend together.

These mental prompts serve as gentle nudges, reminding you to approach life with mindfulness and a holistic perspective. They discourage you from attributing excessive importance to physical possessions, gently underscoring the notion that their real worth lies not in their permanence, but in the experiences and memories they symbolise. This newfound understanding encourages the cultivation of a healthy sense of detachment, thereby unburdening you from unnecessary emotional weight and clearing the path towards a lighter, more contented existence.

It's that magic moment when philosophy blossoms into action. We've unravelled Epictetus' insights, and now it's time to weave them into our lives. The upcoming exercises are your stepping stones, linking deep thought to deep action. Ready to leap? Let's jump from learning to living and cultivate our unique *Theory of Happiness*.

Let's commence this journey with the "Mug Mantra" exercise. As you begin each day with your cherished ritual of enjoying a morning brew, seize this moment for contemplation. Remind yourself that the coffee mug cradled in your hands is merely an object—a vessel for your favourite beverage. Understand that if it were to break, it wouldn't herald an apocalyptic event, but merely a change in the physical state of an inanimate object. This small yet significant morning ritual readies you for a day punctuated with philosophical contemplation, helping you maintain perspective and averting the pitfall of developing excessive attachment to material items.

The "Embrace with Awareness" exercise then invites you to delve into the realm of human relationships. With every heartfelt hug shared with a loved one, engage in a mindful moment to acknowledge life's ephemeral nature. This exercise isn't a morose meditation on mortality, but rather a poignant opportunity to fully appreciate the present moment and the preciousness of human connections. When these moments are suffused with conscious awareness and gratitude, you deepen your bond with your loved ones, truly relishing the joy emanating from shared experiences.

The "Break and Breathe" exercise invites you to select a disposable cup or an expendable piece of old china—something that possesses some, but not a tremendous amount of sentimental value. Under safe conditions, break this object and consciously observe your immediate emotional response. Do you feel a surge of loss or perhaps a wave of aversion to the act of destruction? In that moment, pause, take a deep breath, and recall Epictetus's advice on our attachments to material possessions. This exercise provides a tangible demonstration that our true happiness and contentment are not tethered to the physical objects that surround us. It encourages us to release our attachments to the material world, fostering our internal resilience in the process. Through this practice, we come to the powerful realisation that our sense of well-being is not dependent on external factors but is a spring that bubbles forth from within us.

The "Perspective in Writing" exercise invites you to take pen to paper. Compile a list of the things to which you feel deeply connected. Beside each item, describe how you would feel if it were to vanish abruptly from your life. Then, remind yourself that true happiness does not hang precariously on these objects alone. This exercise assists you in recognising the transient nature of material possessions and gently encourages a paradigm shift. It nudges you to pivot your focus towards life's intangible aspects that offer lasting fulfillment—such as love, kindness, and personal growth.

With these exercises behind us, remember that every decision made today is a step closer to applying Epictetus' wisdom in our daily life. Philosophy is not a purely intellectual pursuit; it's a way of life. Our mission is not just to understand these teachings but to live them. These exercises are your compass, guiding you to your destination. As you journey through, you'll find the path of philosophy isn't just thought but action.

In summary, the philosopher Epictetus underlines the essentiality of routinely revisiting our attachments, ranging from the seemingly mundane objects, like a favourite coffee mug, to the profound ones like our cherished relationships. This perspective isn't promoted to foster a sense of pessimism, but to prepare us for the reality of their impermanence and to guard us from excessive sorrow that arises from unmet expectations.

Epictetus argues that understanding the temporary nature of these attachments doesn't lead us to a cynical detachment. Rather, it provides us with a protective shield against undue emotional turbulence and also augments our appreciation of the ephemeral beauty of life. It nudges us to live in the present, savouring every moment, every connection, and every experience, acknowledging that they are transitory gifts and not everlasting entitlements.

As we incorporate these lessons into our daily mindfulness practices, we fortify our comprehension of Epictetus's philosophy and its practical implications. We begin to view life through a lens tinted with wisdom and introspection, allowing us to react to life's events not with uncontrolled emotion, but with deliberate reflection and understanding.

These practices allow us to subtly shift our paradigms and steadily edge closer towards living a life that resonates deeply with Epictetus's principles. This life is characterised by a delicate balance between our desires and aversions, a profound wisdom that navigates our interactions with the world, and an intense appreciation for the fleeting yet beautiful nature of existence.

In essence, Epictetus's teachings direct us to embrace the impermanent nature of life and our attachments therein. As we engage in mindful contemplation of these lessons, we are not only fortified against potential distress but are also able to extract a heightened sense of beauty from our transient existence. The result is a life lived in accord with Epictetus's principles, a life brimming with balance, wisdom, and a profound appreciation of life's transitory yet captivating allure.

4

Tranquillity Amidst Life's Ripples

When you set about any action, remind yourself of what nature the action is. If you are going to bathe, represent to yourself the incidents usual in the bath—some persons pouring out, others pushing in, others scolding, others pilfering. And thus, you will more safely go about this action if you say to yourself, "I will now go to bathe and keep my own will in harmony with nature." And so, with regard to every other action. For thus, if any impediment arises in bathing, you will be able to say, "It was not only to bathe that I desired, but to keep my will in harmony with nature; and I shall not keep it thus if I am out of humour at things that happen."

Epictetus underscores the critical importance of anticipatory foresight and the strategic adjustment of expectations as essential mechanisms for maintaining a state of inner tranquillity. The practical application of this philosophical principle can be brought to life by picturing oneself at a lively, bustling public swimming pool.

Visualise the symphony of laughter that reverberates across the poolside, punctuated by the dynamic splashes emanating from enthusiastic children engaged in their aquatic escapades. Feel the subtle vibrations of water caused by dedicated swimmers propelling themselves back and forth in pursuit of their fitness goals. Meanwhile, observe the serene individuals reclining poolside, relishing the warm embrace of the sun while luxuriating in a peaceful reprieve from the aquatic antics.

This vibrant mental tableau serves as an effective metaphor, emphasising the need to attune our anticipations to align with the potential realities present in any given situation. Just as a cucumber maintains its refreshing coolness even when steeped in a rejuvenating Pimm's Cup, your overarching goal should revolve around preserving your composed demeanour amidst a milieu that is both dynamic and vibrant, and occasionally punctuated by elements of chaos.

In essence, the lively pool scene underscores Epictetus's teachings on maintaining inner tranquillity by encouraging us to adapt our expectations in response to the multifaceted, sometimes unpredictable nature of life's many scenarios.

Before you embark on any voyage of experience, be it a journey towards the serenity of a bubble bath filled with the scent of lavender, the energetic and sometimes chaotic whirlpool of a family gathering swarming with Aunt Karen's incessant and penetrating questions, or the tumultuous, adrenaline-fuelled adventure of Black Friday sales, solidify this personal declaration: "As I step into [*fill in the blank*], I will steadfastly preserve my tranquillity and poise, regardless of the circumstances that may unfold." This straightforward yet impactful affirmation becomes your guiding star, continually enhancing your ability to maintain a state of serenity and balance, no matter how the landscape of scenarios around you might change or evolve.

Epictetus, with his philosophical wisdom, advises that even when you are confronted with situations that threaten to unsettle your emotional equilibrium - such as the unforeseen incident of a savvy shopper nabbing the last heavily discounted super-sized 4K flat-screen television that you'd set your sights on - your response should be imbued with composed resolve. Gently remind yourself that your ultimate purpose surpasses the transient thrill of any immediate event or material possession. Conceding your composure in such moments would cause you to stray from your true path of inner calm and serenity. By espousing this philosophy, you lay the foundation for a sense of tranquillity reminiscent of a Zen master, enabling you to emanate calm amidst the swirling turbulence of life's inevitable challenges.

The teachings of Epictetus encourage the cultivation of a resilient mindset and a sanctum of inner peace. By accurately discerning the likely future events and mindfully recalibrating our expectations accordingly, we equip ourselves to smoothly navigate the myriad highs and lows of life's oceanic journey with equanimity. Whether we find ourselves amidst the vibrant tumult of a crowded swimming pool, entangled in the spirited dynamics of family reunions, or manoeuvring through high-pressure scenarios like Black Friday sales, we can rely on the wisdom imparted by Epictetus to remain steadfastly centred and composed.

At its core, Epictetus elucidates that maintaining our composure in the face of obstacles and challenges can be a transformative, even transcendental practice. By firmly holding onto our cool and protecting our peace of mind, we not only safeguard our mental wellbeing but also become a shining example to others, demonstrating our ability to weather life's tempestuous storms with grace and resilience. In doing so, we pay homage to the invaluable teachings of Epictetus and foster a state of tranquillity that permeates our daily lives, turning every encounter and experience into an opportunity for serene reflection and understanding.

We now reach that moment where contemplation turns into application. We've dissected Epictetus' teachings, and now it's time to reassemble them into practical, everyday wisdom. The exercises that follow are your toolkit, converting high philosophy into grounded reality. Shall we take the next step? Let's journey from studying to practicing, crafting our personalised *Theory of Happiness*.

THEORY OF HAPPINESS

Let us begin with the "Pool Scene". On encountering a crowded setting, particularly a swimming pool teeming with activity, take a mindful moment to survey the surroundings and adjust your expectations to match the dynamics at hand. Imagine yourself right in the middle of the action, surrounded by the laughter, splashes, and energetic buzz. As you become part of this vibrant tapestry, consciously nurture a sense of calm that remains undeterred amidst the surrounding commotion. Envision yourself as a serene islet amid a bustling sea, unperturbed by the waves of external stimuli. The act of maintaining your composure in such lively environments serves as a living testament to the embodiment of Epictetus's teachings on the cultivation of inner tranquillity.

Proceeding further, engage with the "Aunt Karen Tactic". As you prepare for your next family gathering, visualise the potential challenges that could arise, particularly Aunt Karen's notorious knack for probing questions. Reinforce your commitment to remaining unflustered and steadfast in the face of any pressures that may unfold. Even if Aunt Karen decides to don the hat of "Cupid" and probes into your romantic endeavours, firmly remember your resolution to maintain your equanimity and tactfully steer the conversation away. The ability to respond with tranquillity amidst familial pressures stands as a powerful testament to your inner resilience and an authentic embodiment of Epictetus's teachings.

Next, consider embracing the "Black Friday Zen". When gearing up for a shopping excursion, especially during the whirlwind of a sale season or the pandemonium of Black

Friday, embark on the journey with an unwavering commitment to preserving your peace of mind. As you manoeuvre through teeming stores and hustling shoppers, remind yourself that the ultimate victory is not clinching the most lucrative deals but maintaining serenity throughout the experience. Cultivate an inner haven of tranquillity amidst the external frenzy, moving through the store aisles with grace and composure. Irrespective of the surrounding chaos, your ability to remain centred and unfazed is in perfect harmony with Epictetus's teachings on preserving inner peace amidst changing external circumstances.

Lastly, experiment with the "Cucumber Challenge". For an entire week, incorporate cucumbers into your meals as a symbolic reminder to stay cool-headed, much like a cucumber, regardless of the challenges life throws your way. As you relish the refreshing crunch of cucumber-infused dishes, let the cucumber's crispness symbolise your commitment to preserving inner tranquillity. This imaginative exercise not only injects a dose of fun into your daily routine but also accentuates the philosophy of nurturing and maintaining equanimity in all circumstances, echoing Epictetus's teachings.

As we wrap up these tasks, be mindful that each action taken in line with Epictetus' philosophy takes us closer to a life of wisdom. Philosophy isn't merely an abstract discipline; it's a practical guide. The true value of these teachings is revealed not just in comprehending them but in embodying them. Consider these exercises as your roadmap, leading you towards the life you seek. As you navigate, you'll realise that philosophy is not merely understood but lived. Remember, the secret to inner peace may well be hiding in plain sight — perhaps even within a refreshing cucumber-infused salad or margarita!

To sum it all up, Epictetus emphasises the importance of understanding potential consequences and adjusting our expectations accordingly to maintain inner peace. The philosopher propounds the idea of viewing life akin to a lively public pool, teeming with diverse experiences and unpredictable events.

Just as a public pool encompasses all manner of occurrences —from the excited splashes of children learning to swim to the peaceful glide of the experienced swimmer—so does life with its complex mixture of joys and sorrows, triumphs and defeats, predictabilities, and surprises. Through this analogy, Epictetus implores us to foster a mindset of equanimity, preparing ourselves for the myriad possibilities of life's experiences.

Adjusting our expectations and accepting the unpredictable flow of life allows us to react to life's vicissitudes with a balanced composure, reminiscent of a cucumber serenely floating in a refreshing cocktail. The cucumber, despite the effervescence surrounding it, maintains its cool, buoyant presence, undeterred by the surrounding tumult. This image represents our ideal emotional state amidst the highs and lows of life— serene, composed, and unflappable.

As we internalise and apply this wisdom, we cultivate the ability to respond to life's rollercoaster ride with grace and tranquillity. We learn to swim through the turbulent waters of life, mastering the art of floating in the ever-changing currents with serenity and resilience. Epictetus invites us to dive into the metaphorical pool of tranquillity, learning to navigate life's waves with wisdom and a steady heart.

In essence, there is nothing quite as invigorating as this metaphorical plunge into the pool of serenity, as Epictetus would likely agree. It allows us to retain our calm, no matter how chaotic the outer circumstances may get, leading us to a deeper sense of fulfillment and peace in life. Through these teachings, Epictetus provides us a roadmap towards a balanced life, one characterised by a grounded understanding of life's unpredictable nature and a well-crafted response mechanism that promotes inner peace and resilience.

5

The Art of Perspective

Men are disturbed not by things, but by the views which they take of things. Thus, death is nothing terrible, else it would have appeared so to Socrates. But the terror consists in our notion of death, that it is terrible. When, therefore, we are hindered or disturbed, or grieved, let us never impute it to others, but to ourselves—that is, to our own views. It is the action of an uninstructed person to reproach others for his own misfortunes; of one entering upon instruction, to reproach himself; and one perfectly instructed, to reproach neither others nor himself.

Epictetus imparts an invaluable understanding that often eludes many of us: our inner peace or tranquillity isn't inherently rattled by events themselves, but rather by the lens through which we interpret them. Let's take the universally daunting concept of death, for instance. The goosebumps that crawl up our spine at the mere thought aren't directly induced by the Grim Reaper himself. Instead, they are born from our perception of death as a malevolent, cloak-wrapped figure hovering ominously over our shoulders. This intriguing concept was brilliantly manifested by Socrates. Even when staring death in the face during his trial, he exuded an aura of calmness that stemmed from a serene, unfazed understanding of the end of life.

In the rollercoaster of life, there are bound to be moments when your emotions take a nose-dive into the valleys of discontent, disappointment, or anger. During these low ebbs, it's all too easy to engage in a blame game or 'blame bingo', as I like to call it. It seems almost instinctive to attribute our emotional upheaval to external entities—be it the nosy neighbour, the car that broke down, or even the weather. However, Epictetus offers a golden piece of advice that champions resilience over resentment: resist this tempting pitfall. Rather than casting a judgmental eye on those around you, he advises you to instead turn your gaze inward and embark on a journey of introspection. Scrutinise your own viewpoints and beliefs with the same critical rigour you would apply to a disastrous DIY haircut, one that suggests a lawnmower went on a rogue mission atop your head. It is our interpretations and perceptions, not external events, that truly merit a closer examination.

Epictetus doesn't just provide us with transformative wisdom; he also proposes a unique progression chart for our journey through the School of Stoicism. It's similar to how students progress through various academic levels, except instead of traditional subjects, the syllabus is the art of living. If you find yourself habitually blaming others for your troubles, you're still a novice, enrolled in Stoic Philosophy 101. Once you start to pivot and turn the accusing finger toward yourself, acknowledging your role in shaping your own experiences, you've elevated your understanding to Stoic Philosophy 201. The pinnacle of philosophical enlightenment, however, is a level that transcends the blame game altogether. It is reached when you cease to point fingers, to lay blame, on anyone at all, including yourself. This is the stage where you've ascended to the esteemed status of a black-belt philosophy ninja, one who embodies tranquillity and acceptance.

In our pursuit of this coveted status, we should strive to alter our perspective rather than berating the external world for our displeasure. For instance, if your morning begins with the unpleasant surprise of your toast being charred by your trusty toaster, resist the urge to chide the appliance. Instead, acknowledge that it is your mental construct of "perfect toast" that's the actual mischief-maker. After all, the toaster is simply applying heat, doing its job without malice or intent. You might even learn to find a peculiar charm in a slightly charred slice, which introduces an unexpected crunch and flavour to your morning meal. With this altered perspective, you're not just philosophising—you're philosophising with a side of charred toast! What initially appeared as a culinary mishap has now become a philosophical exploration, turning your breakfast table into a classroom of enlightenment.

Remember, the journey towards enlightenment and tranquillity isn't about changing the world around us, but rather about altering the lenses through which we perceive it. As Epictetus beautifully illustrates, it's not the events but our judgements of them that disturb our peace. So, next time you feel your serenity slipping away, remember to scrutinise your perceptions rather than playing 'blame bingo'. Here's to hoping your philosophical journey is as crispy and enlightening as a slice of charred toast!

Once more, we stand on the brink of inspiration and implementation. We've navigated the maze of Epictetus' thoughts, and now it's time to apply the map to our own terrain. The forthcoming exercises will be your guide, leading from abstract musings to tangible action. Shall we forge ahead? Let's evolve from understanding to living, pursuing our distinct *Theory of Happiness*.

We kick-start this philosophical journey with the "Charred Toast Challenge". This exercise playfully challenges the conventional wisdom of toast-making. For a week, take a leap of faith and adjust your toaster to the 'slightly charred' setting. Each morning, as you sit to enjoy your breakfast, approach the darkened toast not with revulsion, but with a spirit of open-minded curiosity. As you navigate the charcoal edges, question whether the experience is as unpalatable as your initial perception led you to believe. Perhaps, much to your surprise, you might uncover a newfound appreciation for the unique, smoky flavours that dance on your tongue. Even if you don't develop a taste for charred toast, the activity underscores the value of challenging and reassessing our preconceived notions.

The adventure continues with the "DIY Haircut Appreciation" exercise. Muster up the courage for a modest DIY trim — nothing dramatic, just a subtle change that won't make professional hairdressers cringe. As you evaluate your handiwork in the mirror, scrutinise your immediate reaction. Challenge yourself to look beyond the unconventional styling to unearth the silver lining — this could be as simple as acknowledging the bravery it took to hold those scissors. This activity is designed to illuminate how rigid beauty standards can hinder self-acceptance, emphasising the importance of self-love and embracing our unique journey.

Our philosophical tour then leads us to the "Blame Game Detox". Make a solemn pledge to dedicate a whole day to refraining from attributing blame — to others or to yourself — for any mishaps or setbacks that transpire. Pay keen attention to the seismic shift in your perspective when you exclude yourself from the blame equation. This practice fosters personal accountability over your reactions, encouraging responses defined by calmness and clarity, as opposed to frustration or defensiveness.

The grand finale of our experiential expedition is the "Socratic Death Debate". This introspective contemplation of mortality, inspired by the renowned philosopher Socrates, urges us to separate the inescapable reality of death from the fears and cultural perceptions that often shroud it. As part of this profound exercise, jot down any insights that arise, allowing you to deepen your understanding of the nature of life and death, and reconcile with its inevitability.

Having completed these exercises, remember that each effort brings us closer to a life governed by the wisdom of Epictetus. Philosophy isn't just a subject of the mind; it's a compass for action. The real measure of understanding these teachings isn't just in their contemplation but in their execution. View these exercises as your blueprint, constructing your ideal life. As you build, you'll discover philosophy isn't just studied but enacted.

In summary, Epictetus kindly invites us to explore the complex weave of our responses to the multitude of life's occurrences. He urges us to acknowledge that our reactions are often tinted by our interpretations and deeply embedded perceptions, which, like spectacles with coloured lenses, can shape how we view the world and our place within it.

Epictetus underscores the significance of challenging and scrutinising these ingrained perceptions. Just as a jeweller examines a gem under different lights to assess its true value, we must also review our perceptions from multiple angles. By doing so, we can begin to see that they are not infallible truths but mutable viewpoints that can be reassessed and recalibrated.

The philosopher motivates us to initiate a shift in responsibility from external circumstances towards our own perceptions. Rather than blaming the world around us for our feelings of discontent or discomfort, we should turn the mirror inwards, reflecting on how our perceptions may have contributed to these feelings.

This introspective journey, whilst challenging, helps cultivate a profound, inward-looking understanding of ourselves. It enables us to acknowledge our biases and to revise or completely overhaul our perceptions where necessary. In doing so, we learn how to navigate life's choppy waters with a newfound wisdom, developing a balanced approach to interacting with the world around us.

In essence, Epictetus provides us with the tools to engage with life in a more mindful and insightful manner. By continually challenging our perceptions, we can gradually reshape our reactions to life's various events, shifting from passive victims of external circumstances to active participants in shaping our emotional landscapes. This process of internal exploration, guided by the teachings of Epictetus, opens the door to a more thoughtful and meaningful interaction with life.

6

Pixels, Zen, and Surfboards

Be not elated at any excellence not your own. If a horse should be elated, and say, "I am handsome," it might be endurable. But when you are elated and say, "I have a handsome horse," know that you are elated only on the merit of the horse. What then is your own? The use of the phenomena of existence. So that when you are in harmony with nature in this respect, you will be elated with some reason; for you will be elated at some good of your own.

When we think about success and worth, the mental images that come to mind are often materialistic: a shiny, high-powered car that catches everyone's attention or an ultra-HD, 4K, planet-sized TV that sets a new standard for home entertainment. Yet, as we immerse ourselves in the teachings of

Epictetus, we are nudged to reorient our perceptions of success and examine our sources of pride from a different perspective.

Picture this: You're the proud owner of an extravagant vehicle, resplendent, fast, and equipped with high-tech gadgets, echoing an aura of luxury straight out of a James Bond movie. Sitting behind the wheel, you can't help but feel the rush of power and prestige. Yet, Epictetus would encourage you to apply the brakes on this burgeoning pride, for while your car is undeniably impressive, the credit for its marvels belongs to the machine itself, not its driver. It's the result of extraordinary engineering and technological advancements; your boastful proclamation of "Behold my sleek chariot!" merely rides the coattails of your car's coolness.

What then, is the appropriate source of pride, according to Epictetus? He posits that our true worth isn't vested in our material possessions or external achievements. Instead, it lies in our ability to adeptly navigate the complexities of life with grace and equanimity. Envision yourself as a dancer in the grand theatre of existence, effortlessly gliding, twirling, and spinning in harmony with life's ever-changing rhythm. If you're able to pirouette through life's adversities, responding to its ebb and flow with precision and resilience, then that, my friend, is your genuine reason to celebrate. That's your well-deserved cue to crank up your personal applause track and rejoice in your inner fortitude.

Suppose, next time, your pride tempts you to flaunt your extraordinary TV, a marvel of pixel technology that paints breathtaking visuals. Pause a moment, and recognise that while the TV is indeed remarkable, those merits belong to it, not to you. However, if you find yourself skilfully manoeuvring through life's highs and lows, surfing the tumultuous waves of existence like a Zen master, that's undeniably your own achievement! Bask in your capacity to navigate life's uncertainties with wisdom and peace. Let your trumpet of self-praise resound, for it's your inner journey and growth that deserve recognition.

In the grand theatre of existence, our true worth and bragging rights aren't determined by our possessions or external trappings. It's the manner in which we engage with and respond to life's trials. Consider the successful entrepreneur who remains grounded despite abundant wealth, or the artist who persistently creates from an authentic place, regardless of fame. These individuals comprehend that genuine fulfillment and pride are intrinsic, deriving from the personal growth and resilience that enable them to handle life's intricacies.

Epictetus advocates for a paradigm shift in how we perceive accomplishment and satisfaction. He encourages us to shift our focus from external markers of success, such as the vehicles we drive or the cutting-edge technology we possess, to the nurturing of our inner virtues. The emphasis is on our engagement with the world, the manner in which we navigate adversities, and the development of wisdom and tranquillity amidst the challenges life presents. Our genuine cause for pride and satisfaction lies herein.

The philosopher implores us to acknowledge our personal development and inner voyages as our authentic achievements.

The genuine triumph is in gaining mastery over our reactions to our surroundings and life's events. Our material possessions should not be the spotlight of our existence, but rather the individuals we evolve into through our life experiences should take precedence.

Therefore, we are to let go of the yearning for external validation and instead cherish the qualities that truly represent us - a poised dancer amidst the rhythm of life, a Zen master exuding tranquillity, a proficient explorer of life's labyrinth. With each graceful move in this dance of life and each enlightening twist in the maze, take a pause to acknowledge your growth, resilience, and the contentment and purpose you extract from your life's dance.

It's time again to move from theory to practice. We've savoured Epictetus' sage wisdom, now it's time to experience it firsthand. The exercises that follow bridge the gap from ancient philosophy to modern living. Ready to cross the divide? Let's bring Epictetus' philosophy from the theoretical to the practical, shaping our *Theory of Happiness*.

Let's begin with the "Brag-Worthy Chronicles" activity. Over the course of a week, set aside time each day to reflect upon and note down the instances where you've faced life's hurdles with the grace of a professional ballet dancer or the finesse of a world-class athlete. These might be moments when you demonstrated resilience in the face of adversity, or when you persevered through difficult circumstances, or when you exercised wisdom to navigate a tricky situation. At the week's end, sit down with a trusted friend or family member, and share these achievements, not to indulge in self-aggrandisement, but to motivate them on their own personal growth journey. It's about inspiration, not boastfulness!

In the second activity, "Zen Master Surfing", the aim is to cultivate inner peace and resilience. Whenever life tosses you a curveball, imagine yourself as a calm Zen master gracefully riding the waves of existence. Visualise yourself balancing on a surfboard, smoothly navigating life's ups and downs, remaining centred amidst the turbulence. The goal here is not to resist or get attached to outcomes but to embrace life's ebb and flow. This exercise nurtures equanimity, enabling you to confront life's challenges with grace and composure.

Next, we have the "Gadget Fast", where you challenge yourself to resist the urge to flaunt your shiny trinkets or possessions for a full day. Rather than focusing outward, this exercise encourages you to turn your attention inward, shedding light on your personal victories, experiences, or philosophical insights. Use this opportunity to share meaningful stories, lessons learned, or moments of growth with others. This shift fosters deeper connections with those around you and broadens your understanding of life's real treasures.

Lastly, the "Borrowed Brag" exercise helps you cultivate humility. Be mindful of moments when you're tempted to boast about something that isn't your personal achievement, such as a flashy new car. Instead of basking in the car's glory, playfully correct yourself by recognising that it's the car's horsepower or sleek design that deserves the applause, not your merit. This exercise serves as a gentle reminder to focus on personal growth and inner virtues rather than outward, material validations.

At the end of these exercises, bear in mind that every step taken in the spirit of Epictetus brings us closer to living a life of philosophical wisdom. Philosophy isn't just an intellectual exercise; it's an actionable guide. Our goal is not merely to learn these principles but to embody them. Consider these exercises as your toolkit, equipping you for the journey ahead. As you proceed, you'll see that philosophy isn't just known, but experienced.

To encapsulate, Epictetus earnestly encourages us to reconsider the wellspring of our self-esteem. He urges us to shift our source of pride away from the accumulation of worldly goods and the pursuit of external triumphs, and instead focus on truly mastering life's fluctuating and unpredictable journey. This invitation is akin to moving our gaze from shimmering, ephemeral illusions towards the unchanging core of wisdom within us.

Epictetus urges us to comprehend that genuine fulfilment and satisfaction do not reside in the gathering of riches or the achievement of societal prestige, but rather in our capability to deftly sail through the crests and troughs of life with acumen and resilience. Just as a seasoned mariner doesn't pride himself on the ornate decorations of his ship, but rather on his ability to navigate through treacherous waters, we too should focus on developing our inner faculties of resilience and wisdom.

The philosopher astutely reminds us that worldly possessions and outward accomplishments are fleeting and subject to the caprices of fate. In contrast, the cultivation of inner virtues such as wisdom, compassion, resilience, and the alignment of our actions with moral principles form a durable foundation for authentic happiness. These inner virtues, unlike material possessions, are not at the mercy of external forces, but firmly within our control.

By embracing this perspective, we liberate ourselves from the heavy chains of societal expectations. Just as a bird released from a cage soars into the sky, we too can find true freedom and joy in the pursuit of wisdom and self-mastery. This liberation allows us to focus on the harmonious integration of philosophy into our day-to-day lives, turning philosophy from a theoretical concept into a practical tool for living a fulfilling life.

This inward journey invites us to develop personal mastery by scrutinising our character, aligning our actions with our values, and exercising self-discipline. It calls for ethical living that fosters respect and compassion, urging us to uphold fairness in our interactions.

Epictetus implores us to tap into our inner wisdom, a reservoir often overshadowed by the allure of material success. This path to wisdom entails introspection, questioning, and personal growth.

THEORY OF HAPPINESS

This shift in focus is not a mere detour; it's an entirely new journey. It's about forging a resilient spirit that withstands life's tempests, guided by our inner compass towards contentment, peace, and enduring happiness. By venturing inwards and embracing Epictetus's teachings, we become the captains of our souls, navigating through life's storms towards a life of wisdom, fulfilment, and genuine happiness.

7

Prioritising Amidst Distractions

As in a voyage, when the ship is at anchor, if you go on shore to get water, you may amuse yourself with picking up a shellfish or a truffle in your way, but your thoughts ought to be bent toward the ship, and perpetually attentive, lest the captain should call, and then you must leave all these things, that you may not have to be carried on board the vessel, bound like a sheep; thus likewise in life, if, instead of a truffle or shellfish, such a thing as a wife or a child be granted you, there is no objection; but if the captain calls, run to the ship, leave all these things, and never look behind. But if you are old, never go far from the ship, lest you should be missing when called for.

Visualise life as an imposing ocean liner journeying through the infinite waters of time and existence. Each one of us is a passenger on this grand vessel, navigating the unpredictability and challenges that life presents. This journey is not just a random voyage, but an exciting adventure brimming with unexpected turns, trials, and plentiful opportunities for personal development.

Epictetus takes on the role of our skilled guide and compass holder in this metaphor. He shares wisdom and teachings that help us skilfully manoeuvre through the stormy seas of life. He champions the concept of focusing on what lies within our power and developing a sense of acceptance for things beyond our control.

Picture a serene interlude when the ship anchors in a fascinating harbor. This stopover symbolises a temporary hiatus from our sea-bound journey. It offers a chance to walk on firm ground, inhale the refreshing coastal air, and explore life outside the boundaries of our vessel. The harbor, with its myriad of enticing diversions, is akin to the Sirens in Greek mythology, each capable of subtly veering you away from your path.

These distractions could be simple, like beautifully patterned seashells strewn along the shoreline. Each shell, distinctive in its design, tells a tale of far-off lands and tempting sea voyages, urging you to collect them as keepsakes. Alternatively, your senses might be drawn to the irresistible scent of a local food market, its tantalising aroma promising a delightful culinary adventure. Or, you could be enticed by the barista at a local cafe, whose amiable personality and coffee-making expertise invite you into engaging conversations.

While these diversions enrich your journey, adding a vibrant hue to your life's canvas, Epictetus stresses the importance of vigilance. He advises us not to lose sight of our main objective — the ship symbolising our life's central journey. He reminds us that, like sailors who have relied on the North Star for guidance since ancient times, our core priorities should serve as a life compass, guiding our decisions amidst an array of distractions.

Throughout our life's narrative, we encounter an abundance of distractions. Relationships, depicted as unique seashells in our metaphor, often hold a central place. These bonds, whether familial, friendly, or romantic, gift us with a sense of belonging, love, and satisfaction. They enrich our lives, much like the striking seashells add to the allure of the beach.

However, Epictetus nudges us to remain focused on the broader voyage of self-improvement and personal evolution. Life, personified by the captain of our ship, can call upon us to reconnect with our core mission at unexpected times. This call could manifest as a pivotal life event, an exciting opportunity, a sudden hurdle, or a deep-seated realisation that prompts us to reassess our journey's direction.

When such moments arise, Epictetus advises us to be ready to temporarily set aside our shore-side attachments, our relationships, personal achievements and interests. This act doesn't suggest disregard or devaluation of these attachments.

Rather, it emphasises the need to create space for focusing on the grander purpose of our existence.

This could mean making difficult choices or taking actions that unsettle our current circumstances. It could involve moving to a new location for a career opportunity or personal development, embracing tasks that require solitude and introspection, or simply dedicating more time for self-reflection.

Setting aside these attachments does not mean severing them. It's about striking a balance between maintaining these relationships and responding to life's call, allowing us to continue on our journey towards self-improvement. This setting aside is temporary and adjustable, and is not a reflection of the value we place on these relationships or achievements.

When we heed life's call, we aren't abandoning our cherished relationships or accomplishments for good. Rather, we're ensuring they don't tie us too firmly to the harbor, preventing us from continuing our voyage. By doing this, we allow for the ebb and flow of life, creating a delicate balance between our personal connections, achievements, and our overarching journey of personal growth.

This balance allows us not only to nurture our relationships and honour our accomplishments but also to stay attuned to life's call. This state of readiness ensures that we're prepared to rejoin the ship — our journey towards personal growth and fulfilment — when it's time to set sail. This approach equips us to navigate life adeptly, juggling our personal connections, achievements, and the pursuit of our life's mission.

Epictetus's wisdom guides us in every stage of our life's voyage, emphasising the significance of keeping our ship — our core principles and priorities — within sight. This guidance is not confined to a particular life stage; it's a universal reminder to remain alert to life's call, regardless of where we stand in our journey.

By dedicating ourselves to personal growth and the pursuit of wisdom, we're able to fully appreciate the beauty of life's journey. Following Epictetus's guidance allows us to navigate through life with grace, resilience, and a sense of fulfillment. As a result, our life's voyage transforms from a leisurely cruise to an enlightening journey, filled with serenity, storms, personal growth, and a profound understanding of existence and our place within it.

We're back at that pivotal point where philosophy turns into lived experience. We've appreciated Epictetus' wisdom, and now it's time to test these ideas in the laboratory of life. The upcoming exercises are your catalyst, sparking a reaction from philosophical speculation to direct action. Ready to ignite the change? Let's transition from absorbing wisdom to embodying it, powering our own *Theory of Happiness*.

In our "Ship vs. Seashells" exercise, let's delve deeper into the symbolism of your 'ship' representing your top priorities and the tempting 'seashells' signifying distractions that cross your path. Take a moment each day to reflect on the state of your ship and the allure of the seashells. Consider the tasks, commitments, and goals that truly matter to you—the pillars of your life. Then, consciously adjust your perspective and ensure that your focus remains primarily on your ship, keeping your priorities in sight even as the seashells glitter and entice. This exercise encourages self-awareness and a constant realignment with what truly matters in your life.

Now, let's explore the "Captain's Call" exercise, which invites you to embrace discipline and focus. Choose a daily task or responsibility that demands immediate attention—a personal 'captain's call'. When this task emerges, make a conscious commitment to practice discipline by dropping everything else and giving it your undivided attention. By dedicating yourself fully to this task, you cultivate a sense of presence and mastery over your actions. This exercise trains you to discern between what is truly important and what can wait, empowering you to navigate through life's demands with greater efficiency and effectiveness.

In the bustling world of the "Café Quest" exercise, we encounter a multitude of distractions that can easily sidetrack us. Picture yourself on a mission to acquire your daily coffee fix, but be mindful of the seashells along the way—the alluring aromas, conversations, and diversions that might beckon you. The key is to stay focused on your primary mission, keeping the pursuit of your caffeine fix front and centre. By maintaining a steadfast focus on your immediate objective, you develop resilience against distractions and hone your ability to stay aligned with your goals amidst the swirl of external influences.

This exercise cultivates mindfulness and reminds us to stay grounded in our priorities even in the midst of everyday routines.

Finally, let's embark on the "Cinematic Departure" activity—a vivid exercise that taps into the power of imagination. Visualise yourself as the protagonist in an action-packed scene, where life nudges you back to your true priorities. Feel the surge of determination as you let go of distractions and step forward with unwavering focus. Embrace the heroic energy of this mental scenario, embodying the qualities of decisiveness, resilience, and purpose. This exercise serves as a reminder that we have the agency to choose our responses to life's challenges and distractions. By consciously aligning ourselves with our true priorities and courageously taking action, we set ourselves on a path of growth and fulfillment.

As we put these exercises to rest, keep in mind that each action inspired by Epictetus moves us closer to living his teachings. Philosophy isn't just a field of study; it's a living, breathing guide for life. The real essence of these teachings isn't just in their cognition but in their realisation. Let these exercises serve as your guiding path, directing you towards a life of fulfillment and contentment. As you tread, you'll realise that philosophy isn't just conceived but enacted.

To conclude, Epictetus's underlines the importance of maintaining unwavering concentration on our cardinal objectives

THEORY OF HAPPINESS

amidst the captivating diversions that life presents. Epictetus, akin to a seasoned helmsman steering us through life's vast ocean, fervently encourages us to recognise the importance of focusing on elements within our sphere of influence, whilst surrendering control over what lies beyond.

Just as a vessel requires the decisive command of its captain to remain on course amidst turbulent waves and shifting winds, we must harmonise ourselves with life's call. We must continually strive to align our decisions with our core values, acting as compass bearings that guide us towards personal growth and enlightenment. By preserving our commitment to these guiding principles, we foster a sense of congruence and integrity within ourselves.

Epictetus urges us to prioritise the pursuit of wisdom, viewing it not as a mere academic endeavour, but as a practical tool for living. Wisdom acts as our inner compass, helping us navigate the undulating tides of existence with elegance and resilience. It equips us to make judicious choices, to respond to life's challenges with composure, and to derive learning from each of life's experiences, whether they be marked by joy or sorrow.

By remaining true to our priorities and persistently seeking wisdom, we can traverse the journey of existence with a dancer's grace and a boxer's tenacity. This, according to Epictetus, leads us to a profound sense of fulfilment and a richer understanding of life itself. It's akin to discovering a hidden treasure within ourselves, revealing a depth of inner resources and resilience we may have previously overlooked.

In essence, Epictetus's urges us to focus on what truly matters—our inner growth, wisdom, and the art of discerning between what we can and cannot control. By embracing this philosophy, we can turn life's tumultuous sea into a dance floor, gracefully swaying with the ebb and flow, and finding a rhythm that resonates with our deepest values and aspirations. This approach imbues our journey through existence with a sense of purpose, satisfaction, and profound understanding, turning life into a voyage of continuous discovery and growth.

8

Life's Quirky Dance

Demand not that events should happen as you wish; but wish them to happen as they do happen, and you will go on well.

"Find joy in life's demanding gaze", might well have been an axiom voiced by Epictetus, potentially whilst under the scrutinising stare of an indifferent feline companion. His philosophy urges us not to insist petulantly that life must bend to our every desire. Instead, Epictetus advises us to embody the nimble adaptability of an accomplished improvisational comedian, who, when given an unusual and challenging prompt such as 'underwater basket weaving,' can craft it into a captivating, surprising, and uproariously funny performance. When we internalise this mindset, our journey through life becomes as smooth and effortless as the silken coat of a meticulously groomed Persian cat, pampered by the most conscientious of pet owners.

To further elucidate this concept, let's delve into a commonplace scenario—expecting your cat to eagerly chase after thrown objects in the manner of the ever-enthusiastic Border Collie. It swiftly becomes evident that such an endeavour is as practical as attempting to drain the Mediterranean Sea with a pipette—an exercise in futility. Instead of succumbing to frustration or disappointment, we can derive delight in acknowledging the reality of the situation. Your discerning feline friend will almost certainly regard you with an aloof and somewhat contemptuous gaze as you comically scamper after the discarded toy yourself. Accepting, and even revelling in this farcical reality, you're mastering the art of living in a way that few can! In this playful interaction with your cat, you may not score any points in the game of fetch, but you're unquestionably advancing in the grand game of life, courtesy of the insights provided by our cherished philosopher, Epictetus.

And don't overlook the added fringe benefit in this entire cat-fetch scenario. Amid your fruitless fetch efforts, you're inadvertently receiving a cardio workout at no additional charge! Who would have thought philosophy could also encourage physical fitness? The amusement evident on your cat's countenance becomes a motivator, reminding you to find joy in the peculiarities of life. By welcoming life's oddities and embracing its unpredictable nature, you're not merely getting by—you're flourishing. In life's grand theatre, you're not just a puppet but an improvisational artist, adroitly managing unexpected twists and turns. Epictetus serves as your insightful mentor, enabling you to transform the world into your stage. And as Epictetus would affirm, having fun is a vital part of this journey, because isn't that the essence of life?

So, boldly embrace the unforeseen scripts that life provides, and bravely take centre stage. Like an improvisational comedian, you adjust, innovate, and find humour in the most unexpected moments. Picture finding yourself in a situation where you are asked to deliver a speech without prior preparation. Instead of being crippled by anxiety, you draw a deep breath, embrace the absurdity of the moment, and deliver a spontaneous monologue that leaves the audience roaring with laughter. By infusing your existence with a sense of levity and spontaneity, you uncover the true essence of living. Remember, life's grand theatre invites you to be both the performer and the spectator, delighting in the absurdities and finding joy in every scene. With Epictetus as your guide, allow the laughter to permeate your journey, because it's in these moments of delight that you truly come alive.

Therefore, allow life's dance to unfold before you, and with each step, welcome the whimsical twists and turns that emerge. Cherish the moments of humour, find pleasure in the unexpected, and let Epictetus be your sagacious yet jovial companion on this exhilarating journey. Embracing life's eccentric dance will not only bring mirth to your days but will also light the way to a more joyful and fulfilling existence. With a sparkle in your eye and a spring in your step, let the dance commence!

Here we are again, at that crossroad where ideas inspire action. We've explored the richness of Epictetus' teachings, and now it's time to apply this gold to our daily life. The exercises up next are your crucible, transforming ancient thoughts into your modern actions. Ready for the alchemy? Let's journey from intellectual stimulation to experiential enrichment, minting our *Theory of Happiness*.

Let's begin with the "Improv Comedy Stage" exercise. Picture a situation where your carefully planned day takes an unexpected turn. Instead of succumbing to panic or frustration, imagine yourself standing on the stage of a lively improv comedy club. Envision yourself as a skilled improviser, ready to adapt and turn any unexpected twist into a show-stopping performance that leaves the audience in stitches. By embracing the spirit of improvisation, you cultivate resilience, creativity, and the ability to find joy in unexpected situations. This exercise empowers you to navigate through life's surprises with grace and a light-hearted approach.

Now, let's try the "Zen Cat" exercise. Choose an endeavour that feels as futile as teaching a cat to fetch. It could be a personal project, a challenging relationship, or a long-standing habit you wish to change. When things don't go as planned or fail to produce the desired results, channel the equanimity of a cat. Cats are Zen masters in their own right, accepting things as they are, without attachment to specific outcomes. By adopting a cat-like mindset of acceptance and letting go, you can gracefully navigate through life's challenges with serenity and grace. This exercise reminds you to find contentment in the present moment and detach yourself from rigid expectations.

Next, let's explore the "Judgmental Stare" exercise. Find a photo of a cat casting a haughty, judgmental stare. Whenever life veers away from your choreographed plans and frustration begins to build, look at this picture. Allow it to remind you that sometimes it's best to observe and gracefully accept life's dance, rather than trying to control every step. Embrace the power of observation and detachment, gaining valuable insights and perspective without becoming entangled in judgments or unnecessary worries. This exercise encourages you to cultivate a sense of detachment and find peace amidst life's unpredictability.

Lastly, let's celebrate the whimsical with the "Whimsical Oddities" activity. Engage in an activity that is patently absurd but harmless, such as mimicking the act of weaving a basket underwater or creating a silly dance routine in your living room. Delight in the silliness, let laughter bubble up, and revel in the sheer joy of embracing life's whimsical oddities. Always remember that life is often absurd, and it's okay to acknowledge, accept, and even revel in its delightful quirks. By infusing your days with light-heartedness and humour, you cultivate resilience, adaptability, and a deeper appreciation for the beauty of life's tapestry.

Having navigated these exercises, remember that each act influenced by Epictetus brings us closer to living a life of wisdom. Philosophy isn't simply a matter of thought; it's a guide for life. True appreciation of these teachings doesn't lie merely in their understanding but in their application. Regard these exercises as your navigation tools, steering you towards your desired life. As you journey, you'll perceive that philosophy isn't just theorised, but practiced.

To sum it all up, Epictetus's teachings encourage us to do more than just endure life's critical inspections and unpredictable plot twists; they inspire us to truly delight in these experiences. Life, in all its complexity and whimsicality, is not merely a path we tread with caution and reticence, but a vibrant stage upon which we are invited to dance, cavort, and bask in the glow of experience.

The philosopher's wisdom encourages us to appreciate that our ambitions may not always manifest in the manner we envisage. For instance, despite our best endeavours, we might not succeed in transforming our aloof feline companion into an exuberant Border Collie, eagerly fetching thrown balls. However, in Epictetus's view, such perceived failures are not devoid of value. Rather, they offer valuable lessons, afford insights into life's unpredictability, and provide opportunities for growth and self-reflection.

Each misstep, each unrealised goal, instead of being viewed as a setback, can be seen as a notch on the scoreboard of existence. Every experience, whether it aligns with our expectations or deviates from them, enriches us, moulding us into more resilient, adaptable, and empathetic beings. The trials we encounter, the dreams that remain elusive, the ambitions that transform and evolve—each is a chapter in our unique life story, contributing to our individual evolution.

Therefore, Epictetus advises us to embrace the capricious, dance with life's absurdities, and meet its trials with a spirit of adventure and a sense of humour. It is in these moments of levity and acceptance that we realise our true potential and learn to appreciate ourselves, not for our grand achievements, but for our resilience, our adaptability, and our unwavering spirit.

In the grand scheme of life, striving to be the cat's whiskers—aiming to excel and stand out—is not merely about external recognition or success. Rather, it is about embodying courage, maintaining a positive outlook, and deriving satisfaction from our journey, irrespective of its twists and turns. Thus, Epictetus's wisdom inspires us to celebrate our unique path, to find joy in our experiences, and to thrive amidst life's magnificent and often unpredictable theatre.

9

Laughter in Adversity

Sickness is an impediment to the body, but not to the will unless itself pleases. Lameness is an impediment to the leg, but not to the will; and say this to yourself with regard to everything that happens. For you will find it to be an impediment to something else, but not truly to yourself.

Are you ready to challenge your perspective, embrace the dynamic dance of life, and harmonise with its ever-changing tune? Epictetus suggests a potent cognitive shift. This change enables us to understand that while physical ailments such as the common cold can leave our bodies feeling weak, they need not dampen the blazing spirit of our willpower and determination. These inner strengths are not as fixed or rigid as the laws governing our physical world; rather, they are akin to flexible dough, malleable and waiting to be shaped to our advantage.

Thus, even if you are faced with a sprained ankle, causing your leg to be as shaky as an overcooked strand of spaghetti, it shouldn't dampen the explosive display of your lively spirit. Our bodies might be temporarily affected, but our minds, fuelled by the fire of determination, can remain unscathed, continuously striving forward.

To add further depth to this concept, let's immerse ourselves in a hypothetical, whimsical situation—a playful twist of the unexpected. Suppose your internet connection suddenly decides to embark on an unplanned holiday, interrupting your binge-watching marathon of the latest trending Netflix drama. Undeniably, it's a curveball, a spanner thrown into your well-crafted leisure plans. However, this unexpected cyber retreat doesn't have to be the killjoy at your solitary Netflix gathering. Instead, it provides an open platform for your creativity to rally an enthusiastic, fun-loving entourage to keep the party going. Each time life pitches a curveball your way, gently remind yourself with a smile: This might be a temporary glitch, but it's far from an apocalypse. You remain the same resilient, resourceful 'you,' thoroughly equipped to tackle this transient challenge with grace, flexibility, and perhaps even a couple of giggles!

To illustrate this philosophy more vividly, let's navigate into the realm of baking. Imagine you're all set to bake delectable chocolate chip cookies. You've laid out your ingredients, donned your apron, but you discover that your pantry is out of chocolate chips, and the local shops have closed for the night. An ordinary response might be to abandon the mission, but you're no ordinary individual—you're a Stoic-inspired culinary adventurer! Drawing upon Epictetus's teachings, you don't see a roadblock but an opportunity for innovation. With a spark of optimism, you rummage through your kitchen, find oats and raisins, and create a batch of cookies that could give any patisserie in town a run for their money. This anecdote not only encapsulates Epictetus's philosophy of facing life's challenges head-on but also amplifies his encouragement to improvise, adapt, and find delight in life's unexpected twists.

The next time you encounter a challenge, remember that you're not merely enduring a storm; you're also crafting a solo comedy sketch. Life is your stage, and the props can transform at a moment's notice! Embrace this chance to showcase your ability to improvise, adapt, and cultivate a sharp sense of humour. Just as an experienced comedian can skilfully weave unexpected audience interactions into their act, you can transform adversities into distinctive opportunities for growth and laughter. By heartily accepting life's challenges and seeking humour in its peculiarities, you'll tackle obstacles in a way that adds richness, colour, and fulfilment to your journey.

Epictetus advocates an approach to life that is simultaneously light-hearted and profound, where challenges metamorphose into punchlines, and we evolve into skilled comedians nimbly navigating the stage. So, brace yourself for the laughter, the inevitable hiccups, the pearls of wisdom that will emerge, and the sheer joy of living life, Epictetus style! This philosophy isn't just about developing resilience and adaptability; it's about cultivating a buoyant spirit in the face of adversity. With this mindset, you'll unearth a deeper appreciation for life's absurdities, discover an inner fortitude to surmount any hurdle, and transform every setback into a hearty dose of laughter. It's your moment to seize life's microphone and command the stage, not just surviving but thriving amidst the twists and turns of the grand spectacle we call life.

Once again, we find ourselves at that crucial juncture where knowledge becomes practice. We've wandered through Epictetus' philosophy, and now it's time to bring this exploration home. The exercises will act as your compass, defining a path from introspective thinking to intentional action. Shall we embark on our voyage? Let's traverse from acquiring wisdom to embodying it, mapping out our very own *Theory of Happiness*.

Our first exercise is aptly named "Balloon Breaths". This task encourages us to visualise our body as a deflated balloon that we can inflate with each deep breath, a symbolic representation of rejuvenating our spirits in times of stress or despair. Imagine your body, like the balloon, filling up with strength, positivity, and resilience. As you exhale, envision the expulsion of any negative energy or self-defeating thoughts. This exercise is a potent reminder of our inherent capacity to rise above adversities by tapping into our reserves of inner strength and maintaining calm amidst life's tumult.

Following this, we introduce the "Party with Imaginary Pals" exercise. Imagine being in the throes of an unexpected internet outage, stripped of your usual digital distractions. Now, rather than succumbing to frustration, picture yourself dancing with carefree abandon or conversing animatedly with companions conjured from the depths of your imagination. This exercise, though playful, serves to underscore the importance of mindfulness and the potential for joy in simplicity, even when life deviates from our expectations.

We then move on to the "Noodle Strut Challenge", an exercise that beckons us to find humour in adversity. Suppose you've sprained your ankle and are left with an awkward limp. This challenge encourages you to transform this uncomfortable hobble into an exaggerated, comical 'noodle strut'. The premise here is to highlight that humour, when embraced in the face of adversity, can be a powerful catalyst for resilience and a shift in perspective.

The final activity we propose is the "MasterChef Minus Cookies" exercise. Imagine you're preparing to bake a batch of scrumptious cookies only to find you're out of a crucial ingredient, the all-important chocolate chips! This exercise challenges you to leverage your creativity and resourcefulness to concoct a new delicacy, reinforcing the significance of resilience and flexibility in navigating life's unexpected twists and turns.

At the conclusion of these exercises, remember that each choice influenced by Epictetus is a step towards living his philosophy. It isn't enough to understand; we must act. Philosophy isn't solely a mental endeavour; it's a practical way of life. The real impact of these teachings is realised not in comprehension but in action. Take these exercises as your catalyst, propelling you towards a life of wisdom. As you progress, you'll experience philosophy not just as an idea, but as a reality.

In conclusion, Epictetus's profound philosophy offers us a powerful framework for navigating the trials and tribulations of life with resilience and inner strength. By recognising that external circumstances and physical impediments do not define our true selves, we liberate our will and embrace the power to shape our own destinies.

Illness and physical limitations may pose challenges to our bodies, but they do not hinder the indomitable spirit of our will unless we allow them to. Epictetus reminds us that our true essence lies beyond the confines of our physical form, residing in the realm of our volition and inner strength. By internalising this perspective, we shift our focus from the limitations imposed by external factors to the unlimited potential of our own character.

Epictetus's philosophy invites us to transcend the external obstacles that we encounter in life. Instead of viewing ourselves as victims of circumstances, we become active agents, masters of our own narratives. We cultivate the power to respond to adversity with resilience, adaptability, and grace. Like skilled sailors navigating stormy seas, we learn to steer our course with wisdom and tenacity, charting a path of personal growth and self-realisation.

With this newfound understanding, we embrace life's challenges as opportunities for growth and transformation. We no longer fear the storms that may arise, for we have developed the inner resources to weather them. We recognise that the external world may present obstacles and setbacks, but it is our response to these challenges that truly matters. Through our conscious choices and unwavering will, we can navigate the rough waters and emerge stronger, wiser, and more resilient.

By embracing Epictetus's teachings, we embark on a journey of self-discovery and self-mastery. We realise that true happiness and fulfillment do not depend on external circumstances or the absence of adversity. Instead, they arise from within, from the unwavering conviction to live in alignment with our values, to cultivate inner peace, and to pursue personal growth.

Let us, then, embrace the wisdom of Epictetus and strive to live each day with a resilient spirit and an unwavering will. May we find solace in the knowledge that we possess the power to transcend life's challenges and forge our own path to happiness and fulfilment. With this philosophy as our guide, we navigate the ever-changing seas of life with courage, strength, and a profound sense of purpose.

10

Unveiling Your Superpowers

Upon every accident, remember to turn toward yourself and inquire what faculty you have for its use. If you encounter a handsome person, you will find continence the faculty needed; if pain, then fortitude; if reviling, then patience. And when thus habituated, the phenomena of existence will not overwhelm you.

In the sage teachings of Epictetus, we find a perspective that empowers and enlightens: every unexpected barrier that life introduces is not just a hindrance but a golden opportunity disguised as a stumbling block. Rather than conceding to fear and doubt when faced with such spontaneous trials, we're invited to take a step back and self-interrogate: "Which inherent strength within my personal collection can be mobilised to confidently handle this unexpected twist?" Such a profound shift in our perspective forges a pathway towards a stronger, more unyielding approach to life's unpredictable detours.

To fully grasp the dimensions of these personal strengths, let's journey deeper into a variety of scenarios where we can bring to light our inherent resilience. Visualise a situation where you find yourself in the presence of an exceptionally attractive or famous person - an encounter that could potentially lead to a quickened pulse or a flushed face. In such instances, your innate power resides in your self-restraint. This is comparable to the careful control you would exercise while pouring hot coffee into a delicate china cup; you can ensure your words remain steady and eloquent, free from the jittery stumbles of nervousness. Your inner power prevents awe from compromising your self-assured demeanour, transforming you into an island of calm in the stormy sea of emotions.

When you're faced with situations causing discomfort or severe pain, your inner power takes the form of Stoicism. This resilience mirrors the celebrated survival instinct of the cockroach, thriving even in the face of formidable odds. This inner power fortifies you to endure the most challenging conditions, mirroring the tenacity of a desert cactus surviving under the unforgiving sun. As the cactus leverages its internal reserves to flourish amidst adversity, so can you delve into your reservoir of fortitude, standing tall against adversity.

And what about those moments when you are subject to harsh comments or fierce criticism? In these instances, your strength is your patience. With a serene smile, you form a protective shield against these harsh onslaughts. Like a seasoned

Zen master maintaining balance amidst tumult, you permit the harsh words to slip past you, leaving your inner peace untouched. Patience emerges as a robust, impenetrable shield, guarding your tranquillity and ensuring external disturbances cannot penetrate your composed facade.

At its core, the philosophy of Epictetus invites us to become a multipurpose toolkit of life skills. With disciplined practice, a dash of humour, and a generous measure of self-assurance, we can gracefully navigate through life's labyrinth of challenges, boldly declaring, "I am ready for whatever life presents!" The essence of true resilience is not found in avoiding or trivialising trials, but in our capacity to draw from our personal strength toolkit, astutely selecting the ideal tool to confront and overcome obstacles. As we embody this approach, inspired by Epictetus, we learn to not just survive life's tumultuous roller coaster, but to find joy and growth in every twist and turn, leading to a deeper understanding of ourselves and the world around us.

With an enhanced understanding of our personal strengths, we stand on the threshold of a transformative self-discovery journey. We are prepared to encounter whatever lies ahead with grace, wisdom, and an indomitable spirit. Equipped with our toolkit of resilience, we are ready to face every challenge that comes our way, and with every encounter, we remind ourselves of our inherent power to conquer any obstacle. We aren't merely survivors passively experiencing life's challenges, but active conquerors, emerging from each trial with greater strength, wisdom, and a sense of self-accomplishment. This is the essence of living life through the lens of Epictetus: taking charge, embracing challenges, and evolving with every step of the journey.

It's that time again to move from the contemplative to the active. We've basked in Epictetus' wisdom, and now it's time to infuse this sunlight into our lives. The exercises that follow are your prisms, refracting lofty philosophy into a spectrum of daily experiences. Ready to see the colours? Let's evolve from understanding to experiencing, illuminating our *Theory of Happiness*.

Firstly, let's dive into the "Famously Attractive Person" scenario. Don't view this as a dreary exercise, but rather a fun exploration of your superpower of composure. Imagine flipping through a glossy magazine filled with dazzling celebrities or perhaps scrolling through an online photo gallery of your favourite film stars. As you encounter their breathtaking charm, practice maintaining your cool, gently reminding yourself to resist the urge to swoon or gush. Challenge yourself to stay composed and unruffled, even in the face of overwhelming attractiveness. Through this exercise, you will cultivate your superpower of composure, enabling you to exude an aura of confidence and control, especially in situations that might initially leave you flustered or starstruck.

Next up is the "Resilience in Pain" scenario. Embrace the next opportunity to test your superpower of resilience. Maybe

THEORY OF HAPPINESS

you accidentally stub your toe, or you endure the tiny torment of a paper cut. Instead of cursing your luck or mulling over the pain, channel the resilient spirit of a cockroach that survives against all odds. Learn to respond with resilience and strength, using the discomfort as a tool for growth rather than a cause for annoyance. This exercise will fortify your resilience superpower, empowering you to overcome even the most challenging circumstances with grace and fortitude.

Moving on to the "Patience Shield" scenario, envision a situation where someone unjustly criticises or berates you. Instead of giving in to the temptation of a heated retort, practice responding with patience and a knowing smile. Let the superpower of patience shield you from unnecessary conflicts, helping you maintain your tranquillity amidst stormy interactions. This exercise cultivates patience, which not only helps avoid tension but also fosters a deeper understanding and empathy in your interactions with others.

Finally, for building your "Superpower Repertoire", initiate a personal journal dedicated to your evolving toolbox of superpowers. In this journal, note each superpower you discover and how you've developed it, reflecting on your journey and the progress you've made. Use this journal as a wellspring of self-assurance, providing a morale boost when required. Regularly reviewing your inventory of superpowers will serve as a celebration of your unique strengths and abilities, reinforcing your belief in your capacity to face any challenge.

Upon the completion of these exercises, bear in mind that each endeavour steeped in Epictetus' wisdom brings us closer to living his philosophy. Philosophy isn't a static domain of the mind; it's a dynamic way of life. The true power of these teachings isn't simply in knowing them but in practicing them. Use these exercises as your accelerator, driving you towards your ideal life. As you continue, you'll come to see that philosophy is more than thought—it's action.

In our final reflections, let's cast our thoughts back to the wisdom imparted by Epictetus. He enthusiastically propels us towards metamorphosing life's unanticipated adversities into golden moments of opportunity to deploy and refine our personal superpowers. The strategy here is not merely about weathering life's storms passively; instead, it's about heartily embracing them, primed with the perfect instrument from our suite of superpowers. Thus equipped, we can confidently face any challenge that life presents, poised to audaciously exclaim, "Bring it on!"

This philosophical methodology, combined with our unique compilation of superpowers, preps us to continuously navigate life's unpredictable pathways. However, it's not enough to have these superpowers at our disposal; we must exercise them regularly, investing our dedication and perseverance in honing them to reach their full potential. Simultaneously, a dollop of humour can serve as a soothing balm, helping us navigate life's complexities with a light-hearted spirit.

Let's take a cue from Epictetus and remember to face adversity not as a destructive force, but as a transformative one. With each challenging wave we conquer, we further sharpen our skills and grow stronger. We don't merely survive the tumultuous tides; we learn to ride them with grace and agility, transforming them into avenues of growth and self-discovery.

As we continually put these principles into action, we unlock our true potential, paving our way towards profound fulfilment, enhanced strength, and surprisingly, even joy, as we voyage through the whimsical sea of life. It's a continuous journey of discovery, resilience, and growth, where every challenge met is a testament to our inner strength and adaptability. Ultimately, Epictetus teaches us that life isn't about avoiding the storms but learning to dance in the rain.

11

Borrowed Not Lost

Never say of anything, "I have lost it," but, "I have restored it." Has your child died? It is restored. Has your wife died? She is restored. Has your estate been taken away? That likewise is restored. "But it was a bad man who took it." What is it to you by whose hands he who gave it has demanded it again? While he permits you to possess it, hold it as something not your own, as do travellers at an inn.

Here we stand, poised on the precipice of a delightful exploration into Epictetus' unique perspective on impermanence. His wisdom encourages us to refract the spectres of loss and separation through a transformative lens, viewing such moments not as cruel subtractions but as a gracious return of the borrowed. By adopting this empowering perspective, we infuse our partings with resilience and acceptance, softening the edges of loss with the soothing salve of understanding impermanence.

Let's dive into the depth of this philosophy with an all-too-familiar situation. Imagine your young ones, with whom you've shared countless precious moments and life lessons, are now ready to spread their wings. Their once vibrant rooms stand untouched, echoing the reminiscence of their childhood. The instinctive clutch of loss might threaten to tighten around your heart. But wait! Epictetus whispers a heartening counsel in our ears, urging us to perceive this as the rightful return of a beloved library book that was borrowed long-term. Rather than clinging to a sense of loss, we're encouraged to cherish the invaluable narrative that unfolded during their stay under our roof. As we bid farewell to this chapter of our life, we savour the shared growth and experiences, embracing the transition with grace, just as one would appreciate a well-read borrowed book before returning it.

Moving into more challenging territory, consider the heart-rending loss of a life partner. Here, Epictetus offers a steadying hand, reminding us that our 'till-death-do-us-part' agreement has simply run its course. It's not a loss, but the end of a shared lease on love and companionship. The void that threatens to engulf us can instead become a sacred space for honouring the shared journey and cherishing the myriad memories sewn into the fabric of our relationship. As we return this borrowed love, we celebrate the wisdom gained and the life lived, rather than succumbing to despair.

What about those unnerving instances when our possessions are "redistributed" without our consent? Picture waking up to find your prized bicycle no longer parked outside. In these moments, Epictetus's philosophy ushers in a lighter perspective, transforming perceived loss into whimsical benevolence. With this view, we become inadvertent benefactors to the universe, displaying charity in the most unexpected circumstances. This detour into light-heartedness helps us detach from material attachments, reminding us of the transient nature of worldly possessions and their minimal importance in the grand cosmological narrative.

Epictetus invites us to recognise that everything we cherish, everything we believe is ours, is in reality a gracious loan, much like borrowing a cup of sugar from a neighbour. Our existence unfolds as if we're guests in a grand cosmic hotel, where we savour the luxury of life but also recognise the impermanence of our stay. By fully immersing ourselves in this transient experience, we cultivate gratitude for the moments and relationships shared, knowing that they're like the borrowed hotel bathrobe that must inevitably be returned.

Remember, life isn't an all-you-can-stash-in-your-suitcase buffet. Instead, it operates much like a lending service: we borrow, we savour, and then we gracefully return. In moments of apparent loss, let's eschew despair and tune our hearts to the frequency of gratitude. Let's strive to become the universe's most reliable borrowers, always returning our loans on time, much to the delight of the cosmic librarian.

Epictetus's teachings help us unmask the profound wisdom woven into the impermanence of life and the interconnectedness of all things. By embracing this philosophy, we learn to traverse life's winding transitions with grace, gratitude, and a touch of good humour. Every parting becomes an occasion to extend our heartfelt gratitude, accompanied by a cheerful request for a return receipt from the Universe's Lost and Found Department. This philosophy becomes a guidebook, a manual for infusing our lives with acceptance, resilience, and the gentle strength of understanding the cycle of borrowing and returning.

We're back at that compelling moment where thought evolves into action. We've delved into Epictetus' philosophy, and now it's time to channel these currents into our own lives. The exercises that follow will be your conduit, transporting us from intellectual stimulation to life-affirming action. Ready to make the journey? Let's move from conceptual understanding to experiential enlightenment, illuminating our *Theory of Happiness*.

Let's embark on our first exercise, the "Library Book" scenario. This introspective activity asks us to reflect deeply on the relationships that fill our lives, from fleeting acquaintances to enduring companionships. Imagine each individual you cross paths with as a cherished library book, loaned to you by the grand universal library. Each page of these living books unfolds a wealth of knowledge, affection, and experiences. Envision the unique narrative you have co-authored with each individual, the ebb and flow of your shared journey. To fully embody this exercise, take pen to paper and compose a heartfelt thank-you note. Through this act of gratitude, you acknowledge the profound influence each relationship has had on your personal narrative.

Delve into the "Nature's Loan" exercise, a rewarding journey into the heart of Mother Nature. Head outdoors and choose a part of the natural world that resonates with you - a majestic tree, a serene river, or the tranquil canvas of a sunset. Acknowledge the impermanence of these natural elements: the tree will eventually shed its leaves, the river will alter its course over time, the sunset will yield to nightfall. This transience mirrors the nature of a borrowed library book. It's temporary, and its form is destined to evolve and even disappear. But this reality doesn't provoke a sense of loss. Rather, it deepens our appreciation for the fleeting beauty and the wisdom they bestow. Take a moment to articulate your gratitude for these 'borrowed' experiences. This could take the form of writing a short note, or simply speaking words of thanks to the universe for allowing you to witness and learn from these evanescent natural wonders. The intention of this practice is to nurture a heightened awareness of the impermanence of life, applying this understanding to your interactions with people and material possessions. This is not an exercise in mourning transience, but in celebrating the constant flux and the beauty of borrowing and returning - the grand cosmic cycle of life.

The "Generous Donation" activity presents an opportunity to reshape your perspective on unexpected losses of material possessions. Instead of succumbing to a sense of loss, this activity prompts you to embrace the notion that you've inadvertently made a generous contribution to the cosmic treasury. Perhaps your favourite umbrella is now providing shelter to a stranger caught in a rainstorm, or a borrowed book is spreading wisdom in a distant corner of the universe. Discover the whimsy in such situations, picturing the joy your 'missing' items may bring to others. This shift in perspective nudges you towards a mindset of generosity and interconnectedness, softening the edge of loss with humour and acceptance.

The final leg of our philosophical journey is the "Life Hotel" exercise. In this reflective activity, take an inventory of the aspects of your life you 'borrow' from the universe. This catalogue might include relationships, life experiences, cherished possessions, and even personal attributes. Pay homage to the impermanence and transient nature of these borrowed aspects by expressing gratitude for each item. This recognition helps you cultivate a deep sense of appreciation and tranquillity, painting a picture of life as a fleeting yet profound stay in a grand cosmic hotel.

As you engage in these exercises, you find yourself playing an active role in the cyclical dance of borrowing and returning. It's a joyous celebration of the wisdom and personal growth garnered from acknowledging life's ever-changing tapestry. By reframing life not as a hoarding contest but as a graceful performance of borrowing and returning, we imbue our existence with a sense of humour and humility.

With the conclusion of these exercises, keep in mind that every action inspired by Epictetus is a step closer to a life enriched by wisdom. Philosophy isn't merely a mental pursuit; it's a practical map for living. The real worth of these teachings is discovered not just in understanding them but in living them. View these exercises as your guide, leading you towards a meaningful life. As you embark on this journey, you'll find philosophy is not just a subject to study, but a path to follow.

In conclusion, the teachings of Epictetus extend a warm invitation for us to perceive life as an eternal cycle of borrowing and returning. They implore us to redefine our understanding of loss, reframing it as an occasion for gratitude and a graceful act of relinquishment. By recognising the transient nature of all that we hold dear, we acquire the ability to navigate life's transitions with elegance, resilience, and a sprinkle of humour.

Epictetus encourages us to adopt the mindset of grateful borrowers from the universe, acknowledging that everything we possess is merely on loan. This perspective instils in us a sense of wonder and appreciation for each day and every experience. We become attuned to the intricate interconnectedness of all things, recognising our place within the grand tapestry of existence.

Through hands-on practice, we integrate this wisdom into the very fabric of our being. It becomes an inherent part of our perspective, shaping our thoughts, actions, and reactions. As we internalise this profound philosophy, we embark on a journey of personal growth, nurturing a deeper understanding of ourselves, others, and the world around us.

This transformative process allows us to approach life with an open heart, embracing its ever-changing nature and finding solace in the impermanence of things. We learn to let go gracefully, knowing that the act of returning what we have borrowed is not a loss, but an opportunity for gratitude and acceptance.

By living in alignment with these teachings, we cultivate resilience in the face of adversity, embracing life's challenges as opportunities for growth and self-discovery. With grace and resilience as our companions, we move through life's transitions with poise and equanimity, unburdened by attachments and ever open to the wonders that each moment presents.

12

Embracing Life's Chaos

If you would improve, lay aside such reasonings as these: "If I neglect my affairs, I shall not have a maintenance; if I do not punish my servant, he will be good for nothing." For it were better to die of hunger, exempt from grief and fear, than to live in affluence with perturbation; and it is better that your servant should be bad than you unhappy.

Begin therefore with little things. Is a little oil spilled or a little wine stolen? Say to yourself, "This is the price paid for peace and tranquillity; and nothing is to be had for nothing." And when you call your servant, consider that it is possible he may not come at your call; or, if he does, that he may not do what you wish. But it is not at all desirable for him, and very undesirable for you, that it should be in his power to cause you any disturbance.

Epictetus now nudges us towards adjusting our perspectives to enjoy a more relaxed, less anxiety-ridden lifestyle. Epictetus puts forth an alluring argument – that the minuscule sacrifices we make, like the petty frustrations over trivial matters or minor setbacks, are necessary for us to nurture a peaceful spirit. These sacrifices, he contends, far outweigh the strain and materialistic burdens that accompany a life crammed to the brim with incessant activity. By understanding, internalising and practicing this philosophy, we are, in essence, unlocking the door to a new realm – a realm permeated with an elevated degree of tranquillity, contentment, and ultimately, a life that's truly enriched.

As we venture deeper into the gushing fountain of wisdom that Epictetus graciously offers us, we unearth a plethora of practical ways to weave his invaluable principles into the intricate tapestry of our day-to-day lives. Life, in its most authentic form, is essentially an enchanting montage of experiences – some delightful, some distressing, and punctuated with a smattering of minor missteps. You might, for example, inadvertently knock over a bottle of lavishly priced olive oil. Or, you might trudge back home after a gruelling day at work, eagerly looking forward to that last craft beer, only to find it whimsically purloined by an unsuspecting roommate. In these irksome moments, Epictetus's soothing voice echoes in our minds, urging us to not let such trivial slip-ups trigger a cascade of frustration or annoyance. Rather, we should draw a calming breath, let our lips curve into a gentle smile, and view these incidents as insignificant tributes we pay to foster a tranquil spirit. The relentless pursuit of a blemish-free life is as far-fetched as spotting a fantastical unicorn in your backyard. Recognising this simple truth allows us to embrace life's imperfections, occasional fumbles, and enjoy the journey for what it is, without obsessing over the destination.

Now, let's turn our attention to our delightful, yet sometimes maddening, four-legged companions — our faithful dogs. Their antics often serve to lighten our day, although their behaviour might not always align with our expectations. Perhaps your dog has developed a mysterious fondness for chewing on your favourite pair of slippers, inciting a wave of exasperation. Here, we can apply a critical lesson from Epictetus. He proposes that if we permit the actions of beings who live moment-to-moment (much like our dogs) to dictate our emotional state, we are essentially surrendering control to creatures who find joy in activities as basic as sniffing other dogs' rear ends. This insight serves to underscore our human capacity for nuanced thought and resilience. So, when life throws us a curveball, or our dogs delight in causing a bit of mayhem, Epictetus encourages us to laugh at the madness, celebrate the absurdity, and harness our deep reserves of resilience. In doing so, we regain our equilibrium, unearthing the joy and satisfaction that comes from truly cherishing the present moment.

By weaving Epictetus's wisdom into our daily lives, we cultivate a serene perspective. Rather than letting minor mishaps or quirks disrupt our peace, we learn to accept life's imperfections, find humour in unexpected places, and focus on what truly matters. This fosters resilience and adaptability,

THEORY OF HAPPINESS

maintaining tranquillity amid life's chaos. When confronted with minor annoyances, like spilled oil or a mischievous pet, remember to pause, breathe, and respond with grace and humour. Savour these moments of letting go and acceptance; they are the small, profound joys of a relaxed life. This approach fortifies our resilience against life's unpredictability – a timeless gift from Epictetus.

Once more, we're at the threshold where insight paves the way for application. We've absorbed Epictetus' teachings, and now it's time to integrate these lessons into our daily experiences. The following exercises will be your pathway, guiding us from the world of philosophy to the reality of daily living. Shall we embark on this journey? Let's transition from the realm of ideas to the world of actions, contributing to our own *Theory of Happiness*.

Consider the exercise we've fondly termed "Olive Oil Oopsies". Picture a common mishap such as unintentionally toppling over a bottle of olive oil in your kitchen. Rather than succumbing to an immediate rush of frustration, take a moment to consider how this little accident contributes to your overall tranquillity. Perhaps this incident teaches you a vital lesson about the slippery nature of your kitchen tiles when doused in olive oil - an observation you may otherwise have overlooked. On the other hand, maybe the situation compels you to chuckle at the slapstick nature of life, a bit like a scene from a comedy film. By shifting our perspective, we can morph what initially seems like a minor annoyance into an opportunity for learning, introspection, and even laughter.

Next, we have the "Canine Capers" exercise. Here, you're encouraged to recall a recent instance when someone, be it human or pet, acted in an unexpected way. It could be your beloved dog ignoring your command to sit, choosing instead to bound across the park in hot pursuit of a squirrel. Reflect on how their unpredictability adds a dash of excitement to life, akin to your dog's newfound interest in displaying what looks suspiciously like interpretative dance moves in the middle of your living room. By embracing the unique quirks and behaviours of those around us, we become more receptive to new experiences, finding joy in the unpredictable twists and turns of life.

On to the "Fee for Tranquillity" exercise, where you're asked to pinpoint a minor annoyance, such as a tardy, overcrowded bus or a noisy neighbour. Rather than letting this annoyance get under your skin, view it as a small price you willingly pay for inner tranquillity. Can you transform this irritant into an opportunity for relaxation or enjoyment? Does the jam-packed bus give you extra time to indulge in people-watching or to lose yourself in a riveting podcast episode? By altering our perspective, we can spin minor irritants into blessings in disguise that enhance our overall peace of mind.

Lastly, make it a habit to maintain a daily journal as part of the "Serenity Ledger" exercise. Document the day's minor irritations and deliberate on how each contributes to a more relaxed, "chill" life. Perhaps that spilled coffee at work served as a catalyst for an unexpected conversation with the office janitor, who, as it turns out, harbours a keen interest in philosophy. Unearth the silver linings and hidden blessings in everyday annoyances. By keeping a log of these instances, we become more attuned to the positive aspects of life, fostering a greater sense of gratitude and well-being.

As we close these exercises, it's crucial to remember that each endeavour rooted in Epictetus' wisdom is a step towards truly living his philosophy. Philosophy isn't just an intellectual discussion; it's a lifeline for thoughtful action. The real potency of these teachings isn't just in grasping them but in actualising them. View these exercises as your guideposts, directing you towards a conscious life. As you march on, you'll discover philosophy is not just conceived but manifested.

As we conclude our reflections, Epictetus bequeaths us a revitalising outlook on life, encouraging us to see minor mishaps not as impediments but as intriguing patterns woven into our journey's tapestry leading to tranquillity. He inspires us to accept life's capricious nature instead of rebelling against it, educating us to waltz to its impromptu melodies.

Central to his philosophy is the fostering of inner peace—a soulful voyage he entreats us to undertake. On this pilgrimage, serenity blossoms from the rich loam of acceptance and resilience.

Epictetus' wisdom offers us more than a mere prescription for enduring life; it is a charter for engaging passionately with life, to savour its peculiarities and spontaneous moments. By adopting his counsel, we uncover our potential to uphold an unwavering sense of inner peace amidst life's ebb and flow.

Through his philosophical lens, we discern our extraordinary capacity to face life's challenges with balance, to confront its uncertainties with fortitude, and to celebrate its gifts with a heart steeped in gratitude. By immersing ourselves in his teachings, we expose the deep beauty and richness that life presents, even in its simplest moments. We learn to flow with life's currents, seeking comfort in accepting its flaws and joy in exalting its wonders.

In a nutshell, Epictetus' philosophy challenges us to become fully-fledged participants in the dance of life, diving headlong into the journey. By infusing his teachings into our daily lives, we set foot on a transformative path leading to a profound sense of inner calm, resilience, and satisfaction. So let us wholeheartedly welcome this wisdom, sway to life's rhythms, and savour each stride as we traverse the captivating mosaic of existence.

13

Serenity in Life's Circus

If you would improve, be content to be thought foolish and dull with regard to externals. Do not desire to be thought to know anything; and though you should appear to others to be somebody, distrust yourself. For be assured, it is not easy at once to keep your will in harmony with nature and to secure externals; but while you are absorbed in the one, you must of necessity neglect the other.

As we delve deeper into Epictetus' philosophy, we're invited to a masquerade ball where we're asked to dress up as the jester rather than the king. To some, this might seem counterintuitive. After all, who wouldn't want to be the king, commanding respect and admiration? But here, Epictetus shakes his head and laughs, advising us to be content in the fool's motley. He champions the idea of embracing what many would consider undesirable: appearing foolish and dull when it comes to worldly matters. It's as if he's giving us a permission slip to be the person at a fancy dinner party who admits to knowing nothing about fine wines, or the individual at the office water cooler who confesses ignorance about the latest trending Netflix series.

Just picture it: You're strolling through life, happily aloof from the rush and clamour of worldly affairs. While others might fret over not having the latest designer clothes or not being up-to-date with pop culture, you wear your out-of-fashion flannel and whistle 80's tunes with pride. You're like the carefree duck in a pond full of frantic swans. While they elegantly but anxiously preen and parade, you simply float along, occasionally dipping under the water's surface and emerging with a joyful 'quack'. Your focus lies not in keeping up with the swans, but in your own self-improvement journey.

Now let's address the topic of appearing competent and in control. Most of us crave to be perceived as someone who's got it all together. We don our superhero capes, ready to save the world from its troubles. However, Epictetus, always ready with a reality check, urges us to hang up those capes. He advises us to have a healthy scepticism about our abilities. So, even if you've become a virtuoso in playing the symphony of life, Epictetus suggests that there's always another piece to learn, another note to master. Therefore, even though we might appear as somebody in the eyes of others, it's crucial to keep our feet firmly on the ground and to keep ourselves open to learning and growing.

THEORY OF HAPPINESS

In his good-humoured wisdom, Epictetus acknowledges the complexity of maintaining a balance between our internal self and the external world. It's a bit like trying to balance a dancing flamingo on your head while juggling pineapple upside down cakes. Sure, it would make a great party trick, but the chances of being covered in pineapple-flavoured disaster are pretty high. Epictetus sees this and kindly suggests that we focus our attention on the inside rather than the outside. Instead of striving to control everything around us, we could channel our energies towards nurturing our inner peace and growth.

Epictetus' philosophy, delivered with a chuckle and a playful twinkle in his eye, invites us to become joyous 'fools'. He encourages us to prioritise self-improvement and inner peace over worldly acclaim. It's a call to take life less seriously, to dance freely, and to savour the delicious irony of finding wisdom in foolishness. So, let's heed his words, put on our jesters' caps, and get ready for the wonderfully wacky journey of self-discovery that lies ahead!

Again, we reach that point where understanding becomes doing. We've dissected Epictetus' philosophy, now it's time to let these insights shape our actions. The upcoming exercises are your catalysts, enabling the reaction from contemplation to application. Ready to spark the change? Let's shift from the world of thought to the universe of action, fuelling our unique *Theory of Happiness*.

First, we plunge into an activity we'll call "A Day in the Life of a Jester". Here, we'll transport ourselves to a moment when we found ourselves frantically juggling multiple tasks. Picture that day: you're meditating, responding to an avalanche of emails, attending an online workshop, walking the dog, and attempting a Jamie Oliver recipe, all within what feels like a blink of an eye. Remember the sensation of being yanked in numerous directions at once. Now, let's imagine an alternative reality where you placed inner peace on a pedestal over these external tasks. Reflect on this contrast and allow yourself to understand the significance of keeping our internal compass steady amidst the whirlwind of the outside world.

Next, we wander over to the "Inventory of Inner Disruptions". This is where we make a catalogue of the external abilities or traits we've been striving to perfect. This could be anything from mastering Japanese, beating your best marathon time, or cracking the code of...well, coding! Take a moment to ruminate on how these pursuits might have rocked your internal boat. Acknowledging these tremors can reveal the often overlooked sway that our external endeavours can have on our inner tranquillity.

The third stop on our journey is an activity we'll title "Letting the Pineapple Cakes Drop". Here, you're nudged to spot one metaphorical 'pineapple upside down cake' in your life, signifying a duty or responsibility that's triggering unnecessary stress or diminishing your inner serenity. Reflect on how releasing this burden could lead to a broader pathway for tranquillity and calm to wander into your life.

Lastly, we embark on a whimsical and creative task known as "The Fool's Farewell". Let your imagination run wild as you conjure a light-hearted tale or scenario where you bid adieu to your pineapple cake juggling act. You could pass the baton to a master juggler or a circus performer, who could perhaps do more justice to the act than we could. This fun exercise allows us to remember that in the grand circus of life, it is inner peace that deserves the spotlight, not our juggling skills.

Once you've wrapped up these exercises, it's vital to remind yourself that each step taken with Epictetus' philosophy in mind brings us closer to a life steered by insight and joy. Philosophy isn't just a mental workout; it's a roadmap for mindful living. The true essence of these teachings isn't in merely understanding them but in actively implementing them. Look at these exercises as your personal landmarks, guiding you towards a life overflowing with wisdom and tranquillity. As you persist in this journey, you'll discover that philosophy is not just to be contemplated, but to be lived.

As we bid farewell to this exploration of Epictetus' philosophy, it's like we're returning from a magical carnival where the main attractions were inner peace and personal growth. Instead of urging us to try every ride and win every prize at the gaming stalls, Epictetus nudged us towards the peaceful gardens tucked away in a quiet corner. There, he invited us to ponder on the merry-go-round of life, refocus our energies, and embark on a fantastical voyage of self-discovery.

Epictetus, ever the practical philosopher, reminds us to take a break from the hustle and bustle of the fair and indulge in some quiet reflection. It's as if we're sitting on a bench, cotton candy in hand, observing the clamour from a distance. We allow ourselves to realise how much we're driven by external expectations and pressures. This introspection, like spotting a shooting star in the night sky, illuminates the path towards what truly matters: our inner tranquillity.

Armed with this spark of awareness, we're ready to shrug off the invisible backpack filled with societal expectations that's been weighing us down. We become a sort of philosophical Houdini, freeing ourselves from the chains of conformity, and letting go of the need for external validation. We wave goodbye to the crowd's applause, choosing instead to listen to the symphony of our soul.

Moreover, Epictetus, with a playful wink, encourages us to delve into the magical chest of creativity. It might be sketching the fair's Ferris wheel, penning a poem inspired by the laughter and music, or crafting a tune that captures the essence of our carnival journey. This creative exploration offers an intimate space to connect with our deepest selves, offering a wellspring of joy and tranquillity.

But let's not forget, this philosophy isn't a race to the finish line. It's more like a leisurely stroll, where every stumble is a lesson and every pause is an opportunity for growth. If one day we find ourselves carried away by the dazzling lights and the calliope music, it's okay. Tomorrow, the sun will still rise, ready to greet us with a fresh chance to refocus on our inner journey.

Epictetus's wisdom nudges us to swap our chase for the golden ring on life's carousel with a quest for authentic contentment. His philosophy reassures us that the trophy of true happiness isn't housed in a display case of external achievements, but it's found in the heart of our own peace and resilience.

In a nutshell, Epictetus's philosophy is a golden ticket to an extraordinary funfair where the pursuit of inner peace takes centre stage. As we continue to savour this carnival of self-discovery and creativity, we open ourselves to a life bubbling with tranquillity, genuine joy, and fulfilment that outshines any external glitter. So, let's keep our jesters' caps on, enjoy the ride, and revel in the extraordinary journey of being gloriously human.

14

Letting Go For Happiness

If you wish your children and your wife and your friends to live forever, you are foolish, for you wish things to be in your power which are not so, and what belongs to others to be your own. So likewise, if you wish your servant to be without fault, you are foolish, for you wish vice not to be vice but something else. But if you wish not to be disappointed in your desires, that is in your own power. Exercise, therefore, what is in your power. A man's master is he who is able to confer or remove whatever that man seeks or shuns. Whoever then would be free, let him wish nothing, let him decline nothing, which depends on others; else he must necessarily be a slave.

As we journey through the enigmatic terrains of life in pursuit of happiness, it becomes imperative to delve into the uncharted territories of our minds and emotions. It is here, in this nuanced landscape, that we encounter the profound teachings of Epictetus, our astute philosophical guide. Epictetus beckons us towards an enlightening understanding of 'letting go', compelling us to seize our inherent role as the true directors of our lives. He implores us to break free from the burdensome shackles of futile attempts at control, particularly over those elements that reside beyond our influence. Instead, he urges us to channel our efforts towards the territory we truly govern – our personal desires and decisions. This profound shift in focus heralds an era of liberation and empowerment, ultimately illuminating the path to authentic happiness.

In the ebb and flow of our daily lives, we are often swept away by fanciful daydreams where our loved ones, friends, and yes, even our adorable pets, luxuriate in an idyllic bubble of eternal joy and tranquillity, unscathed by the unyielding march of time. Stepping back into the comforting arms of reality, we can make use of Epictetus's sage wisdom as a guiding light. Imagine, if you will, the spectacle of trying to nail jelly to a tree or daringly attempting to strap an eel to a snowboard. Ridiculous as these scenarios might seem, they cleverly illuminate the sheer absurdity of our attempts to grasp what is, in essence, ungraspable. These metaphors may be comical in their depiction, yet they hold a profound truth. In the same vein, the wisdom of Epictetus encourages us to question our often misguided attempts at control, highlighting the necessity of accepting and embracing the uncertain, ephemeral, and often slippery nature of life. Rather than squandering energy on the elusive, Epictetus proposes a transformative redirection of focus. By harnessing our own desires and choices, we can emancipate ourselves from the iron chains of disappointment and frustration that inevitably bind us when we strive to manipulate the winds of external circumstances.

Imagine this common predicament: Have you ever gazed enviously upon a colleague or acquaintance, marvelling at their seemingly flawless existence and secretly yearning to mirror such perfection in your own life? Brace yourself for a serving of reality, steeped in the wisdom of Epictetus. He suggests that this pursuit of vicarious perfection is as fruitful as instructing unicorns to frolic down Main Street in harmonious synchronisation – a whimsical vision that, though charming, is unlikely to materialise. Instead, Epictetus nudges us to recognise our own power, not in orchestrating others' actions but in fine-tuning our desires. By aligning these desires with our true selves, we can derive satisfaction from nurturing them and reflecting our authenticity.

As we forge ahead on this philosophical expedition, we encounter a revelation potent enough to topple the foundations of our conventional perceptions of personal freedom. Epictetus unearths the undeniable truth of our autonomy, emphasising that we alone hold the reins to our desires and fears. You, dear reader, are not merely a passive participant in the theatre of life. You are the scriptwriter, the director, the lead actor – the architect of your destiny, wielding the power to mould your life. Why then, entrust your hopes and fears, the intimate ingredients of your life, to the whims of unpredictable external factors? The analogy is as simple as this: permitting a stranger to dictate your pizza toppings. While you might not detest the resulting culinary creation, it's unlikely to satiate your specific cravings. As an enthusiastic aficionado of pepperoni, why gamble with a potential avalanche of unwanted anchovies? Epictetus compellingly argues that by grasping the reins of our desires and fears, we unlock the door to true autonomy, setting in motion our journey towards fulfilment and happiness.

By accepting Epictetus' profound philosophy, we stumble upon a comforting truth that shatters the illusions of external control. We are not mere puppets, but the master puppeteers of our lives. The trajectory of our journey, the course we chart, is defined by our personal desires and decisions, and not swayed by the unpredictable currents of external circumstances. Through his teachings, Epictetus equips us with a philosophical compass, guiding us away from the fruitless pursuit of controlling the uncontrollable. Instead, he directs us towards the realm where we hold true control, ushering in a sense of liberation. This newfound autonomy clears the path to inner freedom, contentment, and genuine happiness—a path that is ours, and ours alone, to tread.

Here we are, at the juncture where philosophy becomes practice. We've savoured Epictetus' wisdom, now it's time to apply this taste to our own existence. The exercises that follow are your recipe, mixing ancient wisdom into the broth of everyday life. Ready to spice up your life? Let's move from understanding to experiencing, cooking up our own *Theory of Happiness*.

Our expedition begins with the "Wishful Thinking Audit". Consider this as a valuable opportunity to scrutinise your wish list. Compile a comprehensive list of your recurring desires, as wide-ranging as they may be—from yearning for a promotion to wanting your favourite football team to win the championship. After documenting these desires, conduct a self-audit, deciphering which of them hinge on the actions and choices of others. Reflect deeply on these dependencies. Could the longing for a promotion depend on your boss's decision? Perhaps, but could you instead focus on enhancing your skills or widening your knowledge, aspects that are firmly within your control? This crucial shift in perspective is the essence of this exercise—encouraging us to reorient our desires towards areas we can genuinely influence and nurture, thereby inviting a sense of empowerment into our lives.

We then embark upon the whimsically named "Pigs Can Fly Scenario", a delightful detour into the realm of fantasy to examine our often-unrealistic expectations of others. In this parallel universe, pigs, traditionally confined by gravity, display a surprising aptitude for flight, flapping their little wings as effortlessly as the neighbourhood sparrows. As comical as this image may seem, it underscores the stark reality of our sometimes extravagant expectations. Pigs flying might be an amusing concept, but expecting flawlessness from our fellow humans is equally absurd. Through this exercise, we are encouraged to release these unrealistic expectations, promoting acceptance of the beautiful, albeit imperfect, mosaic of human nature.

The journey continues with the "Boss of Me" exercise, nudging us to delve into the recesses of our subconscious and confront a desire or fear that we've unwittingly surrendered control of to someone else. Whether it's a fear of judgement or a desire for approval, this exercise presents an opportunity to reclaim control over these deeply personal aspects. Imagine creating a strategic roadmap, delineating steps to repossess control in that specific area. The exercise encourages us to visualise ourselves asserting our autonomy, making empowered choices, and moulding the outcomes to reflect our authentic desires. The underlying message is empowering—we are not destined to be passive spectators in our lives but the unequivocal authors of our destiny.

Our voyage culminates with the "Desire Controller" exercise. Here, we are asked to single out a current desire that persistently occupies our thoughts, perhaps a longing for recognition or the pursuit of a particular goal. The task is to formulate a strategy to manage this desire, maintaining focus solely on aspects within our control. Just as a master tailor painstakingly crafts a suit to fit perfectly, we can tailor our desires to the contours of our life's unique circumstances. By channelling our energy towards aspects within our purview, we experience a newfound sense of agency and satisfaction.

Having traversed these exercises, bear in mind that each act aligned with Epictetus' wisdom brings us closer to a life reflecting philosophical insights. Philosophy isn't merely an abstract concept; it's a tangible framework for life. The real significance of these teachings isn't only in understanding them but in applying them. Treat these exercises as your beacon, lighting your way towards a life shaped by wisdom. As you navigate, you'll discern that philosophy isn't just examined, but lived.

Wrapping this up, Epictetus teaches us the art of letting go and embracing our true power as the captains of our own lives. Through his teachings, we come to recognise the futility of attempting to control the uncontrollable, and instead, we redirect our focus towards what lies within our realm of influence—our own desires and choices.

Epictetus imparts practical wisdom, providing us with tools that we can incorporate into our daily lives. By engaging in these practices, we embark on a path of self-discovery, autonomy, and fulfillment. We learn to navigate the intricacies of our desires, distinguishing between those that align with our true selves and those that are mere distractions. Through this discernment, we gain the clarity and inner strength to pursue our authentic passions and aspirations.

Embracing Epictetus's teachings liberates us from the burden of excessive control and external dependencies. We release the need to micromanage every aspect of our lives, understanding that true empowerment comes from taking ownership of our own choices and actions. We become conscious creators of our own destinies, shaping our lives in accordance with our values, aspirations, and innermost desires.

In this journey, we witness an extraordinary transformation unfold within ourselves. We experience a deep sense of liberation and empowerment as we relinquish the illusion of control over external circumstances. By nurturing our desires and making conscious choices, we align ourselves with our authentic selves and cultivate a profound sense of fulfillment.

Therefore, my fellow seekers of wisdom, let us embrace the profound revelation bestowed upon us by Epictetus. Let us step into our roles as the masters of our own destinies, releasing the need for excessive control and surrendering to the flow of life. Through the practice of mindful discernment and conscious decision-making, we embark on a remarkable journey of self-discovery and personal growth.

In this pursuit, we uncover the true essence of our being and embrace our inherent power to shape our lives. We become active participants in our own narratives, weaving a tapestry of purpose, autonomy, and fulfillment. With Epictetus as our guide, we unlock the boundless potential within us, unleashing a transformation that radiates throughout every aspect of our existence.

As we navigate the vast expanse of life, may we remember the wisdom of Epictetus and embrace our own agency in shaping our destinies. Let us release the burdens of excessive control and instead focus on nurturing our desires and making conscious choices. By doing so, we step into the fullness of our authentic selves, experiencing liberation and fulfillment. With

Epictetus's teachings as our compass, we navigate the journey of self-discovery, embracing the incredible power we possess to create lives of purpose, autonomy, and personal growth.

15

Feasting with Wisdom

Remember that you must behave as at a banquet. Is anything brought round to you? Put out your hand and take a moderate share. Does it pass by you? Do not stop it. Is it not yet come? Do not yearn in desire toward it, but wait till it reaches you. So, with regard to children, wife, office, riches; and you will some time or other be worthy to feast with the gods. And if you do not so much as take the things which are set before you, but are able even to forego them, then you will not only be worthy to feast with the gods, but to rule with them also. For, by thus doing, Diogenes and Heraclitus, and others like them, deservedly became divine, and were so recognised.

Welcome to the grand exploration of Epictetus's banquet, a philosophical banquet teeming with vibrant and diverse life experiences that symbolise the dynamic opportunities life presents.

Sit yourself down at a lavishly adorned dining table, where an enticing spread of mouth-watering dishes awaits your attention. Each dish, in its unique culinary character, represents a distinct facet of life's opportunities and experiences. Let's consider the creamy mashed potatoes, their velvety texture and comforting taste perhaps symbolising the reassuring and comforting aspects of our lives, like close-knit relationships or a stable career. As this dish of familiarity comes your way, feel free to relish a generous helping. Savour the taste, the comfort it brings, and the feelings of contentment it evokes.

But this banquet of life isn't just about enjoying what's served to you. It's also about reciprocating, passing the gravy boat along to your fellow diners, sharing the flavoursome sauce that adds depth to the meal. This act, while small in a literal sense, carries significant implications for how we live our lives. It's about acknowledging others' needs, respecting their desires, and cultivating an environment that fosters mutual enjoyment. The person who hoards the gravy, be it at the dining table or life itself, is far from admired. Their actions spoil the harmony of the communal feast, much like those who monopolise opportunities and resources create discord in the symphony of life.

Similarly, let's explore the fiery allure of the spicy chicken wings, a vibrant dish that may serve as a metaphor for audacious and thrilling opportunities life occasionally presents. These may lie tantalisingly out of reach, evoking an impulsive urge to lunge across the table, to seize the moment before it escapes. But Epictetus urges patience, a virtue echoed through the ages. Remain present, engaging in the rich tapestry of dialogue and experience unfolding around you. Trust that these enticing opportunities, like the spicy chicken wings, will find their way to you when the time is right.

The banquet table's limits extend far beyond its physical boundaries, becoming a microcosm for our lives. From the depths of personal relationships to the lofty heights of our career aspirations, and the vast landscape of our financial pursuits, the 'banquet' mindset encourages us to embrace life's myriad possibilities. By adopting this mindset, we are not only guests but also the maestros of this grand banquet, orchestrating our destiny and engaging in enlightening discussions that expand our perspectives.

Now, let's venture further into the philosophical feast. Epictetus introduces a deeper layer: the concept of restraint and self-discipline. Envision a monk in a sweet shop, surrounded by endless confectionery yet remaining calm, composed, and in control of his desires. By embodying this level of discipline, we can ascend to a celestial league, joining the ranks of revered philosophers like Diogenes and Heraclitus, who not only preached but genuinely lived these virtues. This discipline, this divine self-control, delivers a satisfaction that outlasts and outshines the fleeting pleasure of even the most sumptuous dessert.

In essence, Epictetus's philosophy encourages us to realise that true fulfilment and inner peace lie not in ceaselessly pursuing our desires but in mastering the art of self-control. By applying discipline and moderation to our actions and desires, we elevate ourselves, stepping onto a higher plane of existence. This journey to self-mastery requires patience, curiosity, and respect for timing as we navigate through life's rich buffet. As we savour each moment's richness, cultivate gratitude, and make choices that align with the greater good, we find deep joy in the harmonious symphony of shared experiences. We don't merely partake in life's grand banquet; we become a pivotal part of it, fostering a balanced and fulfilling existence.

Once again, we're at the stage where comprehension ushers in application. We've navigated the seas of Epictetus' wisdom, now it's time to dock these insights into our harbor. The exercises that follow are your anchor, grounding philosophical notions into the reality of modern living. Ready to set sail? Let's voyage from knowledge to practice, steering our *Theory of Happiness*.

The curtain rises with our first exercise titled "Life's Buffet Simulation". Picture yourself at life's grand buffet, where every experience or challenge you encounter over the course of a week is a tantalising dish ready to be sampled. Perhaps the sticky toffee pudding represents a sticky situation at work, or the plate of bountiful salad mirrors the rich tapestry of your personal relationships. Whichever dish lands on your plate, the trick is to observe your reactions and adjust them in alignment with Epictetus's sage advice. By consciously tailoring our responses, we begin to savour the depth, richness, and complexity imbued in each morsel of life's grand buffet.

Following this, we dive into the "Patience Game". It is human nature to eagerly anticipate things, our minds often teetering on the brink of tomorrow, casting long shadows on the present. In this exercise, we invite you to harness the power of patience. Be it yearning for a promotion or the sweet apple pie that caps a hearty meal, resist the urge to fast-forward time. Instead, breathe, ground yourself in the present, and learn to appreciate the blessings you currently hold. This exercise paves the way to contentment and fosters a nurturing habitat for gratitude to flourish.

Next, we encounter the "Celestial League Tryouts". In this engaging exercise, we ask you to pinpoint a temptation or desire that often sways you off your path. Maybe it's the pull of the smartphone during a conversation, or the siren call of that extra slice of cake when you're already full. Whatever it is, commit to sidestepping this temptation for a set period. Revel in the emancipation that unfurls from practicing self-discipline, savouring the sweet taste of liberation from transient pleasures.

Lastly, there's "The Celestial Playlist", a delightful exercise where you imagine yourself as a celestial DJ, curating a playlist for a divine gathering of enlightened beings. This is more than just a compilation of songs; it's a mirror to your soul. Reflect on how your chosen melodies mirror your current mindset and values. How does the rhythm of your life resonate with these tunes? This exercise encourages you to delve into your internal rhythms, allowing you to better align your choices with your authentic self.

Upon wrapping up these exercises, keep in mind that every choice steeped in Epictetus' philosophy is a step closer to a life enriched with wisdom. Philosophy isn't simply an intellectual pursuit; it's a practical guide for living. The true power of these teachings lies not just in comprehending them but in embracing them. View these exercises as your milestones, guiding you towards a mindful life. As you press on, you'll discover that philosophy isn't just learned, but lived.

To summarise, Epictetus's teachings encompass the profound notion of perceiving life as a grand banquet. He advocates for the practice of moderation and patience, urging us to embrace shared experiences and cultivate self-control. Through his philosophy, we are reminded of the importance of considering the needs of others and patiently awaiting opportunities, rather than impulsively chasing after them. By fully immersing ourselves in life's experiences and appreciating the intricate tapestry they weave, we are invited to partake in the banquet of life with a genuine sense of awe and gratitude.

In the grand scheme of things, Epictetus's philosophy serves as a guiding light, encouraging us to cultivate moderation, patience, and gratitude as we engage in life's magnificent feast. He beckons us to savour each bite-sized experience, relishing the exquisite company of others, and nurturing the belief that our desires will manifest in their perfect time. Through the practice of self-restraint and mindful awareness, we lay the foundation for a fulfilling and meaningful existence, ensuring our place at life's abundant banquet table, where contentment awaits.

Let us raise our glasses in celebration of the precious moments we have and the vibrant tapestry of life that unfurls before us. Let us savour each delectable moment, embracing the richness of the present and the boundless possibilities that lie ahead. With Epictetus as our guide, we embark on a journey of mindful indulgence, where every experience becomes a source of nourishment for our souls. In this banquet of life, let us cultivate moderation, patience, and gratitude, cherishing the intricate flavours and textures that intertwine to create a symphony of existence.

In the banquet of life, let's nourish not just our senses, but also our heart's virtues. Honouring Epictetus, let's embody moderation, patience, and gratitude, cherishing each moment. By valuing life's richness and our connections, we elevate our existence to a divine feast. Let's partake mindfully and appreciatively, deserving of the divine.

16

Harmonising Empathy

When you see anyone weeping for grief, either that his son has gone abroad or that he has suffered in his affairs, take care not to be overcome by the apparent evil, but discriminate and be ready to say, "What hurts this man is not this occurrence itself—for another man might not be hurt by it—but the view he chooses to take of it." As far as conversation goes, however, do not disdain to accommodate yourself to him and, if need be, to groan with him. Take heed, however, not to groan inwardly, too.

We now step onto the stage of a transformational journey aimed at refining our emotional intelligence and mastering the art of empathetic support. Our esteemed philosopher and life coach, Epictetus, will conduct us through the symphony of wisdom surrounding the art of empathetic resonance.

Envision someone in the grip of sorrow's storm, their emotions churning like an ocean in the throes of a tempest. They may be grappling with the poignant farewell of their child departing for university, an event that has emptied the nest and filled the heart with echoing silence. Alternatively, they might be confronting a significant professional setback, an event that has tumbled their meticulously arranged world into disarray.

However, before we plunge ourselves into this sea of emotional turbulence, Epictetus ushers in a moment of philosophical clarity: it's not the event itself that triggers these torrents of tears, but rather, the individual's perception of it. What one person perceives as a calamitous storm could be merely a drizzle to another, underscoring the inherently subjective nature of our emotional responses.

Navigating the intricate world of human interaction and friendship often demands a careful balancing act, akin to a tightrope walker's daring feats above an awe-struck crowd. Yet, in Epictetus' orchestra, he doesn't advocate for emotional Stoicism or the repression of feelings. Although it's vital to offer a compassionate ear and share in communal grief when appropriate, Epictetus suggests we consider it like a duet in a karaoke session. We are there to provide moral support and harmonise, not to mimic their sorrowful rendition of "My Heart Will Go On" note-for-note. Indeed, repeating every discordant note might culminate in a metaphorical exodus from the karaoke bar, defeating our noble intent of offering solace.

Now, imagine a friend passionately belting out the lyrics, "Every night in my dreams, I see you, I feeeeeeel you," in a key that grates on the ears. In your role as a supportive friend, the aim isn't to echo their dissonance but to provide a steadying hand, seizing moments of harmony and gently guiding them back on track—preferably in such a subtle way they remain blissfully unaware of your guidance.

Just as a skilled duet partner complements their singing partner's style without overshadowing it, your empathetic presence should synchronise with their emotional state, providing a soothing counterpoint to their emotional symphony. In preserving your emotional stability, you provide a calming presence and aid them in regaining their emotional equilibrium. The goal is to strike the right chord: offering comfort and guidance, all the while honouring and respecting their unique emotional journey.

When we encounter a friend ensnared by emotional distress, Epictetus advises us to resist the impulse to be swept into their emotional maelstrom. Stay anchored in your own emotional stability, offering comfort and support while keeping a firm grip on your individual perspective. Empathising with their pain is natural, but surrendering completely to their emotions risks undermining your ability to provide the support they need. In the same way that you wouldn't mirror their off-key singing, it's paramount not to replicate their emotional turmoil. We must acknowledge their experiences and emotions but maintain our clarity of mind and emotional equilibrium.

Mastering this art of empathetic resonance requires a blend of delicacy, self-awareness, and a deep understanding of Epictetus's philosophy. It involves striking a delicate balance between offering empathy and preserving personal boundaries. By tuning into others' emotions whilst ensuring our emotional stability, we can extend meaningful support and understanding. This mindful approach helps foster deeper connections, paving the way for a safe space for others to express themselves authentically.

As we venture forth on this transformative journey, let us always remember: the true beauty of empathetic support lies not in perfect replication, but in the harmonious symphony we create together.

We now reach the phase where thinking evolves into acting. We've waded through Epictetus' teachings, now it's time to let these insights ripple into our actions. The exercises that follow are your lifeline, connecting the depth of philosophy to the surface of daily life. Ready to make a splash? Let's transition from theorising to actualising, buoying our unique *Theory of Happiness*.

The "Mirror Not Sponge" challenge encourages us to respond empathetically when friends open up about their sorrows, while maintaining our emotional boundaries. This exercise transforms us into reflective mirrors, bouncing back empathy and understanding without soaking up the anguish of others. We're not designed to be emotional sponges, absorbing all the despair around us. Instead, we need to serve as mirrors reflecting empathy, thereby supporting others without drowning in their sea of grief. This exercise provides an invaluable shield to protect our emotional wellbeing while still offering meaningful support.

Next, we embark on a light-hearted journey in the "Karaoke Practice" challenge. Picture a lively karaoke session. Your duet partner misses a few notes, but instead of replicating their off-key warbling, you subtly guide the performance back on track. This musical metaphor extends to real-life emotional scenarios. It asks us to offer emotional support, to be there for others while retaining our emotional stability. Like a skilled duet partner who adjusts their voice to complement their singing mate, we can empathise without getting swept up in their emotional whirlwind.

The third exercise, the "Indifferent Incidents Diary", invites us to pen down experiences that have a significant impact on others but barely cause a ripple in our emotional reservoir. This simple act of documenting varied emotional reactions underscores the subjectivity of emotional responses. We learn that our emotional landscapes are profoundly individualistic, moulded by our unique experiences and perspectives. Reflecting on these disparities illuminates the intricacies of human emotions, fostering empathy, and deepening our understanding of others.

Our final expedition takes us to the "Emotional Cannonball" exercise. Imagine a series of bodies of water, each signifying a different emotional intensity. Standing on the edge, you choose your immersion level: a deep dive into turbulent emotions or a cautious toe-dip. This visualisation offers a valuable framework for setting emotional boundaries, providing a toolset to navigate emotional waters with resilience and balance. Much like deciding our level of immersion in water, we can determine how deeply we engage with emotionally intense experiences.

As we conclude these exercises, remember that each action guided by Epictetus brings us closer to a life suffused with wisdom. Philosophy isn't just a cerebral endeavour; it's a compass for thoughtful action. The true potency of these teachings doesn't lie merely in understanding them but in embodying them. See these exercises as your roadmap, charting the course towards a life defined by wisdom. As you journey, you'll understand that philosophy isn't just intellectual, but integral.

In conclusion, we have delved into the intricate interplay of shared emotional experiences, emphasising the importance of preserving our individuality while finding harmonious connections with others. As we embark on a journey of growth and learning, we equip ourselves with the necessary tools to forge meaningful relationships, fostering a deep understanding of others while safeguarding our own emotional well-being. By integrating Epictetus's teachings into our lives, we gain valuable insights into the art of balanced empathy and the transformative power of emotional resilience.

Epictetus's wisdom reminds us of the vital significance of maintaining emotional equilibrium. This balanced approach allows us to cultivate profound and empathetic connections without losing sight of our own emotional boundaries. By applying these teachings in our daily lives, we nurture our emotional intelligence, establish healthy personal limits, deepen our comprehension of diverse emotional responses, and offer meaningful support to others without becoming overwhelmed by their emotional burdens.

In essence, Epictetus invites us to embrace the delicate dance between empathy and self-preservation. As we navigate the intricate tapestry of shared emotions, let us carry with us the invaluable lessons we have learned—lessons that enable us to authentically connect with others while preserving our emotional stability. By internalising these teachings, we cultivate a profound sense of balance, enabling us to gracefully and wisely navigate the labyrinth of emotions that life presents us with.

May our journeys blend compassion and self-care, fostering deep connections while nurturing our emotional health. Guided by Epictetus, we honour individuality and interconnectedness, weaving empathy and self-preservation into an emotionally resilient tapestry. Embrace the power of balanced empathy, enriching both our relationships and ourselves.

17

Navigating Life's Grand Theatre

Remember that you are an actor in a drama of such sort as the Author chooses—if short, then in a short one; if long, then in a long one. If it be his pleasure that you should enact a poor man, or a cripple, or a ruler, or a private citizen, see that you act it well. For this is your business—to act well the given part, but to choose it belongs to another.

Let's now delve into the philosophy of Epictetus, not by leafing through dusty philosophical manuscripts, but by embracing the lively, energetic realm of a theatre narrative. In the great spectacle that is life, picture yourself as an active participant, not merely a bystander – you are a performer.

Whether you're a seasoned thespian, or an aspiring debutant stepping onto the stage of existence, your experiences – your victories, challenges, and learnings – bestow upon your character a unique depth that a pre-written script could never embody. Your life isn't a rehearsal. It's the main event. Your actions and experiences lend your character a distinct and authentic feel that transcends any playwright's imagination.

Pause for a moment as you step onto this cosmic stage, your heart beating in sync with the rhythm of life. Take a look around you, taking in the grandeur of this cosmic amphitheatre. You are a key player in this incredible narrative, a narrative not authored by you, but by a grand designer who writes the story of life. Indeed, life is an enthralling play, engaging and packed with unexpected twists.

The grand theatre of life offers a variety of roles—some significant, others seemingly minor, but all leaving a mark. You might be in the spotlight for a short but powerful cameo, creating a lasting impression, like a spark lighting up the night sky before vanishing, leaving only awe behind. Your actions in this brief moment can spark inspiration and cause spectators to reflect long after the stage lights dim and the curtains fall.

You might be the lead in an epic tale, with your life unfolding like a riveting drama packed with highs and lows. This journey doesn't just shape your destiny, but also influences the lives of those connected to yours.

Picture yourself as a tenacious underdog, wrestling with challenges and standing victorious. Your story could motivate others by showing that victory is possible, even in the face of adversity. You could also be that delightful comic relief, the clown whose hilarious antics bring joy and laughter to everyone, reminding us all to seek the humour in life's twists and turns.

Further imagine yourself as a high-flying executive, making industry-reshaping decisions in lofty boardrooms. Then again, perhaps you're an Average Joe, leading a life filled with mundane tasks punctuated by moments of simple joy, such as cooking instant noodles to perfection. Regardless of the magnitude of your role, it's vital in the grand narrative of life.

Here's where Epictetus's wisdom comes into play: see yourself not as the puppet master controlling the story, but as a passionate actor. Your aim isn't to control the story but to wholeheartedly accept the role given to you and perform it to the best of your abilities. From the start to the end, understand your role's nuances, embrace its strengths and weaknesses, and bring its unique qualities to life with authenticity and courage.

Keep Epictetus' wisdom close to your heart as you embark on this extraordinary journey. Your task isn't to rewrite your script, but to embrace your given role and perform it with gusto. So, tighten your metaphorical acting boots, step onto the grand stage of life with determination, and prepare for the performance of a lifetime. Remember, life isn't just about surviving—it's about fully living each role and making every act count.

Here we stand again on the border where reflection becomes action. We've wandered through Epictetus' philosophy, now it's time to plant these seeds into our life's garden. The exercises that follow are your gardening tools, embedding the wisdom into the soil of daily existence. Ready to harvest? Let's move from cognition to cultivation, growing our own *Theory of Happiness*.

Our first stop on this exercise tour is "The Role-Play Game". This imaginative activity invites you to craft a diverse range of roles on individual slips of paper. These roles can range from the heroic figure of a caped superhero to the courageous underdog, the wise elder, or the comedic jester. The full spectrum of life's rich tapestry is your oyster. Once you've compiled your roles, you will randomly select a slip, and your task for the day is to fully embody the chosen character in their attitudes, mannerisms, speech, and actions. By immersing yourself in a role that may be different from your usual self, you're not just kindling the sparks of creativity, but you're also expanding your capacity for empathy, as you momentarily step into someone else's shoes.

Next, we invite you to take part in "The Unexpected Audition". Picture life's unexpected events – be it a challenging work assignment that's landed on your desk or a sudden personal conflict – as auditions for roles you never anticipated playing. Instead of meeting these situations with trepidation or apprehension, view them as unique opportunities to showcase your adaptability, resilience, and strength. Let these moments stand as testament to your improvisational skills, your courage, and your grace under pressure.

We then journey to the "Standing Ovation Challenge", a weekly commitment to excel in a performance worthy of a hearty round of applause. Each week, identify a personal goal that demands your utmost dedication and commitment, a role that challenges you to rise to the occasion. This goal might involve learning a new skill, overcoming a fear, or resolving a personal conflict. Embrace this opportunity to shine, and when the week draws to a close, celebrate your achievement with a well-deserved standing ovation.

To round off our list of exercises, we propose an "Unplanned Improv" night with your nearest and dearest. This fun-filled activity involves assigning unanticipated roles to each participant, culminating in an impromptu performance filled with laughs and surprises. Immerse yourself in the joyful unpredictability of the moment, and later, take a moment to reflect on the experience, contemplating how it felt to embrace and perform these spontaneous roles. This exercise fosters a sense of camaraderie and playfulness, as well as flexibility and quick-thinking, which are invaluable traits in life's grand theatre.

At the end of these exercises, it's key to remember that every step inspired by Epictetus is a stride towards a life enlightened by wisdom. Philosophy isn't just a theoretical discourse; it's a pragmatic guide for life. The real strength of these teachings isn't just in grasping them but in translating them into action. Consider these exercises as your guide, leading you towards a more enlightened life. As you move forward, you'll comprehend that philosophy isn't just a subject, but a way of life.

As we conclude and you return to the grand stage of life, it is essential to recall Epictetus's guiding words. While you might not always have the privilege of choosing your part in the grand narrative of life, you possess the remarkable power to deliver a performance that is both genuine and impactful. With unwavering confidence, an unwavering commitment to authenticity, and a readiness to breathe life into each role, you can approach the stage of life with purpose and passion.

Embrace the unique journey that lies before you, delving into the depths of your character and exploring the boundless possibilities of your existence. Let your performance radiate with inspiration, uplifting not only yourself but also those fortunate enough to witness your artistry. Remember that it is not solely about the role you play but the way in which you bring it to life.

Embody the teachings of Epictetus as you navigate the ever-changing scenes of your life's play. Infuse your actions with integrity, empathy, and a profound sense of purpose. With each interaction and decision, aim to make a lasting impact, leaving a positive imprint on the hearts and minds of those who share the stage with you.

And when the curtains finally close, take a bow, acknowledging the beauty and significance of your contribution to the grand masterpiece that is life. Reflect on the journey you have undertaken, the growth you have experienced, and the connections you have forged. Celebrate the courage it took to step onto the stage, embracing both the challenges and the triumphs that have shaped your performance.

Therefore, my fellow actors of existence, go forth with confidence, passion, and an unwavering commitment to authenticity. Break a leg as you embrace the role you were destined to play, allowing your performance to illuminate the hearts and minds of others. May your presence on life's grand stage be a testament to the power of human expression and the transformative impact of living with purpose. Let your every act and word resonate with the depth of your character, for in doing so, you elevate the collective spirit of humanity. Bravo, my fellow thespians, as you embody the timeless wisdom of Epictetus and embark on a journey of self-discovery, growth, and profound happiness.

18

Balancing Chaos

When a raven happens to croak unluckily, be not overcome by appearances, but discriminate and say, "Nothing is portended to me, either to my paltry body, or property, or reputation, or children, or wife. But to me all portents are lucky if I will. For whatsoever happens, it belongs to me to derive advantage therefrom."

Ready yourself to unlock your inner reservoir of strength and resilience, for we are about to set sail on an unconventional journey that will capture the imagination of even those who find their daily lives profoundly intertwined with the avian kingdom. Allow your mind to take wing, transporting you into the stirring midst of a raven's domain. Its calls, bone-chilling in their intensity, reverberate with uncanny notes, potent enough to awaken the creative muse of master story-teller Alfred Hitchcock. One can easily imagine him drawing on such inspiration to weave the narrative of a spine-tingling sequel to his classic, 'The Birds'.

However, before the raven's dissonant aria can unsettle your tranquillity, let's turn to the teachings of our Stoic philosopher, Epictetus. In the face of this jarring avian serenade, imbue within yourself a mantra of persistence and optimism: "This clamour does not portend my downfall. On the contrary, I stand as the undaunted optimist, the resplendent sunbeam that penetrates even the most ominous, darkest clouds. Whether I am grappling with a tempestuous storm or a blistering heatwave, whether my path crosses with scornful crows or melodious canaries, I possess the remarkable ability to transform adversity into triumphant victory".

At the heart of this philosophy is not the mere act of drowning out life's dissonant sounds, but rather the more creative endeavour of reshaping them. Could the crow's relentless cawing not be an urgent alarm bell, a noisy nudge pushing us to tackle tasks that have been gathering dust on the shelves of procrastination? Or perhaps it's nature's unconventional method of serenading us with a boisterous, albeit strident, live symphony for our auditory pleasure. The choice is ultimately yours—to tune into the frequency of positivity and elevate its resonance until the raw, grating caws slowly transmute into a motivational anthem that invigorates your spirit.

Visualise the crow's harsh calls as emblematic of life's many hurdles and tribulations. Instead of allowing them to discourage or overwhelm us, we can opt to regard them as propellants for personal evolution and transformation. Just as the crow's startling caw disrupts our complacency, catapulting us into a heightened state of awareness, life's challenges too can jolt us into action. They can coerce us to face procrastinated tasks with resolve and determination. This paradigm shift enables us to reinterpret disturbances as opportunities for growth, empowering us to flourish even amidst adversity.

The crow's cawing also serves as nature's poignant reminder of life's unpredictable dynamism and diversity. It might lack the mellifluous sweetness of the canary's song or the soothing lullaby of the dove's coo, but it is a unique and genuine testament to the world's rich tapestry of sounds. By receiving this raucous chorus as an orchestration of nature's notes, we can foster a sense of awe and wonder even amidst the most dissonant and unexpected moments. This shift in perception encourages us to wholeheartedly embrace the present, to express gratitude for the varied hues of life's experiences, regardless of their initial jarring manifestation.

The inherent power to reshape our perception of the crow's caw, or indeed any life's challenges, resides within each one of us. It's a transformative ability, a mental agility, that we can harness to bring a nuanced shift in our outlook. The crow's caw, a mere auditory sensation, can be a morning alarm, a melody, or a discordant noise, all depending on the listener's chosen perspective.

Similarly, when faced with life's challenges, we possess the capacity to heighten the resonance of positivity and resilience within us. We can consciously decide to fuel our internal echo chamber not with sounds of defeat but with a resounding, uplifting rhythm of perseverance.

We are granted the option to adopt an optimistic mindset, a mindset that paints trials not as intimidating obstacles but as stepping stones. These stepping stones, albeit a little rough underfoot, can lead us across the turbulent river of hardships to the lush greens of new prospects, untapped opportunities, and personal growth.

Every challenge we face, every hardship we endure, can serve as a mason's chisel, shaping our character and refining our spirit. The friction may cause temporary discomfort, but the end result is a polished gem, our resilience, reflecting the radiant spectrum of our personal growth and triumph.

It is within our hands, our minds, and our hearts, to transmute the seemingly discordant chords of life into a harmonious symphony. A symphony that may begin with the raw cacophony of struggle but eventually settles into an uplifting melody that sings the triumphant verses of our growth, our resilience, and our victory. This harmony is the real music of life, echoing with the tones of trials and the refrains of triumph. It's up to us to conduct this symphony, to choose the notes and orchestrate the melodies that will define our life's soundtrack.

We're back at the turning point, where contemplation transforms into practice. We've feasted on Epictetus' wisdom, now it's time to metabolise these nutrients into our lives. The upcoming exercises are your enzymes, breaking down the complex philosophy into digestible actions. Ready for the process? Let's transition from ingestion to assimilation, nourishing our *Theory of Happiness*.

The first exercise on this transformative journey is the "Flip the Script Game". This exercise invites us to view life's obstacles through a fresh lens, seeking out the silver linings that are often concealed beneath the surface. Imagine, for instance, the aggravation that ensues when you encounter a flat tyre during your commute home. Instead of capitulating to frustration, perceive this momentary pause as a serendipitous opportunity to savour the beauty of a glorious sunset. Such natural spectacles are often overlooked in the perpetual haste of our modern lives. This reframing exercise helps us in metamorphosing a potentially vexing situation into a tranquil moment of reflection.

The "Dance Off the Jitters" exercise introduces a playful way to manage anxiety. When engulfed by a wave of anxious energy, we are challenged to channel this into an impromptu dance. This exercise allows us to transform our nervous energy into an expression of joy and vitality, thereby liberating us from the clutches of anxiety. By engaging in this exercise, we can turn stress into a catalyst for creative expression, reminding us that we are capable of controlling our emotional responses and restoring our mental balance.

The "Positivity Jar" exercise invites us to cultivate a habit of recognising the positive outcomes that emerge from unexpected or challenging situations. Each day, we jot down one such positive experience and place it in a jar. Over time, this jar metamorphoses into a tangible testament to our resilience and resourcefulness, a collection of personal triumphs that we can revisit during moments of self-doubt or despair. This activity reinforces the idea that every challenge harbours within it an opportunity for personal growth and progress.

Our final exercise equips us with "Optimist's Glasses". These metaphorical glasses are not worn on our noses, but rather fitted onto our minds. They enable us to peer beyond the superficial difficulties presented by life's obstacles, unearthing hidden opportunities for self-improvement and personal development. The "Optimist's Glasses" empower us to perceive every situation, no matter how challenging, as a potential avenue for growth and learning.

Having completed these exercises, bear in mind that each action anchored in Epictetus' wisdom moves us closer to a life steeped in philosophical insights. Philosophy isn't a purely intellectual exercise; it's a practical guide for meaningful living. The true significance of these teachings isn't only in understanding them but in living them out. Treat these exercises as your compass, pointing the way towards a life of wisdom. As you persist, you'll realise that philosophy is not just analysed, but actualised.

As we bring this to a close, let us take a moment to reflect on the sagacious wisdom of Epictetus. Life's symphony, with its myriad experiences, may at times be filled with discordant squawks and cacophonous cries. However, it is our responsibility to uncover the underlying rhythm amidst the noise, to identify the hidden opportunities that lie veiled within each setback, and to discern the latent positivity amidst the chaotic melee.

Epictetus's teachings highlight the empowering potential of shifting our perspectives towards life's trials and tribulations. He invites us to seek out positivity even in the face of adversity, encouraging us to view setbacks not as insurmountable impediments, but rather as unconventional pathways that lead to unseen opportunities for growth. It is through this conscious choice to align ourselves with resilience and positivity that we acquire the remarkable ability to transmute even the most grating and dissonant notes of life's symphony into a harmonious anthem of victory and personal development.

By embracing Epictetus's philosophy, we equip ourselves with the tools to navigate life's challenges with grace and fortitude. We learn to cultivate a resilient mindset, capable of reframing setbacks as valuable learning experiences and catalysts for growth. Instead of succumbing to despair or allowing negativity to consume us, we adopt a proactive approach that seeks out the silver linings and transformative possibilities within every situation.

Through this intentional perspective shift, we unlock the capacity to transform adversities into catalysts for personal evolution. We come to recognise that beneath the surface noise and chaos, there lies a hidden tapestry of wisdom, strength, and opportunity. By actively seeking out these hidden gems, we tap into our innate power to shape our own narratives and create a symphony of triumph and growth.

Therefore, let us heed the wisdom of Epictetus as we navigate the symphony of life. With a steadfast commitment to resilience and a positive outlook, we embrace the challenges and dissonance as invitations for growth and transformation. We harmonise the seemingly discordant notes of life, skilfully weaving them together to create a powerful and triumphant melody. As we journey through the orchestra of existence, may we realise the empowering potential that lies within us to transmute adversity into personal strength, turning life's trials into opportunities for fulfillment and personal growth. Let us conduct this symphony of life with resilience, courage, and a profound appreciation for the transformative power of embracing life's challenges.

19

Dancing with Invincibility

You can be unconquerable if you enter into no combat in which it is not in your own power to conquer. When, therefore, you see anyone eminent in honours or power, or in high esteem on any other account, take heed not to be bewildered by appearances and to pronounce him happy; for if the essence of good consists in things within our own power, there will be no room for envy or emulation. But, for your part, do not desire to be a general, or a senator, or a consul, but to be free; and the only way to this is a disregard of things which lie not within our own power.

As we continue the journey to become masters of our own destinies, picture yourself strolling into an 'All You Can Eat' contest at your favourite local pizza parlour. The air is thick with the scent of cheesy delight and your confidence is soaring, almost as if you have a bottomless pit for a stomach that can compete with the never-ending depths of a cosmic black hole. This is akin to life's battles where the crux is knowing when to take up arms and when to step back. You approach the pizza buffet just like life's myriad challenges, applying discernment in your choices, picking the battles you know you can triumph over. In both cases, it's about knowing your strengths, your weaknesses, your limits, and then using this understanding to carve out a victorious path for yourself.

Next, envision someone basking in the limelight, receiving waves of admiration like a parched desert eagerly absorbing the first rain of monsoon. It's an innate human tendency to feel a twinge of envy, like a tiny seed threatening to sprout into a rampant green-eyed monster. However, before capitulating to this universal impulse, take a moment to breathe deeply, engaging your internal Zen mode. Remember, true happiness blooms from the fertile soil within you; it doesn't rely on external validation or material acquisitions. This serene state of being blossoms when your actions and thoughts are in harmony with your deeply-held values. Instead of inviting envy to cast a shadow on your peace, savour the richness of your unique journey. Honour the path paved with personal experiences and lessons, for it navigates you towards a fulfilling destination shaped by your aspirations.

Epictetus propounds the idea of shifting our desires away from the captivating aura of power, charm, and wealth that often surrounds prominent figures. Instead, he recommends focusing on a deeper, more rewarding target - freedom. This freedom isn't a guest at the glamorous banquet of external success but dwells within the quiet solitude of our thoughts, emotions, and reactions. It's the art of handling life's hurdles with graceful equanimity, unperturbed by the whirlwinds of external circumstances. By concentrating our energy on nurturing resilience, fostering gratitude, and enhancing self-awareness, we unlock the true essence of freedom. It's a treasure found not in the glistening mirage of transient worldly allurements but within the inner recesses of our being.

Staring at the towering mountain of infinite desires can be as daunting and precarious as an uninvited wrestling match with a grizzly bear. The odds may appear overwhelming, and disappointment might lurk menacingly in the shadows. However, when we refocus our gaze towards the more navigable mound of achievable aspirations, the terrifying grizzly bear combat metamorphoses into a friendly tussle with a teddy bear. This analogy is not meant to trivialise our aspirations, but to underscore that the essence of success isn't tied solely to the fulfilment of external desires. Rather, it lies in our ability to cultivate inner virtues, make significant personal strides, and maintain equanimity in the face of life's inevitable challenges. The pursuit of personal growth, nurturing of enriching relationships, and mastering our reactions - these become the milestones that redefine victory in life's grand game.

By wisely choosing our battles, focusing on inner development, and ensuring our actions resonate with our core values, we step closer to invincibility. We uncover a deeper understanding of victory, one that transcends superficial achievements to embody a state of genuine contentment, purpose, and authenticity. Epictetus's teachings illuminate the path to this inner victory. Like a lighthouse guiding lost ships towards safe shores, they beckon us to embark on an enriching journey towards self-mastery and fulfilment.

Once more, we reach that spot where thought gives rise to action. We've dived deep into Epictetus' wisdom, now it's time to surface these treasures into our reality. The exercises to follow are your treasure map, charting the course from profound depths to practical applications. Ready for the adventure? Let's sail from wisdom acquisition to wisdom application, enriching our *Theory of Happiness*.

First up on our interactive agenda is the "Battle-Chooser Bonanza". This exercise invites you to establish a daily habit of selecting a challenge you're supremely confident of conquering. It could be as uncomplicated as resisting the seductive allure of the snooze button, or as ambitious as preparing a nutrient-rich kale salad for lunch. The core premise is to pick a challenge that aligns with your personal ambitions and values. By intentionally deciding on battles where the likelihood of victory is high, you not only get to savour the gratification of success, but you also cultivate a sense of self-belief and resilience that radiates into all other areas of your life. The goal is not solely to enjoy the triumphant outcome but also to relish the celebratory dance that follows, commemorating your adeptness at gracefully navigating life's myriad challenges.

Our next stop is the "No Green-Eyed Monster Fiesta". Imagine dedicating an entire day to celebrate a life devoid of envy, a life where jealousy is conspicuously absent. As you immerse yourself in the love, joy, and prosperity that already colour your life, any traces of the green-eyed monster will recede, much like a timid wallflower that inadvertently stumbled into a vivacious Zumba class. This exercise encourages you to foster gratitude and appreciation for your blessings, thereby promoting a mindset of abundance rather than scarcity. By refocusing your attention on the blessings and achievements sprinkled throughout your life, you forge a positive and empowering perspective that lifts your spirit and bolsters your overall well-being.

Now, let's unlock our creativity with the "Freedom Manifesto". Seize your favourite pen and a sheet of paper and begin to list all the things within your control that contribute to your sweet, cherished freedom. Reflect on elements like your Stoic demeanour when facing adversity, your adaptable attitude that warmly welcomes change, and your unwavering commitment to personal growth and self-improvement. This exercise nudges you to introspect on areas where you hold influence and encourages you to take charge of your life. By acknowledging and nurturing these qualities, you lay the foundation for a sense of freedom that rises above the transitory nature of external circumstances. It's your bespoke guide to liberation, a personal recipe for independence that empowers you to flourish and live life on your own terms.

Finally, let's put the "Chill Out Chant" to the test. Whenever you find yourself caught in the relentless hamster wheel of worry over something beyond your control, resort to a soothing mantra as your safety valve. Play with phrases like "I am the maestro of my actions and reactions" or "I control my vibe; I'm the DJ of my life." While it might sound cheesy, think of it as the extra dollop of mozzarella on your wisdom pizza—a delightful and empowering topping. This exercise invites you to cultivate a sense of inner peace and resilience when facing adversity. By consciously redirecting your thoughts and affirming your agency, you break free from worry and anxiety, thus enabling you to navigate life's challenges with an enhanced sense of ease and tranquillity.

As we wrap up these tasks, remember that each endeavour guided by Epictetus' teachings is a step towards a life illuminated by wisdom. Philosophy isn't merely a mental discipline; it's a guide for thoughtful living. The true value of these teachings isn't just in learning them but in living them. See these exercises as your map, leading you towards a wise and meaningful life. As you press on, you'll come to see that philosophy is not just contemplated but enacted.

In summary, Epictetus imparts profound teachings that invite us to redefine the concept of invincibility. It is not about overpowering physical challenges, but rather about discerning and selecting our battles wisely. By aligning ourselves with values that resonate deeply within us and focusing our energy on aspects within our sphere of influence, we cultivate a sense of personal empowerment and agency that transcends mere physical strength. This way of thinking not only sets the stage for success but also nurtures a profound inner strength and resilience.

Moreover, Epictetus emphasises the importance of directing our attention towards elements that are within our control. By shifting our focus to our responses, attitudes, and ongoing self-improvement, we can alleviate unnecessary worries and anxieties. This deliberate choice to prioritise the aspects of life that we can influence fosters a sense of inner peace, contentment, and satisfaction.

Lastly, Epictetus urges us to passionately pursue freedom, not as an external state governed by circumstances, but as an inner liberation from the bonds of societal expectations and irrational fears. This inner freedom, he asserts, is a priceless treasure that enriches our lives with profound depth and meaning. By transcending the limitations imposed by external forces and liberating ourselves from the shackles of societal pressures, we unlock the true essence of our being and embark on a journey of self-discovery and self-actualisation.

To encapsulate, Epictetus's teachings illuminate the path to genuine invincibility. It lies in the mindful selection of battles, the conscious cultivation of controllable factors, and the passionate pursuit of inner freedom. Embracing these teachings empowers us to navigate life's challenges with grace and adeptness, cultivating a sense of contentment, equilibrium, and unwavering strength. By internalising these principles, we awaken the potential within us to lead lives of purpose, fulfilment, and genuine invincibility. As we embrace these teachings, we unlock the doors to a life coloured by resilience, wisdom, and an unyielding spirit that transcends external circumstances.

20

Reframe, Pacify, Pause, Soothe

Remember that it is not he who gives abuse or blows, who affronts, but the view we take of these things as insulting. When, therefore, anyone provokes you, be assured that it is your own opinion which provokes you. Try, therefore, in the first place, not to be bewildered by appearances. For if you once gain time and respite, you will more easily command yourself.

Let's embark on a deeper exploration of Stoicism, a philosophical sanctuary where cutting remarks are blunted and your inner peace holds firm, immovable against the tide of external insults or affronts. Imagine yourself in the midst of a bustling scene: a disrespectful jibe is thrown your way, or perhaps an impolite individual launches a poorly executed affront towards you. Your instinctive reaction might be a swell of resentment, a potent surge of emotion driven by the primal need to uphold your dignity and respect.

However, it's in this crucial moment, teetering on the precipice of indignation, that the insightful wisdom of the Stoic philosopher Epictetus whispers to your heart. He gently reminds us that it's not the one causing the disruption that unsettles your peaceful waters. Rather, it's your personal interpretation, your mental processing of their uncivil behaviour that stirs the calm surface of your emotional sea. In reality, you wield the power to reframe their distasteful words or disrespectful actions into trivial incidents, robbing them of any profound influence or impact on your emotional well-being.

The next time your tranquil mind stands threatened by an unruly tempest, take a moment to recalibrate your internal equilibrium. Do so with the precision and calm of an experienced sailor deftly adjusting his sails amidst a storm. Consider the instigator of the disruption as nothing more than an overzealous child, full of sound and fury, but ultimately as harmless as a gentle summer rain. Always bear in mind, it's your reaction—or more specifically, your conscious non-reaction—that lends power to their actions.

Before the vortex of anger sweeps you up, remember to gift yourself a moment to pause, to quieten the stirring turmoil within. Breathe deeply, count slowly to ten, let each number pull you further from the precipice of anger. Better still, transport your mind to a place of serene beauty—a pristine sandy beach where palm trees rustle gently in the wind, a hammock sways invitingly, offering respite and relaxation, and a cool, tropical drink promises sweet relief from the heat. Let this soothing mental escape embrace your spirit, providing a calming refuge for your burgeoning emotions, diffusing them before they can erupt.

As you navigate the seas of life, always remember that you are the master of your emotional vessel. You're the seasoned conductor of your feelings, skilfully directing the symphony of your reactions, dictating the tempo, the volume, the rhythm. No one can snatch the baton from your grasp unless you willingly surrender it. Your crucial role is to maintain your composure amidst adversity, to increase the resilience within you, to navigate through life's unpredictable squalls with a steadfast grace that refuses to buckle under pressure.

In dealing with life's challenges, sprinkle a touch of lighthearted grace over your experiences. By doing so, you build a fortress of tranquillity around your mind, your emotions. Your radiant resilience and calm poise becomes a beacon for others, as infectious as a beautifully composed piece of music that warms the heart and stirs the soul.

Epictetus's teachings provide a sturdy foundation, reminding us that insults and provocations can only shatter our inner peace if we extend them an invitation. A stoic mindset, coupled with the practice of reframing, offers a formidable arsenal. It equips us to strip insults of their poison, viewing them through a lens of benign humour rather than anger or outrage.

The act of mentally transforming a verbal assault into a harmless jest can dramatically alter their emotional impact on you. Our reactions, or the deliberate absence of them, shape the significance we grant to these experiences. By mastering our composure and harmonising with our inner strength, we retain control over our emotions, over our responses. We become adept at navigating life's choppy waters with an elegance and grace that makes even the most storm-tossed sea seem like a calm pond on a summer's day.

We arrive again at the threshold where knowledge becomes practice. We've journeyed through Epictetus' philosophy, and now it's time to incorporate these discoveries into our daily lives. The exercises up next are your compass, guiding you from profound insights to pragmatic actions. Ready to embark? Let's venture from understanding to living, shaping our unique *Theory of Happiness*.

Let's begin our exploration with the "Rubber Duck Technique". Confronted with an insult, you are encouraged to envision it as a rubber duck quacking mid-flight. Picture the antagonist cocking their arm back, their eyes gleaming with mischief, and then hurling a vivid, neon-coloured duck in your direction. This amusing mental exercise serves as a potent tool to defuse tension, enabling you to face insults with a grin rather than a grimace. By reshaping the affront into something light-hearted and harmless, the sting of the insult is effectively diminished, allowing you to sustain your composure and rise above the negativity.

Next on our agenda is the "Count to Ten Challenge". Instead of bracing for the emotional impact when faced with a verbal assault, take a moment to inhale a deep, calming breath and consciously count to ten. With each number, visualise a layer of annoyance evaporating, as ephemeral as a rabbit disappearing into a magician's hat. This practice provides a metaphorical 'cooling down' period, a pause that allows you to regain control of your emotions and respond with enhanced clarity. By the final count, you'll discover your anger has diffused, making room for a composed and thoughtful response.

Don't overlook the significant effect of "Happy Place Visualisation". Close your eyes and imagine a setting that embodies your ultimate tranquillity and contentment — it could be a sun-drenched beach, a serene, snow-capped mountaintop, or a snug corner in a bustling coffee shop. When the pressures of life mount, press your mental escape button and transport yourself to this peaceful haven. Let the imagined warmth or the crisp air fill your mind, calming your thoughts and restoring your inner Zen. This mental sanctuary provides a vantage point from which to regain perspective and recentre amidst the turbulence of daily life.

Finally, we explore the transformative potency of "Laughter Therapy". Even during the most challenging moments, life offers a humorous side waiting to be discovered. When you feel the pressure rising, redirect your focus to find humour in your situation. Recall a ludicrous anecdote or envision the individual you're interacting with donning oversized clown shoes and a bright red nose. The more absurd, the better! Laughter serves as a powerful antidote for stress, capable of dispelling tension, triggering the release of endorphins, and connecting us with a sense of inner joy. Embracing levity in the face of adversity not only protects your tranquillity but also radiates positive energy, enhancing the collective mood.

Upon the completion of these exercises, keep in mind that every act imbued with Epictetus' wisdom takes us closer to a life guided by insight. Philosophy isn't merely about thinking; it's about doing. The real import of these teachings doesn't lie just in comprehending them but in applying them. Consider these exercises as your signposts, guiding your path towards a life of wisdom. As you journey on, you'll discover that philosophy isn't just about pondering, but about practicing.

As we draw our exploration to a close, the enduring wisdom of Epictetus stands as a beacon, illuminating the way to nurture inner tranquillity even in the face of adversity. His teachings instruct us to deftly reframe perceived insults and provocations, empowering us to view them as benign, or even comical. The process of visualising insults as inflatable rubber ducks harmlessly being hurled towards us, or envisaging the disrupters as overzealous toddlers, helps to reshape our emotional landscape. By retaining our composure, we ensure our serenity remains unbroken, fortifying us to confront life's inevitable challenges with an unwavering resilience and grace.

Epictetus's profound words echo in our minds: "it is not he who gives abuse or strikes, who insults, but the view we take of these things as insulting." This profound insight establishes the foundation for a life filled with joy, harmony, and a steadfast sense of tranquillity that remains undisturbed by external disturbances.

Epictetus guides us to navigate life's complex paths with an unshakeable commitment to preserving our inner peace. His teachings challenge us to shift our perspective, recognising that the potential for insult lies within us, not in the actions or words of others. Cultivating a light-hearted, even playful, outlook enables us to dissociate from the negative impact of these supposed affronts. This altered perspective ensures that we meet any potentially disruptive encounters with equanimity, possibly even amusement, preserving our sense of inner tranquillity.

As we incorporate Epictetus's teachings into our everyday lives, we begin a transformative journey towards a life infused with joy, marked by resilience, and safeguarded by an unshakeable tranquillity. In the face of adversity, we harness the power of reframing, visualising affronts as harmless and inconsequential, and their perpetrators as innocent, over-energetic children. Their actions hold little significance in our quest for peace and happiness.

By adopting this philosophy, we foster a life of joy that is not tethered to the opinions and actions of others. We realise that true tranquillity dwells within us, readily accessible in the midst of life's trials and tribulations. Guided by Epictetus's wisdom, we chart a course illuminated by resilience, grace, and an unwavering dedication to maintaining our inner peace. Harnessing the transformative power of our perspectives, we craft a life that radiates joy and harmony, reducing any potential insults to mere whispers in the wind.

21

Befriending the Monsters Within

Let death and exile, and all other things which appear terrible, be daily before your eyes, but death chiefly; and you will never entertain an abject thought, nor too eagerly covet anything.

We now journey into the delightful and shadowy maze of the human psyche - a charming spectacle we might affectionately term the 'Carnival of Shadows'. As this carousel begins to spin, you may feel a niggling sense of unease, akin perhaps to the first time you tried to assemble flat-pack furniture without the instructions. But fret not! This is not an expedition into the heart of darkness, but rather an opportunity for a friendly chinwag with some of our most primal fears, including the granddaddy of them all: death.

Epictetus, our philosophical tour guide on this odyssey, offers us a treasure map. However, instead of X marking a chest of gold doubloons, it leads us towards an intimate acquaintance with our fears. Foremost among these is death. Now, at this point, you might be wondering if Epictetus has taken leave of his senses but stay with me here. He's not suggesting we develop a fondness for black clothing and melancholic poetry, or even purchase a season pass to the local graveyard. His proposition is to understand death as a natural, inescapable part of life and, by doing so, to remove some of its ominous presence.

Consider this less a scream-inducing roller coaster ride through a haunted house, and more a quirky afternoon tea party with your fears. The name of the game here is familiarity. The more crumpets you share, the more chatter you engage in, the less terrifying they become. Your fears might even reveal their eccentric and intricate personas that add a dash of colour to the grand tapestry of life.

Take, for example, the fear of public speaking, often experienced as a sensation comparable to navigating a minefield while blindfolded. Superficially, it might seem insurmountable. Yet, if we dare to peer beneath the surface, we often find it rooted in a deep-seated craving for approval and a fear of judgement. By acknowledging these underlying concerns, we can develop strategies to enhance our self-confidence, improve our communication skills, and ultimately harness this once incapacitating fear as a springboard for personal growth.

Likewise, consider the fear of failure. Often, it might feel like an enormous gorilla ready to pounce at the slightest whiff of risk. Yet, if we stop, take a step back and observe this gorilla from a safe distance, we see that it's fuelled by a fear of disappointment and the desire to maintain status. Understanding this allows us to redefine what success means to us, encourages us to embrace the lessons embedded in failure and equips us to bounce back stronger.

Fear of death, though undeniably more profound, follows a similar pattern. It lurks in the shadows, like a detective mystery novel filled with complex twists and turns. Its roots are usually tangled up in a web of unfulfilled dreams, untapped potentials, and unexpressed love. Confronting and untangling these can propel us into a deeper appreciation for life and its fleeting beauty, transforming this intimidating fear into a motivating force to live our lives to the fullest.

So, let's embark on this transformative journey of self-discovery and fear transformation. We're not just looking to put on a brave face or ignore our fears; that would be like putting a Band-Aid on a water leak. We're aiming for a complete overhaul of our understanding and perception of fear, transforming it from a looming phantom into a well-understood companion.

As we step into this grand hall of shadows with our torches held high, we illuminate these fears and invite them to join us in the light. We confront them, understand them, and ultimately control them. In doing so, we clear the path towards a life steeped in authenticity, resilience, and personal growth. We become composers of our own symphony of courage, where each note resonates with our fearless spirit, harmonised with an underlying melody of contemplative wisdom.

We stand at that pivotal point where wisdom turns into action. We've unravelled Epictetus' teachings, and now it's time to weave them into the fabric of our existence. The forthcoming exercises are your loom, connecting ancient wisdom to contemporary reality. Shall we begin weaving? Let's transition from understanding to living, crafting our own *Theory of Happiness*.

Our opening act, the "Backstage Pass Visualisation", invites you to close your eyes and imagine your fears not as looming nightmares concealed in the shadows but as rockstars, flamboyant and larger-than-life. Picture yourself striding towards them with bold assurance, offering a firm handshake, and capturing a cheeky memento with a quick selfie. Through this humanisation of our fears, we extract them from their dark lairs, and in doing so, their power over us diminishes. Suddenly, our once paralysing fear of snakes may resemble an eccentric glam rock band clad in sequined costumes, their threatening hisses swapped for the thrilling riffs of electric guitars.

Next on our line-up is the "Daily Concert Ritual". Each day, select one fear to star centre stage within the concert hall of your consciousness. As the performance unfolds, a gradual sense of familiarity begins to supersede your initial apprehension. The fear that previously provoked icy shivers down your spine now translates into a melodic anthem, resonating with your fortitude and resolve. Who could have imagined that a fear of heights could metamorphose into a triumphant aria of courage and resilience?

Stepping up next is the "Laughing at the Spiders Challenge". Your quest, should you choose to accept it, is to seek out the hidden comedy lurking within each fear. Visualise a heavy metal band comprised entirely of menacing spiders, their eight legs ensnared in their webbing, stumbling over each other in a hysterically choreographed ballet of humorous chaos. As their attempts to provoke fear fumble and falter, their ominous aura fades away, replaced by your laughter reverberating through your entire being. In this moment of joyous levity, you recognise that laughter possesses the power to dissipate even the darkest shadows, bathing them in a radiant glow of illumination.

Our closing act is the "Making Friends Exercise." Find a comfortable space, grab a pen and paper, and jot down all your fears, regardless of their magnitude. Then, engage with each fear, acknowledge its existence, and find its silver lining. This isn't about dismissing your fears, but about transforming them into opportunities for growth. Fear of public speaking? View it as an impetus to improve your presentation skills. Fear of spiders? It can heighten your awareness in spider-prone areas. Repeat this for each fear, pairing it with a potential positive outcome. Now you've transformed the intimidating entities into manageable ones, with a personalised tool for understanding and dealing with your fears. Revisit this list whenever needed and continue to redefine your relationship with your fears.

As we conclude these exercises, bear in mind that each step inspired by Epictetus brings us closer to a life of insight and wisdom. Philosophy isn't just about intellect; it's about action. The true value of these teachings isn't just in understanding them, but in living them. View these exercises as your lantern, illuminating the path towards a wise life. As you proceed, you'll come to understand that philosophy isn't just discussed, but lived.

As we draw the curtains on this part of our journey, we are left with an enriched understanding of the pivotal role of confronting our fears and transforming them into allies. We've envisaged our fears as intriguing, complex characters, no longer hidden in the shadows but standing centre-stage in the theatre of our minds, ready for a detailed exploration.

Imagine these fears as vibrant, complex characters each making their entrance under the spotlight. Dressed not in monstrous masks but in outfits that mirror their true complexities and eccentricities. Each character, a unique blend of traits, hints at underlying desires, insecurities, and hopes. They demand not terror, but understanding, not avoidance, but engagement. By doing so, we dismantle the forbidding exterior of our fears and look at them with a blend of curiosity and newfound respect, lessening their hold over us.

In our day-to-day lives, we could establish a routine of dedicating each day to unravelling one such character, one fear at a time. Whether it's the fear of rejection that dances with dramatic flair or the fear of failure that performs with a sombre grace, or even something as seemingly benign as the 'eight-legged wonder' fear, we spend time deciphering its story, understanding its root causes, and formulating a way to address it. By doing so, we demystify our fears, empowering us to formulate a tactical response to them, thereby reducing their impact on our tranquillity.

Moreover, let's not forget to appreciate the lighter side of our anxieties. Laughter, as we all know, can be a potent tonic to our fears, lessening their grasp on our psyche. By teasing out the comedy in our fears, we ease the associated stress and usher in a sense of relief and calm.

These methodologies serve to reframe our emotional responses to fear, nurturing an internal oasis of peace and equipping us with the tools to weather life's squalls with resilience and aplomb. This approach offers both immediate relief from the crippling weight of fear and sows the seeds for long-term emotional resilience and mental fortitude.

In conclusion, let's continue to allow this symphony of wisdom and personal development to guide us on this enlightening odyssey of self-discovery. By embracing our fears as insightful mentors, we dive deeper into the realms of our psyche, nurturing a profound self-awareness and emotional evolution. In this harmonious composition, every note and pause becomes a learning opportunity, preparing us to navigate the symphony of life with courage, elegance, and resilience. Let us go forth, fearlessly exploring and growing, as we continue to compose our unique masterpieces of life.

22

Facing Uncertainty

If you have an earnest desire toward philosophy, prepare yourself from the very first to have the multitude laugh and sneer, and say, "He is returned to us a philosopher all at once"; and, "Whence this supercilious look?" Now, for your part, do not have a supercilious look indeed, but keep steadily to those things which appear best to you, as one appointed by God to this particular station. For remember that, if you are persistent, those very persons who at first ridiculed will afterwards admire you. But if you are conquered by them, you will incur a double ridicule.

The odyssey towards Stoicism, eloquently portrayed by Epictetus, is strikingly similar to a demanding road trip across a wild, untamed landscape, riddled with inevitable obstacles such as potholes and bumps. Like how a physically gruelling journey requires a robust vehicle and a tenacious spirit, so does your philosophical exploration necessitate a robust commitment and unwavering mental resilience. As you traverse this rocky road, anticipate doubters to tailgate your every move towards enlightenment, leaping at every chance to question your pursuits. Their taunts, artfully camouflaged as good-natured jabs like "Lo and behold, our fresh philosopher!" or "What a startling, sudden awakening!", may linger, attempting to instil a sense of self-doubt.

In such predicaments, it's vital to bear in mind the sage guidance of our philosophical virtuoso, Epictetus. He advises us not to retaliate with aggressive intellectualism or wield our philosophical knowledge as a medieval knight would a sword in battle. Instead, Epictetus encourages us to greet such scepticism with tranquillity and a steadfast belief in our philosophical convictions. Consider embracing your principles with the unyielding tenacity of a barnacle clinging to a ship's hull, treating them as divine wisdom bestowed from the celestial banquet in the lofty heights of Mount Olympus. Interestingly, the act of persistent Stoicism in the face of scepticism often results in a surprising reversal of roles. The cynics who once questioned your philosophical journey may soon marvel at your determination and steadfast belief, becoming unexpected supporters rather than critics.

However, the journey is not without its philosophical plot twists. Succumbing to the jeering and doubt tossed in your direction can be as detrimental as veering off course on a challenging road trip, potentially leading to your ridicule. Philosophy, far from being a cosy fireside chat, can be more likened to a roller coaster ride, filled with exhilarating peaks of insights, sharp turns of realisations, and swift descents into valleys of self-doubt. This path demands a robust philosophical constitution, not meant for those who are weak of heart or easily unsettled.

In the intricate maze of philosophical exploration, doubters often assume the role of a minotaur, their bewitching taunts reverberating through the corridors of our thoughts. According to Epictetus, navigating this labyrinth is a vital part of our expedition towards sagehood. Much like the hero overcoming arduous trials in a mythical quest or dodging the wrath of a fearsome dragon guarding a coveted treasure, facing these naysayers becomes an evaluation of our resilience. Imagine setting foot on a steep mountain trail, teeming with physical hurdles and mental adversities. As you ascend, fellow climbers may question your decision to undertake such a rigorous journey, casting doubts on its worthiness. But in these challenging moments, it's crucial to remain focused on your mission and trust in your chosen path's wisdom. By demonstrating an unwavering resolve in the face of doubt, you validate your commitment to embracing the transformative power of philosophy.

The wheels of philosophical inquiry should never cease turning. Instead, persist in your journey, viewing the obstacles along the way as stepping stones towards growth. Think of these challenges as vantage points, presenting stunning vistas of your evolving wisdom. Each encounter with scepticism and doubt serves to refine your understanding, enhancing your wisdom. Much like a river forging its path through rugged terrain, you too navigate through robust currents of doubt and scepticism, shaping your philosophical path, and emerging with an enriched sense of self and purpose.

Keep in mind that challenges serve as a crucible, refining our character and solidifying our commitment to wisdom. Thus, it's essential to savour the roller coaster ride of philosophical exploration, embracing the exhilarating peaks of enlightenment as well as the sobering troughs of doubt. Each twist and turn on this ride presents an opportunity to build resilience and cultivate a profound understanding of the world and oneself. Don't let the winds of scepticism deter you; instead, let them drive you forward. For it is often in the face of uncertainty and doubt that the blossom of wisdom radiates the most brilliantly.

Here we are, back at that magical junction where philosophy translates into practice. We've soaked up Epictetus' wisdom, and now it's time to wring these lessons into our lives. The exercises up next are your sponge, absorbing the essence of philosophy and squeezing it into everyday experiences. Ready to get soaked? Let's transition from wisdom-absorption to wisdom-expression, hydrating our unique *Theory of Happiness*.

Our maiden voyage, the "Impress Me Symphony", encourages us to commence each day with a heartfelt acknowledgement of an action or decision that ignites a spark of pride within us. It might be as simple as acknowledging an unnoticed act of kindness, like helping an elderly neighbour carry their shopping, or recognising a positive step toward personal growth, such as resisting the temptation to procrastinate. Just as the dawn chorus of birds sets a peaceful and inspiring tone for the day, our self-appreciation symphony lifts our self-esteem to the VIP box at life's grand opera, far above the judgments of others in the stalls below.

Next on our journey is the "Self-Talk Show". In this exercise, we set aside a few valuable minutes each day for an intimate chat with our inner selves. Visualise ourselves as the charming host of our own late-night talk show, our face gently illuminated by the cosy amber glow of a desk lamp. Like a popular TV show host making witty and inspirational remarks, we use this opportunity to acknowledge our progress, spur ourselves on for future challenges, and share a laugh or two about the quirky moments on our philosophical journey. This activity helps in understanding that the most stimulating conversation is often the one we have with ourselves.

Following this enlightening self-chat, we march on to the "Pep Up Parade". In this activity, we revisit a familiar scenario where we've often tried to impress someone else – it could be a boss, a friend, or a loved one. However, we infuse this scenario with a refreshing twist. We brainstorm ways to impress ourselves within the same situation, thus sparking moments of self-validation. Instead of a parade showcasing the expectations of others, we shape it into a jubilant procession of self-fulfilment and contentment. We shift our focus from seeking external approval to fostering a garden of self-satisfaction.

Our philosophical voyage concludes with a vibrant "Philosophy Fiesta". This exercise encourages us to celebrate our leaps and bounds as budding philosophers. Whether it's a giant leap towards mastering indifference towards external validation, or a cautious step in formulating an effective rebuttal in a philosophical debate, each milestone, no matter how big or small, deserves a jubilant toast. Just as one might celebrate conquering a steep hilltop hike with a triumphant cheer, we rejoice in our strides towards wisdom and personal growth.

As we bring these exercises to a close, remember that every effort infused with Epictetus' teachings is a stride towards a life of wisdom. Philosophy isn't simply a mental exploration; it's a toolkit for living. The real essence of these teachings is unveiled not just in their study but in their application. Treat these exercises as your guidebook, charting your path towards a life imbued with wisdom. As you journey forward, you'll realise that philosophy isn't just pondered, but practiced.

In summary, our extraordinary odyssey towards Stoicism navigates us through a wild, untamed landscape of scepticism and doubt, guided by the radiant lantern of Epictetus's teachings. Along this enlightening road trip, we not only learn the art of resolutely hugging our philosophical beliefs but also deftly turn sceptics into admirers. Despite wrestling with the gusts of doubt and the quicksand of derision, we pull ourselves from these challenges with a renewed sense of purpose and a profound understanding of our philosophical principles.

Our journey to attain wisdom runs across terrain pockmarked with uncertainties and questioning voices. Yet, guided by the beacon of Epictetus's wisdom, we plough forward, steadfast in our commitment to our philosophical principles. As we encounter sceptics and naysayers, we face their doubts with unwavering conviction, transforming their scepticism into admiration. The winds of doubt that aim to snuff out our flame of wisdom find themselves no match for our resolute spirit.

With each step along this transformative journey, we square off with the quicksand of derision, refusing to be consumed by its negativity. Instead, we emerge from its depths with a reinvigorated sense of purpose and an unshakeable commitment to our philosophical ideals. The challenges we meet serve to reinforce our resolve, highlighting the importance of remaining true to our beliefs, even when adversity blows our way.

What initially appear as formidable hurdles gradually morph into stepping stones of growth. Our encounters with doubt and scepticism thrust us forward, filling us with a wellspring of knowledge and resilience. We welcome these challenges as opportunities for personal and intellectual development, using them to broaden our reservoir of wisdom and solidify our resolve. Each obstacle we conquer becomes a testament to our steadfast commitment to the pursuit of truth and enlightenment.

As we persevere on this mesmerising journey of philosophical exploration, we carry with us the lessons learned, the victories savoured, and the wisdom garnered. Epictetus's teachings act as our compass, guiding us through life's intricacies and reminding us of the transformative power of philosophical inquiry. We approach each twist and turn with a sense of purpose and a heightened appreciation for the profound depths of wisdom that lie ahead.

23

Impress Yourself

If you ever happen to turn your attention to externals, for the pleasure of anyone, be assured that you have ruined your scheme of life. Be content, then, in everything, with being a philosopher; and if you wish to seem so likewise to anyone, appear so to yourself, and it will suffice you.

Imagine the spectacle of standing at the heart of a grand and resplendent stage. The spotlight illuminates you, transforming your presence into a radiant beacon of brilliance against a backdrop of shadowy obscurity. With the poise of a ballet dancer and the dynamism of a breakdancer, you twirl, jump, and spin, juggling vibrant spheres in a mesmerising fusion of agility and dexterity. The captivated audience watches in wide-eyed anticipation, their collective breath held, their applause echoing like a rhythmic heartbeat. Every clap, every cheer, becomes a dose of adrenaline, propelling you to strive harder, perform better, and dance with amplified passion. This metaphorical spectacle may seem eerily familiar as it mirrors the intricate choreography of our daily lives where we're perennially performing for societal approbation. Yet, when the applause of the audience puppeteers your performance, guiding your actions and choices, you're left precariously balancing on a metaphorical tightrope with no safety net in sight.

Fear not, for we have Epictetus, our philosopher extraordinaire from the annals of ancient wisdom, presenting a solution as comforting as a safety trampoline poised beneath your philosophical tightrope. His counsel, as luminous as a finely polished gem, is to cherish and nourish your inner philosopher. Strengthen your bond with this internal sage through meditation and intellectual inquiry. Let it become your reliable ally during introspective musings under the starlit canopy of the midnight sky. As you brace yourself to showcase your wisdom and intellectual prowess, remember, the audience you need to captivate and impress the most is none other than yourself. Why? Because during this philosophical journey, you're not just the lead performer mesmerising the crowd with your bravura spectacle, but also the most discerning critic seated in the front row. Your self-evaluation and self-approval wield the unique power to sculpt your philosophical journey, influencing its course and outcome.

As you embark on this intellectual exploration, flaunting your wisdom like a finely-tailored ensemble, ensure your gaze remains locked on the most crucial critic – yourself. The self-awarded standing ovations and enthusiastic applause offer a value that surpasses any external validation. Make impressing yourself the golden standard, the cardinal principle. Remember, in the grand ballroom of your personal philosophy, the magic of a captivating performance lies in your self-validation.

With wisdom as timeless as the stars, Epictetus advises us that the journey towards self-improvement and wisdom isn't a grand spectacle for others to enjoy or critique. Instead, it's a deeply personal quest, an intimate journey where your judgement and approval serve as the benchmark of success. Embrace the duality of your role as both the performer and critic, and let your internal applause become the melody that guides your philosophical dance. Seek validation from the depths of your own being, not from the mercurial external world, for it's in this self-approval that you'll find profound satisfaction and a sense of fulfillment like no other.

Remember that the applause from the external world can be capricious and unpredictable, fluctuating with the whims of societal trends and ever-changing expectations. It's like a sporadic breeze that can either fill your sails or leave them flapping aimlessly. In contrast, the applause that resounds from within your own heart, from your deepest self, remains steadfast and enduring.

This internal applause doesn't sway with the tide or falter at the first gust of opposition. It's a consistent rhythm, a drumbeat that propels you forward, providing validation and reassurance even when the external applause fades to silence. It is this internal affirmation that should be your guiding beacon, your North Star, as you navigate the often rugged, but enriching, terrains of philosophy.

As you absorb, contemplate, and integrate each new philosophical insight, refining and deepening your understanding of both the self and the universe, this inner applause reverberates louder. It is this self-approval, this inner satisfaction, that truly fuels your journey. Each stride you take, each revelation you uncover, is met with a standing ovation from the most important critic of all - yourself. It provides the wind beneath your philosophical wings, invigorating your journey towards self-realisation, wisdom, and, ultimately, the manifestation of your best self.

It's that moment again when philosophy turns into action. We've navigated the seas of Epictetus' teachings, and now it's time to anchor these insights in our everyday lives. The following exercises are your anchor, grounding lofty philosophy in the reality of daily living. Shall we drop anchor? Let's journey from exploration to settlement, anchoring our own *Theory of Happiness*.

We commence this engaging journey with the "Impress Me Routine". This simple exercise encourages you to begin each day by performing an act that brings about a sense of personal pride. It doesn't have to be grand or elaborate. For instance, you might choose to begin your day by preparing a healthy breakfast, keeping your living space tidy, or offering assistance to a neighbour in need. The focus is on self-appreciation and acknowledging personal achievements, no matter how modest. Such self-affirming activities serve to reinforce your self-esteem, reminding you that you are the most important cheerleader in your life. Celebrating your personal victories, regardless of their size, helps cultivate a sense of empowerment, reinforcing the understanding that your self-worth and self-approval are paramount, far outweighing any external validation.

Next on our agenda is the "Self-Talk Show". Imagine hosting your own talk show, wherein you are both the star guest and the effervescent host. Find a serene spot, perhaps with a comforting hot beverage, and engage in a conversation with yourself. During this self-dialogue, commend yourself for the progress you've made, encourage yourself to face upcoming challenges, and even share a few light-hearted philosophical anecdotes to keep the tone buoyant. By carving out a safe space for introspection, you foster a positive inner dialogue, which is essential in supporting your philosophical evolution.

Then, join the ranks in the "Pep Up Parade". Imagine a situation where your initial objective is to impress someone else. Now, challenge yourself by flipping the scenario. Consider how you could alter your actions to impress yourself instead. This mental gymnastics not only builds cognitive flexibility but also serves as a reflective mirror, shedding light on your motivations and aspirations. It gently nudges you towards an empowering realisation – authentic validation originates from within. By shifting your focus towards impressing yourself, you realign your life's priorities, fostering a sense of self-contentment and fulfilment.

Finally, it's time to let your hair down at the "Philosophy Fiesta". Host a jovial celebration to honour your philosophical milestones. Each stride you've made, be it mastering indifference towards external validation or crafting an impactful argument in a philosophical debate, deserves to be commemorated. This 'fiesta' serves as your self-awarded medal of honour, acknowledging the strides you've made on your journey towards wisdom and personal growth.

At the end of these exercises, keep in mind that each step steeped in Epictetus' wisdom is a leap towards a life enriched by philosophy. Philosophy isn't merely a scholarly pursuit; it's a practical compass. The genuine potency of these teachings is discovered not just in understanding them but in actualising them. Consider these exercises as your itinerary, guiding you towards a wiser way of living. As you press on, you'll comprehend that philosophy isn't just explored, but embodied.

In conclusion, Epictetus's resounding directive resonates within the depths of our souls: the voice of the most influential critic is none other than our own. Therefore, let us firmly lace up our philosophy trainers and stride forward with unwavering determination on the exhilarating path of wisdom and self-discovery. In this profound journey, we embrace the power of self-approval and self-validation, for it is within the chambers of our own judgment that the true essence of philosophical fulfilment resides.

As we encapsulate the teachings of Epictetus, we are reminded that the quest for wisdom is an internal odyssey. It is a journey where self-judgment and self-approval serve as the ultimate measures of our success. By dedicating ourselves to impressing our own discerning selves, rather than merely seeking external applause, we unearth a wellspring of profound satisfaction and fulfilment. Embracing the dual roles of performer and critic on our philosophical expedition, we focus our attention on the resounding applause emanating from within, refining our understanding and igniting the flames of wisdom and self-realisation.

Epictetus invites us to centre our attention on our inner dialogue, shifting our focus from the fleeting applause of external critics to the steadfast applause of our own souls. This shift in perspective allows us to recognise that our own judgment holds the greatest weight in the pursuit of philosophical fulfilment. It is through the alignment of our actions, beliefs, and values with the applause of our inner critic that we unlock the true potential of our journey.

Embracing the role of both performer and critic, we embark on a dance of self-discovery and growth. As performers, we strive to express our philosophical insights and live in alignment with our values. As critics, we engage in thoughtful introspection, evaluating our own thoughts, actions, and progress. Through this symbiotic interplay, we refine our understanding, deepen our insights, and propel ourselves forward on the path of wisdom and self-realisation.

The journey towards wisdom is not about seeking validation or praise from others, but about seeking self-approval and finding resonance within ourselves. By cultivating a strong sense of self-judgment and self-validation, we tap into a wellspring of confidence, clarity, and purpose. We free ourselves from the whims and opinions of external critics, finding solace and fulfilment in the unwavering applause of our own hearts.

Let us heed Epictetus's timeless wisdom and embark on this awe-inspiring journey of self-discovery and philosophical exploration. Tighten the laces on your philosophy trainers, for the path ahead is exhilarating and transformative. Embrace the power of self-approval, for it is through our own judgment that we unlock the gates to true philosophical fulfilment. With every step we take, let the resounding applause of our inner critic propel us forward, guiding us towards wisdom, self-realisation, and an enriched understanding of ourselves and the world around us.

24

Being a Nobody

Let not such considerations as these distress you: "I shall live in discredit and be nobody anywhere." For if discredit be an evil, you can no more be involved in evil through another than in baseness. Is it any business of yours, then, to get power or to be admitted to an entertainment? By no means. How then, after all, is this discredit? And how it is true that you will be nobody anywhere when you ought to be somebody in those things only which are within your own power, in which you may be of the greatest consequence? "But my friends will be unassisted." What do you mean by "unassisted"? They will not have money from you, nor will you make them Roman citizens. Who told you, then, that these are among the things within our own power, and not rather the affairs of others? And who can give to another the things which he himself has not? "Well, but get them, then, that we too may have a share." If I can get them with the preservation of my own honour and fidelity and self-respect, show me the way and I will get them; but if you require me to lose my own proper good, that you may gain what is no good, consider how unreasonable and foolish you are. Besides, which would you rather have, a sum of money or a faithful and honourable friend? Rather assist me, then, to gain this character than require me to do those things by which I may lose it. Well, but my country, say you, as far as depends upon me, will be unassisted. Here, again, what assistance is this you mean? It will not have porticos nor baths of your providing? And what signifies that? Why, neither does a smith provide it with shoes, nor a shoemaker with arms. It is enough if everyone fully performs his own proper business. And were you to supply it with another faithful and honourable citizen, would not he be of use to it? Yes. Therefore, neither are you yourself useless to it. "What place, then," say you, "shall I hold in the state?" Whatever you can hold with the preservation of your fidelity and honour. But if, by desiring to be useful to that, you lose these, how can you serve your country when you have become faithless and shameless?

In a world teeming with societal expectations and relentless pressure to transcend the average, one can find themselves questioning their worth and living under the spectre of becoming a 'nobody'. Yet, my dear reader, let me assure you that your worth is not delineated by external standards dictated by societal whims or a deceptive measure of honour. You were not thrust into this world with a label plastered on your forehead, awaiting judgement from a capricious jury to assign your value. Your worth is intrinsic, a self-determined treasure evaluated based on principles that you have personally established.

Have you found yourself tossing and turning in the dead of night, grappling with the yearning to frequent glittering social events or amass a legion of followers on social media? Epictetus, our revered philosopher, would gently remind us that these pursuits do not delineate our life's purpose. We aren't circus performers, bound to perform death-defying stunts in society's circus, nor are we destined to be packed into the clown car of societal expectations. The true essence of our existence is illuminated in the unyielding quest for self-improvement and growth. Our worth glistens in our unwavering commitment to personal betterment, self-advancement, and the cultivation of virtues.

One might fret that adopting a modest lifestyle might deprive friends of life's finer comforts. However, it's vital to correct this misapprehension. You aren't commissioned with the duty of dispensing wealth and prestige to others like some mythical genie summoned from a lamp. Such expectations are as far-fetched as expecting a goldfish to belt out tunes in a Broadway show. Your role in others' lives doesn't entail gratifying their materialistic desires. Instead, it lies in being a steadfast and reliable companion. The value you impart to your relationships isn't measured by material acquisitions or grand experiences, but by the sincerity of your empathy, the support you offer, and the genuine care you extend.

As life unfurls, opportunities that seem to align with your values and principles may beckon. Yet, it's essential to pause and contemplate whether chasing these opportunities requires sacrificing your principles for material gains or ephemeral rewards. Genuine success nestles comfortably in the consonance between your deeds and your values. Instead of obsessively seeking external validation or bartering your self-worth, emphasise leading a life that resonates with your core beliefs. This synchronicity paves the path towards authentic fulfilment and a deep sense of accomplishment.

In the grand theatre of life, each individual has a unique role to play. One need not aspire to emulate the likes of a tech prodigy or a coffee mogul to feel valuable or relevant. Your worth isn't determined by drawing comparisons to figures like Elon Musk or the reigning coffee king. Each of us contributes to society's intricate tapestry in our distinctive ways. Being an upright citizen, treating others with respect, and leading a life marked by integrity and honesty are what truly render you invaluable. Your influence might not be spotlighted or universally celebrated, but it carries weight and meaning nonetheless.

Thus, liberate yourself from the burdensome shackles of unrealistic expectations and embrace the liberating truth that you are enough just as you are. Direct your energy towards personal growth, living a life that is in harmony with your values, and nurturing meaningful relationships. In doing so, you'll unearth a sense of happiness and fulfilment that far surpasses the transitory allure of external validation or societal recognition. Remember, in life's grand performance, the quality of your character and the authenticity of your actions carry true weight and worth.

We're back at the crossroads where philosophy meets practice. We've been savouring Epictetus' wisdom, and now it's time to cook these ideas into our everyday life. The exercises to follow are your kitchen, taking raw wisdom and turning it into a meal for the soul. Ready to cook? Let's transition from learning to living, preparing our own *Theory of Happiness*.

First on our list is the "You Rock Visualisation". In this exercise, imagine yourself as the main character in a high-definition virtual reality story, embodying the very best version of yourself. Perhaps you're a good listener, an empathetic friend, always ready to lend an ear. Or maybe you're the neighbour who's never too busy to lend a hand, or the employee who takes on challenges with unabating enthusiasm and diligence. Just a few minutes each day, steep yourself in this mental panorama, highlighting your best traits. Celebrate moments where you've displayed kindness, generosity, or wisdom, and let these memories reinforce your faith in your potential. It's like a personal highlight reel playing on a loop, strengthening your belief in your inherent good.

Moving forward, the "Role Play" exercise urges you to catalogue the various roles you play in life. You might be a friend, a family member, a neighbour, an employee, or a citizen. With each role, contemplate how you could raise the bar and surpass expectations without losing sight of your integrity. As a friend, for example, you could choose to provide unwavering support during challenging times, standing by your comrades with empathy and understanding instead of getting drawn into the petty realm of gossip or trivial entertainment. Through such mindful decisions, you not only improve the quality of your relationships but also contribute positively to the wider societal milieu.

Our third exercise is "Dignity over Dollar", which prompts you to imagine a situation where significant material gains threaten to sway your moral compass. Instead of succumbing to the allure of financial benefits, navigate a path that helps you retain your self-worth. Let's say, for instance, you're offered a promotion that would require you to usurp credit for a colleague's hard work. Rather than tarnishing your integrity, you could graciously decline the proposition, demonstrating your allegiance to fairness and honesty. By doing so, you embody the principles of Stoicism and serve as a moral beacon to those around you.

Lastly, get into the habit of conducting regular "Honour Checks", akin to a personal weekly review session. It's a dedicated time for introspection, where you evaluate if you've compromised your core values for surface-level benefits. If you find instances where you've bartered away your honour, apply Stoicism's wisdom to devise a robust plan safeguarding your integrity for the future. This practice of self-examination and self-correction fortifies your character, empowering you to align your deeds with your values and lead an authentic and morally consistent life.

As we close out these exercises, recall that every endeavour inspired by Epictetus brings us closer to a life led by wisdom. Philosophy isn't merely an intellectual game; it's a life strategy. The true essence of these teachings lies not just in knowing them but in living them. Treat these exercises as your guide, leading the way towards a life defined by wisdom. As you forge ahead, you'll discern that philosophy isn't just an abstraction, but a lived reality.

In conclusion, Epictetus's timeless wisdom highlights the significance of focusing on what we can control and not being overly concerned with external factors or seeking validation from others. He encourages us to prioritise our own honour, integrity, and self-respect over external measures of success.

Epictetus challenges the idea that we should prioritise gaining power or recognition in society, reminding us that such things are beyond our control and should not define our worth. Instead, he urges us to cultivate our own virtues and be of consequence in the aspects of life that we have influence over. By maintaining our fidelity and self-respect, we can find true fulfilment.

Furthermore, Epictetus challenges the notion that we should compromise our own honour and integrity to assist others or meet societal expectations. He argues that it is unreasonable and foolish to sacrifice our moral principles and well-being for the sake of material assistance or social status. True assistance comes from being a loyal and honourable friend, not simply providing material possessions.

He also reminds us that our responsibility lies in fulfilling our own duties and obligations, rather than feeling obligated to meet the needs or desires of others or our country. He encourages us to focus on being the best versions of ourselves and making a positive contribution aligned with our values and integrity. By doing so, we can serve others and have a meaningful impact without compromising our own moral compass.

In essence, Epictetus's teachings guide us to maintain our honour and integrity, focus on what we can control, and prioritise our own virtues and character. By embodying these principles, we can genuinely serve others and make a positive difference in the world.

25

The Social Spotlight

Is anyone preferred before you at an entertainment, or in courtesies, or in confidential intercourse? If these things are good, you ought to rejoice that he has them; and if they are evil, do not be grieved that you have them not. And remember that you cannot be permitted to rival others in externals without using the same means to obtain them. For how can he who will not haunt the door of any man, will not attend him, will not praise him, have an equal share with him who does these things? You are unjust, then, and unreasonable if you are unwilling to pay the price for which these things are sold, and would have them for nothing. For how much are lettuces sold? An obulus, for instance. If another, then, paying an obulus, takes the lettuces, and you, not paying it, go without them, do not imagine that he has gained any advantage over you. For as he has the lettuces, so you have the obulus which you did not give. So, in the present case, you have not been invited to such a person's entertainment because you have not paid him the price for which a supper is sold. It is sold for praise; it is sold for attendance. Give him, then, the value if it be for your advantage. But if you would at the same time not pay the one, and yet receive the other, you are unreasonable and foolish. Have you nothing, then, in place of the supper? Yes, indeed, you have—not to praise him whom you do not like to praise; not to bear the insolence of his lackeys.

Embarking on the journey of social navigation can often appear as an intricate and taxing task. Let's imagine, you find yourself amidst a lively gathering, the room pulsating with a myriad of engaging characters. Over by the intricately carved mantelpiece, one individual, possessing an enigmatic charm, effortlessly draws the crowd's attention. Another, with an uncanny knack for timing, grabs the last savoury canapé off the silver platter, invoking the envy of the less fortunate. Yet another, who seems as unremarkable as an average potato in a bin of truffles, suddenly becomes the centre of whispers and sidelong glances due to a thrilling tale shared in hushed tones.

These scenarios, as enchanting as they might seem under the warm glow of candlelight, may lure those who seek the thrilling rush of social dominance. However, it's crucial to question - do these circumstances genuinely resonate with your personal beliefs and ambitions? If not, there's no cause for despair. This divergence, far from being a setback, may indeed be a hidden blessing. Your steadfast commitment to your authentic self enables you to evade the tempting yet fleeting distractions often associated with such gatherings. Epictetus, in his sagacious insight, confirms that you incur no harm in such circumstances. Instead, your integrity stands tall and steadfast, much like a lighthouse weathering a stormy sea.

Now, what about those who aspire to mingle with the social elite, enchanted by the dazzling allure of the high-profile tapestry? For these individuals, it's essential to prepare for the intricate dance of networking, the fine art of offering commendation without resorting to flattery, and the daunting task of checking one's ego. It's all too easy to lament the lack of extravagant benefits associated with these circles if one is reluctant to adapt to their norms or risks undermining personal values. The situation is akin to desiring a gourmet sandwich but balking at the price tag - a stern yet undeniable reminder that every choice carries a consequence, a lesson that Epictetus consistently emphasises.

To bring this concept to life, let me walk you through an imaginary trip to a fresh produce market, an environment Epictetus might have relished. Imagine a vibrant head of lettuce, its dew-dappled leaves offering an inviting freshness, all for just a pound. Another customer, enticed by the lettuce's appeal, buys it, while you decide to keep your pound. It's crucial to understand that neither of you has been short-changed or disadvantaged. Your fellow shopper now owns the lettuce, but you retain the value equivalent to the lettuce—your unspent pound, a powerful asset in its own right. This straightforward analogy sheds light on Epictetus's principle that our choices are inherently personal and should align with our individual values and priorities.

Epictetus's insights on aligning choices with personal values extend beyond mundane shopping decisions and into the intricate tapestry of our social lives. Consider a scenario where you don't receive an invite to a high-profile dinner party. Upon reflection, you might realise that you didn't invest in building a substantial relationship with the host. If you're content with this outcome—missing the party—it speaks volumes about your priorities. However, if you desire to be part of such social gatherings but are unwilling to commit the necessary social capital, waiting for an invitation to magically appear becomes an exercise in futility.

On the flip side, there's an inherent joy in choosing not to fawn over individuals you find less appealing, or not having to bear through mundane small talk and forced humour. As Epictetus might have quipped, "savour this freedom. It's an invaluable luxury". Recognising and leveraging our power of choice in social scenarios enables us to cultivate authentic connections, invest energy in relationships that align with our values, and foster a sense of liberty and satisfaction. This is the essence of embodying Epictetus's philosophy in the dazzling theatre of our daily lives.

It's that time again to move from pondering to performing. We've cherished Epictetus' insights, now it's time to reflect these lessons into our daily actions. The exercises that follow are your mirror, reflecting philosophical wisdom into practical living. Ready to see your reflection? Let's shift from introspection to manifestation, reflecting our unique *Theory of Happiness*.

The first endeavour is the "Chameleon or Authenticity?" exercise. Consider the different social situations you're in or aim to be a part of. Imagine yourself at a bustling cocktail party or a professional networking event. Pay close attention to your behaviours and interactions. Are you a social chameleon, changing colours to blend in? Or are you standing tall in the authenticity of who you are? This exercise nudges you to determine if your social behaviours align with your personal values, exemplifying Epictetus's lessons on authenticity and personal integrity.

Next, let's move to a more tactile, real-world exercise, whimsically dubbed "The Lettuce Lottery". It starts with a simple trip to your local grocery shop or market. Select an item - a head of lettuce, for example - and assess its worth to you. Is it worth its price, or would you rather retain your money? Extend this thought experiment to your social life. Are the perks of certain social engagements worth the "price" of admission, whether that's time, effort, or the compromise of your values? If not, recall Epictetus's wisdom: you're still holding the value, albeit in a different form.

Our next exercise, "The RSVP Riddle", calls for a bit of imaginative role play. You're expecting an invitation to a desirable social event, but as time ticks away, it becomes clear that no invitation is forthcoming. Instead of succumbing to disappointment or indignation, use this opportunity for reflection. Have you truly invested in a relationship with the host or is your desire tied only to the event's benefits? If it's the latter, consider if you're prepared to pay the "social price" for such gatherings in the future. If the answer is no, bask in the freedom that Epictetus encourages - the freedom of conscious choice.

Finally, consider the "The Epictetus Exchange". Visualise your social interactions as a vibrant marketplace, where words and actions are the currency. Each interaction is a transaction - what are you willing to offer, and what do you hope to gain? Are these social "trades" in harmony with your values and personal integrity? By picturing your social interactions as an animated exchange, you encourage a mindful approach, promoting genuine connections in line with Epictetus's teachings.

Having completed these exercises, it's essential to remember that every action rooted in Epictetus' wisdom is a stride towards living his philosophy. Philosophy isn't simply a thought exercise; it's a lifestyle guide. The real power of these teachings is not just in their comprehension but in their embodiment. See these exercises as your lodestar, guiding you on the journey towards wisdom. As you journey, you'll recognise that philosophy isn't just a subject, but a life practice.

As we come to the end of this exploration, we reflect on Epictetus's profound teachings that encourage us to approach social dynamics with wisdom and self-awareness. In a world where comparisons and external validations abound, he reminds us of the futility of seeking happiness and self-worth through the preferences and opinions of others. Instead, he invites us to find solace and strength in our own integrity and personal growth.

Epictetus challenges us to examine our reactions when we perceive others being preferred before us in various social settings. He asks us to consider whether those things that others seem to possess are truly good or evil. If they are good, he advises us to rejoice in their good fortune, recognising that their happiness does not diminish our own. On the other hand, if they are deemed as evil, he urges us not to be grieved by their absence in our lives. In essence, he reminds us that our well-being should not be contingent on the external circumstances or possessions of others.

Furthermore, Epictetus emphasises that if we desire to rival others in externals, such as the attention and courtesies they receive, we must be willing to employ the same means to obtain them. He asks us to reflect on how we can expect to have an equal share with someone who diligently attends, praises, and ingratiates themselves with others if we choose not to engage in such behaviours. To expect the benefits without paying the price is deemed unjust and unreasonable.

In conclusion, Epictetus's teachings guide us towards a deeper understanding of the complexities of social dynamics.

He invites us to cultivate genuine relationships based on mutual respect and understanding, rather than seeking validation or competing for external rewards. By embracing these teachings, we free ourselves from the need for excessive approval or the burden of conforming to societal expectations. We find contentment in the choices we make, the connections we foster, and the values we uphold. Let us embrace this wisdom as we navigate the intricate dance of social interactions, finding fulfillment in the authentic connections we forge and the meaningful contributions we make to the lives of others.

26

Calm Amidst the Chaos

The will of nature may be learned from things upon which we are all agreed. As when our neighbour's boy has broken a cup, or the like, we are ready at once to say, "These are casualties that will happen"; be assured, then, that when your own cup is likewise broken, you ought to be affected just as when another's cup was broken. Now apply this to greater things. Is the child or wife of another dead? There is no one who would not say, "This is an accident of mortality." But if anyone's own child happens to die, it is immediately, "Alas! how wretched am I!" It should be always remembered how we are affected on hearing the same thing concerning others.

Life is often depicted by philosophers and poets alike as 'nature' or 'fate'. An apt metaphor for life is that of an experienced film director, one who meticulously shapes the narrative arc of our existence. Just as an acclaimed auteur navigates the highs and lows of a cinematic masterpiece, life guides us through a labyrinth of experiences. Yet, life isn't the sort of director who announces its intentions through the booming voice of a megaphone, instead, it imparts its lessons subtly through events and experiences. It's through our reactions to these instances that we receive a reflection of our perceptions, behaviours, and our overall comprehension of the world.

Consider the endearing story of the neighbourhood child, an unintentional expert in ceramic destruction. This tiny whirlwind of energy possesses an almost supernatural talent for shattering crockery. The child's performance unfolds in a predictable routine: each time he clumsily lets go of a cup, we're greeted by the familiar soundtrack of ceramic meeting floor, followed by the sight of the once-whole cup splintering into a myriad of fragments. Observing this spectacle, we may allow ourselves a soft chuckle, pat the child sympathetically, or offer the parents a soothing word of comfort. Shaking our heads with a knowing smile, we might sigh, "Well, c'est la vie!" This French phrase, meaning "Such is life," is an acknowledgement of life's inherent unpredictability and its often messy reality. It's through these minor disruptions that we understand this accident as a trivial mishap that doesn't carry significant weight in the grand scheme of our existence.

Let's shift the lens to another scenario. On a dreary Monday, burdened by the weight of worldly concerns, you accidentally chip your favourite cup. The moment that your cherished coffee companion meets its untimely end, your typical morning suddenly transforms into an epic saga of loss. The tranquil sanctuary of your home feels invaded by the calamity of a treasured object's demise. You find yourself caught in the throes of an emotional tempest, your lamentation echoing the grandeur of a Shakespearean tragedy.

This theatrical reaction would certainly earn an amused eyebrow raise from Epictetus. He would argue that your grand display of sorrow stems from an identical 'oops' moment as when the neighbourhood child dropped a cup. The key difference here lies in your personal attachment to the broken object. Epictetus' advice would encourage a more composed response to such an event. You should recognise the event as one of life's unexpected turns and understand that the cup, despite its emotional significance, shares the same destiny as any other object—the recycling bin.

Taking this exploration of reactions to minor mishaps further, let's delve into the more challenging terrain of profound human experiences, specifically the devastating loss of a loved one. When we learn of such a loss affecting someone else, we naturally adopt solemn expressions, lower our voices to gentle whispers, and offer comforting words of wisdom, such as, "Such is the natural order of things. Death, as painful as it is, remains an inevitable part of life."

Yet, when we are personally faced with this painful reality, we often find ourselves overwhelmed with shock, grief, and confusion. We grapple with existential questions, question the fairness of the universe, and perhaps in moments of deep sorrow, cry out, "Why me?!" This contrasting response, while natural and human, starkly deviates from the Stoic acceptance we advocate when others face similar tragedies.

During such moments of personal distress, it is crucial to remind ourselves of the wisdom we readily offer to others. We must acknowledge that the comforting truths and philosophical insights we share in times of others' need are equally valid when we navigate our own adversities.

We're all fellow voyagers aboard the same existential vessel, which we could whimsically dub The S.S. Life Happens. This grand ship doesn't discriminate based on privilege or status. There are no VIP lounges or economy sections—only a common deck where all passengers face the same peaks and troughs, the same unpredictability of the vast sea of life's experiences.

Regardless of our individual roles or circumstances on this existential journey, we must remember that the insights we share during others' hardships are not just words to be discarded when we face our own trials. These insights form the cornerstone of our life philosophies, intended to be lived and embodied in our day-to-day existence. When we extend comfort, empathy, and wisdom to those around us, we must also remember to show the same compassion and understanding to ourselves in times of difficulty.

By acknowledging our shared humanity, embracing life's unpredictable nature, and applying the wisdom we offer others to our own situations, we arm ourselves to navigate life's ups and downs with resilience, grace, and perspective. This process can foster a deeper understanding that we are not alone in our struggles. Rather, we are all fellow passengers on this grand journey, weathering the same storms and basking in the same sunlight aboard The S.S. Life Happens.

Here we are, at that intriguing intersection where philosophy and action converge. We've drunk deeply of Epictetus' wisdom, now it's time to let this wisdom flow into our daily lives. The upcoming exercises are your river, carrying the water of wisdom from the source to the sea of action. Ready to flow? Let's move from drinking in knowledge to living it out, flowing towards our own *Theory of Happiness*.

Our first assignment on this joyous philosophical journey is appropriately titled "The Cup Catastrophe". Picture this: You're enjoying your morning tea when suddenly, in a disastrous turn of events, your cherished cup slips from your grasp and shatters into a hundred pieces on your kitchen floor. Before you surrender to the desire to let out a heartrending cry worthy of an Italian opera's grand finale, try a different approach. Simply shrug, perhaps give a bemused chuckle, and proclaim, "Well, c'est la vie!" The essence of this task is to remember that even as your cup is reduced to ceramic smithereens, life remains wonderfully and absurdly unpredictable, and sometimes, these minor mishaps are an integral part of the ride. You might find it almost impossible to keep a straight face while executing this exercise!

Next on our agenda, we've got the delightful exercise titled "The Stoic Switcheroo". It's quite a fascinating process: you encounter an inconvenience – a stubborn traffic jam, an elusive sock playing hide-and-seek, or the tragically comic scenario of your toast deciding to take a gravity-induced dive butter-side down. Take a deep breath and visualise the same vexing incident occurring to someone else. What sort of thoughtful advice would you dispense? Now, picture yourself standing before a mirror, locking eyes with your own reflection, and delivering that same counsel to yourself with a generous dollop of self-compassion. This practice works wonders in fostering empathy, not just towards others, but equally towards yourself. It's a gentle reminder to not be overly harsh with ourselves when life throws a spanner in the works.

Moving forward, we explore the intriguing exercise of "Role Reversal". Imagine you're grappling with a personal setback, perhaps a major disappointment or loss. Now, envision yourself donning the role of a wise, empathetic friend penning a heartfelt, comforting letter of condolence to you. Pay attention to the choice of words, ensuring they convey sincerity without being mired in excessive sentimentality. What kind words of consolation would this friend extend? Write them down. This task is a powerful way to tap into your innate wellspring of wisdom and strength, prompting you to provide yourself with the same comforting support you'd generously extend to a dear friend in their hour of need.

Lastly, we present to you "S.S. Life Happens". This exercise is all about reflection. As your day comes to a close, consider one event that didn't quite pan out as you had planned. View this hiccup not as a calamity, but as a wave expertly navigated by the sturdy ship that is your life – The S.S. Life Happens. Embrace the highs and lows, the unexpected twists and turns of your day, and take comfort in the knowledge that each experience, no matter how seemingly insignificant, contributes to the richness of your journey.

At the close of these exercises, keep in mind that each effort made under Epictetus' philosophy is a step towards an enlightened life. Philosophy isn't simply theoretical; it's practical. The real strength of these teachings doesn't lie in understanding alone but in their implementation. Consider these exercises as your GPS, directing you towards a wise and fulfilled life. As you carry on, you'll discover that philosophy isn't just a matter of discussion, but of action.

In conclusion, Epictetus urges us to adopt a consistent and compassionate perspective towards life's inevitable ups and downs. He invites us to embrace a mindset of equanimity and empathy, treating our own misfortunes with the same understanding and acceptance we readily extend to others.

Epictetus's teachings remind us that life is a collective voyage, and we are all passengers aboard the S.S. Life Happens. Just as we offer words of solace and reassurance to a neighbour whose cup has broken, Epictetus encourages us to offer the same grace and acceptance to ourselves when our own cups shatter. By cultivating a sense of detachment from the outcomes and a compassionate response to our own misfortunes, we navigate the seas of life with resilience and grace.

Let us remember that our experiences are not isolated events but part of a broader human tapestry. When we face adversity, we can choose to view it as a natural occurrence, a casualty that is bound to happen on this shared voyage. By adopting this broader perspective, we cultivate emotional resilience and find solace in the knowledge that we are not alone in our challenges.

Drawing from Epictetus's wisdom, we don the hat of a Stoic philosopher, embracing the "c'est la vie" attitude that acknowledges the impermanence and unpredictability of life. We learn to respond to our own misfortunes with a calm acceptance, recognising that they are an inherent part of the human experience. In doing so, we release ourselves from the burden of unnecessary suffering and allow ourselves to move forward with courage and fortitude.

As we journey through the peaks and valleys of life, let us embrace the shared humanity that binds us all. Let us extend the same empathy and understanding to ourselves that we readily offer to others. By aligning our reactions with the teachings of Epictetus, we navigate life's challenges with a sense of equilibrium and perspective.

In summary, the philosophy of Epictetus reminds us that our reactions to life's events hold immense power in shaping our overall well-being. By adopting a compassionate and accepting stance towards our own misfortunes, we embrace the essence of our shared human journey. So, let us navigate life's ebb and flow with resilience and empathy, knowing that each wave and gust is an opportunity for growth and self-discovery.

27

Life's Labyrinth

As a mark is not set up for the sake of missing the aim, so neither does the nature of evil exist in the world.

Standing at the edge of a monstrous labyrinth, you're struck not just by its daunting scale, but also by its intricate and spaghetti-like design. It's a head-scratcher of a maze that could give a bowl of linguini a run for its money! Now, your reasons for being here aren't some sort of quirky fascination for brainteasers, or a peculiar hankering to be lost. Neither is it purely for the adrenaline kick that would impress a die-hard roller coaster fan. No, your reasons are far more substantial. You're here with a bulldog determination to take on this labyrinthine titan, guided by your mental compass, and you're keenly fixated on the ultimate reward: the labyrinth's heart, a treasure trove of personal revelations and "aha!" moments that await like a pot of gold at the end of a rainbow.

Picture this labyrinth as a metaphor for our lives, faithfully mirroring its wild roller-coaster ride of complexities, sudden twists, and unpredictable surprises. Each labyrinthine corridor reflects the countless decisions that life flings at us like an over-excited tennis ball machine, directing us towards a kaleidoscope of outcomes, some delightful, others, well, let's just call them 'character-building'. In the same way, life constantly nudges us to make choices, confront obstacles, and ride its whirlwind, all with the aim of personal growth, deeper understanding, and the grand adventure of discovering our true selves.

Epictetus, encourages us to view life's speed bumps in a new light. These barriers aren't just cosmic banana peels that cause us to spill our morning cuppa in dismay. They're not some celestial jesters playing practical jokes at our expense. No, these challenges deserve a more thoughtful and deeper interpretation.

Life's hurdles, just like the labyrinth's unexpected twists and hidden corners, aren't pesky roadblocks but golden opportunities for growth and self-improvement. They've been carefully scattered across our path, much like breadcrumbs in a fairy tale, to provoke us into confronting them, learning valuable life lessons, and celebrating our victories, no matter how small they may be. Each obstacle we conquer acts as a stepping stone towards cultivating resilience, boosting self-awareness, and evolving into the best version of ourselves, like levelling up in a video game.

When navigating life's labyrinth, remember Epictetus' sage advice. The aim isn't to get caught up in a twisty maze that'd make a contortionist's head spin. Instead, we should adjust our strategy, turn to our moral compass, and press on. Just as a map is essential for finding your way out of an actual labyrinth, our personal values, guiding principles, and wisdom from past missteps form the compass that guides us through life's labyrinth.

Life isn't a mean-spirited maze that enjoys watching us stumble; rather, it's akin to an adventure-packed journey that encourages us to navigate with purpose, determination, and resilience. As we get familiar with life's labyrinthine nature, we bolster our resilience and fine-tune our knack for making choices that ring true with our inner selves. Mastering each challenge endows us with strength and insight, improving our understanding of ourselves and the world around us.

When you find yourself on the threshold of life's labyrinth, remember, you're armed with an arsenal of courage, determination, and wisdom. Dive headfirst into this journey, explore the diverse routes, and let this maze-like adventure be a transformative experience. Allow it to reveal the hidden gems within you, fostering self-discovery and personal growth. Life's labyrinth is not a foe to be beaten, but a journey to be undertaken, a story to be written, and a victory to be savoured.

Epictetus's wise words remind us that challenges are not in our path to make us miss our aim, but to guide us towards it. The labyrinth isn't designed to trap us, but to facilitate our journey to its heart. Similarly, life's obstacles aren't there to trip us up; they are guideposts pointing us towards self-realisation and personal growth. As Epictetus said, "As a mark is not set up for the sake of missing the aim, so neither does the nature of evil exist in the world". So, lace up your adventure boots and let's tackle this labyrinth!

We have reached that pivotal moment when understanding morphs into action. We've roamed the landscapes of Epictetus' wisdom, now it's time to integrate these vistas into our life's journey. The exercises up next are your guideposts, directing us from philosophy to praxis. Ready for the expedition? Let's transition from sightseeing to pathfinding, journeying towards our unique *Theory of Happiness*.

Our first mental workout, "Inner Maze Mapping", takes an inventive spin on problem-solving. Let's put it in perspective. Imagine your life's current challenges as a sprawling labyrinth, a complex maze with high, vine-covered walls. Picture yourself standing at the entrance, fully equipped with a map and compass, the early morning sun casting long shadows. In this task, you're an intrepid explorer, fearlessly venturing into the labyrinth, not with trepidation, but with a determined and unwavering focus on your ultimate goal - finding the solution to your problem. Rather than getting consumed by the labyrinth's puzzling intricacies, your objective is to concentrate on the destination, plotting your route with strategic precision. Picture the sense of achievement you'll feel when you successfully navigate the labyrinth, emerging triumphantly at the other end, overcoming each twist and turn, to ultimately reach your goal. This exercise sharpens your strategic thinking and ensures you stay solution-focused, even when faced with life's most daunting labyrinths.

Next, we invite you to engage in the "Maze Memoir", a week-long journey of introspective journaling. Each day, record the obstacles you encounter, documenting the whirlwind of emotions evoked, thoughts provoked, and wisdom gleaned from each challenge. This mindful act serves not just to hone your emotional intelligence but to also ignite the illuminating flame of self-reflection. After a week of this consistent practice, sit in a quiet corner, reviewing your entries. You might find that you've navigated more labyrinths than you initially perceived, a testament to your natural resilience and uncanny ability to adapt and grow. It's a compelling narrative that speaks volumes of your strength and endurance, which you might otherwise overlook amidst the chaos of life's labyrinth.

Our third cerebral challenge, "Epictetus' Navigator", champions the philosophy of mindfulness when grappling with life's dilemmas. Upon facing a new obstacle, take a mental pause and ask yourself, "Am I getting ensnared in the problem, or am I dedicatedly focusing on finding a solution?" This mindful moment of introspection allows you to preserve clarity in the midst of life's convoluted mazes. It's like temporarily stepping away from the labyrinth, perching on a hilltop, gaining a bird's eye view, and then strategising your path forward with renewed perspective.

Lastly, we present "Maze Mythbuster". Identify a recurring issue that's been gnawing at your peace of mind, and jot down three reasons why this isn't a cosmic conspiracy designed to impede your progress. Instead, view it as a golden opportunity for growth and learning. By reshaping your interpretation of these persistent challenges, morphing them from treacherous labyrinths into stepping stones, you catalyse a seismic shift in your mindset. You welcome new horizons for personal development, setting yourself on a path of optimism and constructive thinking.

Upon the conclusion of these exercises, remember that every step taken following Epictetus' wisdom is a leap towards a life of clarity. Philosophy isn't solely about intellectual analysis; it's a practical guide to living. The true essence of these teachings lies not just in their understanding but in their practice. Use these exercises as your guideposts, marking your path towards wisdom. As you traverse this path, you'll comprehend that philosophy isn't just a theory, but a lived experience.

To conclude, our exploration of Epictetus's philosophy unveils a transformative understanding that challenges and hardships are not malevolent forces designed to hinder our progress. Rather, they are integral components of the intricate tapestry of life, serving as catalysts for growth and self-improvement.

Epictetus reminds us that just as a target is not set up to be missed, the nature of evil does not exist in the world with the sole purpose of inflicting harm upon us. Instead, life presents us with a series of tests and trials, intended to sharpen our skills, deepen our understanding, and forge our character.

In embracing this perspective, we shift our perception of adversity. We no longer view it as a cruel imposition but as an opportunity for self-transformation. With each challenge we face, we are provided with the chance to learn valuable lessons, develop resilience, and uncover hidden strengths within ourselves.

Epictetus's philosophy encourages us to approach life's journey with a sense of curiosity, embracing both its triumphs and tribulations. We recognise that the obstacles we encounter are not barriers to our happiness but stepping stones towards personal growth and self-realisation.

As we navigate the labyrinthine path of life, we develop an unwavering resilience and an indomitable spirit. We learn to adapt, persevere, and thrive in the face of adversity. By embracing the challenges that come our way, we harness the transformative power they hold and emerge stronger, wiser, and more fulfilled.

In summary, Epictetus's teachings guide us to realise that life's challenges are not to be feared or avoided but embraced as opportunities for growth. By shifting our perspective, we recognise the inherent potential within every obstacle and approach them with courage, resilience, and a commitment to self-improvement.

Let us embark on this journey with open hearts and minds, ready to face life's trials as opportunities for personal transformation. May we navigate the labyrinth of existence with the wisdom of Epictetus as our guide, forging a path that leads to true happiness, resilience, and an unwavering sense of inner peace.

28

Your Mental Kingdom

If a person had delivered up your body to some passer-by, you would certainly be angry. And do you feel no shame in delivering up your own mind to any reviler, to be disconcerted and confounded?

Let's embark on a captivating journey through the boundless terrains of our minds, a vast expanse ripe with potential, waiting to be explored and harnessed. Imagine yourself not as a mere traveller, but a sovereign monarch ruling over this expansive domain. As a monarch, you bear the honour and responsibility of shaping and governing your mental kingdom, much akin to the diligent efforts of a Zen gardener meticulously tending to their garden, or a dedicated resort team working tirelessly to infuse tranquillity within their realm. Like these steadfast stewards, we too must treasure our minds with the same degree of unwavering commitment and care.

Consider your mind as a sacred sanctuary, a hallowed enclave where your thoughts, aspirations, and dreams take centre stage. Here, they perform the riveting drama of your life, drawing applause, evoking introspection, and offering valuable insights. Within this sanctuary, establishing and reinforcing a sturdy shield against disruptive forces is paramount. Much like the vigilant watchman at the gates of a fortress, you stand tall and resolute, prepared to hoist the "Not Welcome" sign at the first sign of negativity. Embrace this profound duty of safeguarding and strengthening your mental fortress, for it's within these well-fortified walls that an essential harmonious environment thrives—an environment that is indispensable for your overall well-being and happiness.

Let's take a moment to reflect on the meticulous care and patience required to maintain a Zen garden. Picture a gardener gently dragging a rake across the sand, each stroke carving intricate patterns, symbolic of the thoughtful arrangement of thoughts and emotions. The garden's delicate balance demands constant care: the careful pruning of bonsai trees to maintain their form, the nurturing of lotus blossoms to ensure their vibrant bloom. Our minds echo this very call for vigilance. Wield your mental broom to sweep away any lingering cobwebs of apprehension and self-doubt. Prune the prickly branches of harmful thoughts and cherish your inner serenity —akin to a delicate lotus blossom—encouraging it to unfurl in its magnificent glory. After all, a garden overrun by unsightly weeds loses its allure, just as a mind cluttered with negativity undermines its potential for peace and joy.

As we delve deeper into the concept of fortifying our mental territories, let's appreciate the significance of positive influences. Like a discerning host who thoughtfully curates a guest list, inviting only those who radiate positivity and enthusiasm, we must also exercise selectivity when allowing influences into our mental sanctuary. Surround yourself with individuals who embody optimism and cheer, those who uplift your spirits, spur you forward, and motivate you to unlock your fullest potential. Choose companions, mentors, and role models who radiate positivity, champion your personal growth, and encourage you to realise your dreams. By consciously curating the company we keep within our mental kingdom, we cultivate an atmosphere that nurtures our well-being and incites happiness.

Furthermore, it's crucial to monitor the information and media we expose ourselves to, as they exert a significant impact on our mental state. Akin to a balanced diet that fuels our physical bodies, a wholesome mental diet nourishes our minds. Seek out books, podcasts, and articles that infuse positivity, foster personal growth, and bolster resilience. Engage in activities that elevate and inspire you, whether that's appreciating soulful music, indulging in creative endeavours, or basking in the tranquillity of nature. By consciously choosing positive influences, we contribute towards fortifying our mental kingdoms, reaffirming our commitment to maintaining a serene and joyful state of mind.

In this vast kingdom of the mind, where thoughts hold sway and emotions ripple across like waves in an ocean, it's our responsibility to create an environment that's conducive to our well-being and happiness. Let's take on this task with fervour, ready to cultivate our mental kingdom into a haven of peace and joy. Ultimately, the quest for happiness sets sail from the harbour of our minds. It's within this mental sanctuary, cradled in the comfort of our thoughts and perceptions, where we'll unravel the enigma of authentic joy and contentment.

We're back at the precipice where contemplation transforms into application. We've gazed at Epictetus' wisdom, now it's time to use this vision in our lives. The upcoming exercises are your spectacles, focusing philosophy into everyday clarity. Ready to see clearly? Let's shift from looking to seeing, shaping our unique *Theory of Happiness*.

Our journey commences with an intriguing exercise, the "Mind-Palace Role Play". This imaginative endeavour paints a vivid scenario where an unsolicited detractor attempts to infiltrate the calm precincts of your mental fortress with their disquieting negativity. Let's liken this mental intruder to an unruly guest trying to gate-crash a meticulously planned party. As the host of your mental soiree, you rise to the occasion, nimbly crafting an apt and perhaps even wittily humorous riposte. This response serves as a metaphorical door-slam, assertively reminding the unwanted visitor and yourself of your sovereign

reign over your thoughts and emotions. This exercise fortifies the walls of your mental kingdom, underlining the inviolable fact that the power to shape your reactions and maintain tranquillity is exclusively yours.

Next in our itinerary is a delightful indulgence, the "Stoic Stand-Up". Picture yourself as a stand-up comedian, entrusted with the task of regaling your audience with a comedic recounting of a past incident—an event when an uninvited disruptor attempted to unsettle your tranquillity. In narrating this tale, allow your innate comedic flair to shine. Exaggerate the incident, sprinkling dashes of absurdity and layers of humour. Think of this exercise as serving a dual purpose: amplifying the laughter quotient while concocting a potent deterrent against those who threaten to disturb your peace. The central teaching of this amusing routine is the power to find humour in challenging situations, thereby utilising a light-hearted approach to defuse negativity.

Now, let's make way for the "Mental Doorman". This mental exercise presents you with a unique opportunity to inaugurate each day with an empowering vision: a formidable yet friendly doorman stationed dutifully at the entrance of your mental kingdom. Just like a seasoned bouncer who meticulously controls entry into an exclusive club, this guardian symbolises your resolution to safeguard your mind from undesirable influences. Envisage this doorman as an embodiment of your unyielding resolve to protect your mental realm, allowing entry to only positivity and the choicest vibes, while banishing any negative intruders who dare to approach. This mental tableau serves as a potent daily reminder of your authority in determining the influences that permeate your mental kingdom, reinforcing your commitment to preserving a serene and joyous atmosphere.

Our exploration concludes with the "Epictetus's Comic Strip", an exercise that invites your imagination to take flight. Embark on a creative escapade to design a comic strip encapsulating your triumphant stand-offs against the metaphorical 'peace pirates', those trying to disrupt your tranquillity. Adorn your pictorial narrative with hues of humour and wit, portraying yourself as the unyielding hero who bravely defends the serene realm of the mind. By transforming these encounters into a comic strip, you celebrate your victories against disruptive elements, creating a vibrant testament to your ability to nurture and protect your mental sanctuary.

As we finish these exercises, remember that every endeavour in line with Epictetus' teachings brings us closer to a life enlightened by wisdom. Philosophy isn't a mere mental exercise; it's a compass for living. The true power of these teachings lies not just in intellectual understanding but in active practice. Consider these exercises as your North Star, guiding you towards a life of wisdom. As you press forward, you'll realise that philosophy isn't just about intellectual understanding, but active living.

In summation, Epictetus's philosophy serves as a rallying cry, compelling us to take a proactive stance in guarding our most precious possession—our minds. Just as a skilled gardener tends to their plants, carefully weeding out the unwanted and nurturing the growth of the desired, we too must diligently cultivate our mental landscapes. We have the agency to shape our thoughts, emotions, and reactions, creating an inner sanctuary that radiates with positivity, resilience, and unwavering peace.

Imagine yourself as the unwavering gatekeeper of your mental realm, standing tall and resolute against the onslaught of negative influences. As the custodian of your mind, you possess the power to choose which thoughts and beliefs you allow entry, and which you turn away. Embrace the role of the discerning curator, inviting only those elements that invigorate and inspire, while steadfastly rejecting those that undermine your well-being.

By mindfully reinforcing our mental strongholds, we fortify the foundation of our inner sanctuaries. Surround yourself with constructive influences—inspiring books, supportive relationships, uplifting music, and nurturing environments. Immerse yourself in the beauty of nature, engage in creative pursuits that fuel your passions, and seek out experiences that bring you joy and fulfillment. In doing so, you create an atmosphere that nurtures and supports your growth, fostering a sense of harmony and balance within.

Guided by Epictetus's wisdom, let us march forward on this noble expedition, reclaiming our sovereignty over our minds. Through our daily practices of self-reflection, mindfulness, and intentional choice-making, we forge a path that leads to tranquillity and happiness. As we traverse the ever-changing landscape of life, we remain steadfast in our commitment to protect and nourish our mental realms, recognising that true happiness lies not in external circumstances, but in the resilience and serenity of our inner selves.

With each step forward, we become architects of our own well-being, co-creators of a life filled with purpose, contentment, and authentic joy. Embracing the teachings of Epictetus, we awaken to the boundless possibilities that lie within us and tap into the immense power to shape our own happiness.

Let us embark on this transformative journey, hand in hand with Epictetus as our guide, forging ahead with courage and determination. As we guard our mental fortresses, we cultivate a sacred space where negativity withers away, and the seeds of self-empowerment and inner peace can take root and flourish. May the philosophy of Epictetus continue to inspire us to embrace our role as guardians of our minds and may our pursuit of happiness be a testament to the enduring strength of the human spirit.

29

Choice and Commitment

In every affair consider what precedes and what follows, and then undertake it. Otherwise, you will begin with spirit, indeed, careless of the consequences, and when these are developed, you will shamefully desist. "I would conquer at the Olympic Games." But consider what precedes and what follows, and then, if it be for your advantage, engage in the affair. You must conform to rules, submit to a diet, refrain from dainties; exercise your body, whether you choose it or not, at a stated hour, in heat and cold; you must drink no cold water, and sometimes no wine—in a word, you must give yourself up to your trainer as to a physician. Then, in the combat, you may be thrown into a ditch, dislocate your arm, turn your ankle, swallow an abundance of dust, receive stripes [for negligence], and, after all, lose the victory. When you have reckoned up all this, if your inclination still holds, set about the combat. Otherwise, take notice, you will behave like children who sometimes play wrestlers, sometimes gladiators, sometimes blow a trumpet, and sometimes act a tragedy, when they happen to have seen and admired these shows. Thus, you too will be at one time a wrestler, and another a gladiator; now a philosopher, now an orator; but nothing in earnest. Like an ape you mimic all you see, and one thing after another is sure to please you, but is out of favour as soon as it becomes familiar. For you have never entered upon anything considerately; nor after having surveyed and tested the whole matter, but carelessly, and with a halfway zeal. Thus some, when they have seen a philosopher and heard a man speaking like Euphrates—though, indeed, who can speak like him?—have a mind to be philosophers, too. Consider first, man, what the matter is, and what your own nature is able to bear. If you would be a wrestler, consider your shoulders, your back, your thighs; for different persons are made for different things. Do you think that you can act as you do and be a philosopher, that you can eat, drink, be angry, be discontented, as you are now? You must watch, you must labour, you must get the better of certain appetites, must quit your acquaintances, be despised by your servant, be laughed at by those you meet; come off worse than others in everything—in offices, in honours, before tribunals. When you have fully considered all these things, approach, if you please—that is, if, by parting with them, you have a mind to purchase serenity, freedom, and tranquillity. If not, do not come hither; do not, like children, be now a philosopher, then a publican, then an orator, and then one of Caesar's officers. These things are not consistent. You must be one man, either good or bad. You must cultivate either your own reason or else

*externals; apply yourself either to things within or without you—
that is, be either a philosopher or one of the mob.*

Imagine standing at the edge of a precipice, the pounding heartbeat in your chest the only sound louder than the echo of anticipation that reverberates in your ears. You're about to take the plunge into the exhilarating unknown, embarking on a daring bungee jumping adventure. Perhaps you find yourself in a kitchen instead, the smell of baked goodness filling your nostrils as your heart drums a nervous rhythm in your chest. Your task: to craft the perfect soufflé - an edible masterpiece that stands tall and proud, defying gravity and critics alike. Or, in the arena of dreams, you visualise yourself standing on an Olympic podium, a shiny gold medal swaying from your neck as the deafening applause of the crowd fills your senses. The adrenaline rush from these ventures is as invigorating as a high-speed boat ride zipping across a placid, crystal clear lake.

Yet, as you stand intoxicated by this rush of anticipation, Epictetus, our philosophical companion, advises a slight pause. His voice, like a calming breeze, emerges from the whirlwind of your thrill-infused thoughts. He beseeches us not to hurl ourselves recklessly into the allure of these enticing adventures. He advises us to pause, to take a deep, grounding breath, and to thoughtfully consider the potential risks and rewards associated with our pursuits. Such careful contemplation can help us evade potential pitfalls that might lead us down a rocky road to the ominous town of Disappointmentville.

The smorgasbord of life brims with glittering opportunities, each one flashing its enchanting façade, its thrilling allure, and its shadowy underside. The glossy promises of these ventures kindle our imagination, stoke the flames of desire, and nudge us towards the unknown's tantalising thrill. However, with every expedition, every venture, comes an often-overlooked companion - the less glamorous side of the coin: the demands of sacrifice, the relentless persistence needed, and the expectation of robust resilience.

Take, for instance, the beguiling dream of Olympic gold. The intoxicating image of standing atop the victory podium, the applause resounding in your ears, is indeed a captivating picture. But to ascend this pinnacle of triumph, a formidable climb awaits you. The journey towards Olympic glory demands significant sacrifices. Envision trading Friday night pizza parties for gruelling training sessions, replacing tempting beach days with unwavering discipline, and foregoing impromptu social gatherings to remain focused on the gold. What's more, despite such sacrifices, the spectre of defeat looms large, casting an unsettling shadow over the many hours of exertion, sweat, and dedication invested in this pursuit. The glamour of the golden dream suddenly tarnishes slightly when observed through this realistic lens.

In light of such potential challenges, it's vital to approach any new venture as you would a marathon. You wouldn't start a long-distance run without lacing up your shoes, setting a comfortable pace, and prepping your body and mind for the road ahead. Similarly, launching yourself into a new endeavour without the necessary preparation risks landing you among the whimsical dreamers, those who flit from one fleeting ambition to another, changing their life's trajectory as often as they change their socks.

Epictetus cautions us against such fickle behaviour, emphasising the significance of commitment in the pursuit of any ambition. He warns that each dream we chase will inevitably demand some sacrifices, including renouncing certain comforts, enduring hardships, and even tolerating the occasional good-natured jibes from peers who may not understand our chosen path. To prevent falling into the trap of becoming a "jack of all trades, master of none", it's vital to carefully choose a path and channel all our energies into mastering it, notwithstanding the challenges it may present.

For instance, let's consider you're drawn to the path of philosophy, intrigued by the allure of profound insights and the promise of inner peace. An admirable choice indeed! But remember, even this path is strewn with thorns. Choosing to tread the philosophical trail might require forgoing certain worldly pleasures, bearing the bemused expressions of those unfamiliar with your pursuit, and perhaps feeling somewhat detached from the mainstream whirl. Yet, if the quest for wisdom, insight, and tranquillity strikes a deep chord within you, brace yourself for a journey that promises to be profoundly transformative. If, however, philosophy doesn't stir your passion, don't despair. Follow the path that truly resonates with you and dedicate yourself to it fully. The point is to commit wholeheartedly to your chosen path, rather than meandering aimlessly from one trail to another, left feeling directionless and devoid of purpose.

By meticulously considering the demands, sacrifices, and potential rewards of the paths before us, we equip ourselves to make more informed decisions that align with our deepest desires. Whether our chosen path involves chasing adrenaline-fuelled adventures, dedicating ourselves to mastering a complex craft, or delving into the profound depths of philosophy, the key is to embrace the journey with unwavering commitment and intentional action. This approach empowers us to relish life one slice at a time, rather than attempting to sample every dish on life's expansive buffet. Epictetus, in his characteristic witty style, reminds us that while we can't experience every aspect of life, we can fully engage in the experiences that resonate deeply with us, leading to a more fulfilling and meaningful existence.

Once again, we're at the pivot where thought turns into action. We've danced with Epictetus' philosophy, now it's time to let this rhythm guide our steps. The exercises to follow are your dance floor, where you translate the rhythm of philosophy into the dance of daily life. Ready to dance? Let's move from philosophy to practice, choreographing our own *Theory of Happiness*.

First up, we have "Role Roulette", an experiment in experiential philosophy. For one week, immerse yourself in the world of a philosopher. Replace your evening Netflix marathon with a contemplative engagement with philosophical heavyweights like Nietzsche or Plato. Exchange your typical morning jog for a thoughtful walk, with your mind churning on life's grand mysteries. As you lunch, instead of the usual chat, stir up conversation on the purpose of existence. This transformation might make you feel like a modern-day Socrates, tangled up in profound questions about life and reality. The goal here isn't to turn you into a full-time philosopher, but to encourage introspection and deeper engagement with life's big questions.

Next, we dive into "Passion Freeze Tag". Imagine a notice board filled with vibrant sticky notes, each one representing a role or dream you've fancied at some point in your life. Against each role, jot down the necessary skills, potential sacrifices, rewards, and perhaps the not-so-glamorous side of each role. Scan through these notes and pause when you spot a role that sparks a compelling sense of commitment, despite the potential sacrifices and challenges. It's possible that you've just stumbled upon a passion that aligns perfectly with your authentic self, a beacon lighting your way forward in life.

We now move to "Epictetus's Scale of Choice". For this, picture a traditional weighing scale. On one side, place the aspiration or goal you wish to achieve, and on the other, place all the potential sacrifices, challenges, and behavioural changes you'd have to make to achieve that goal. If the scale tips in favour of your goal despite the weight of the challenges, then you have a genuine commitment towards it.

Lastly, we venture into the "Reality Check Relay", a self-guided tour through your interests. Pick a hobby or pursuit that catches your fancy. Dive deep into understanding its many facets - the time and financial commitments, the possible challenges, and the pitfalls. After this thorough exploration, if your spirit still blazes with a strong zeal to pursue this hobby, then you've successfully passed the reality check. You're ready to set sail on this new adventure with an unflinching sense of commitment and enthusiasm.

Having navigated through these exercises, bear in mind that every choice inspired by Epictetus is a step towards a life filled with wisdom. Philosophy isn't merely a contemplative exercise; it's a practical roadmap for life. The real value of these teachings lies not just in their study but in their application. See these exercises as your compass, steering you towards a life that embodies wisdom. As you advance, you'll recognise that philosophy isn't just about cognition, but about action.

In closing, let us draw upon the wisdom of Epictetus and reflect on the profound implications of his teachings. Life, with all its intricacies and possibilities, presents us with a myriad of paths to explore. However, Epictetus reminds us that true fulfillment lies not in the pursuit of fleeting desires and superficial engagements, but in the deliberate selection of a purpose that resonates with our core values and aspirations.

Just as a discerning connoisseur selects the finest ingredients to create a remarkable feast, we too must approach life's offerings with thoughtfulness and intentionality. It is not about indulging in every passing fancy or chasing after every fleeting opportunity, but about choosing our endeavours wisely and committing ourselves to a meaningful and purposeful path.

Epictetus's message resonates deeply in a world filled with distractions and superficial pursuits. He urges us to resist the temptation to be swept away by the current of popular trends and shallow aspirations. Instead, he invites us to consider our true nature, our unique strengths and capabilities, and to embrace the path that aligns with our authentic selves.

By carefully assessing our own capacities and understanding the sacrifices that come with each pursuit, we gain clarity on what truly matters to us. We must be willing to make sacrifices, to invest time, effort, and discipline, and to face the inevitable challenges and setbacks that accompany our chosen path.

In embracing Epictetus's philosophy, we become architects of our own destinies. We embark on a journey of self-discovery and self-mastery, recognising that true fulfillment lies not in the accumulation of external accolades or material possessions, but in the alignment of our actions with our inner values and principles.

Let us remember that we cannot be everything to everyone, nor can we pursue every path simultaneously. It is a conscious decision to commit to a particular way of life, to cultivate our own reason, and to pursue the virtues and ideals that resonate deeply within us.

Epictetus's wisdom urges us to be mindful of our choices and to accept the consequences that come with them. We may be misunderstood, face opposition, and endure hardships, but in staying true to our chosen path, we find the serenity, freedom, and tranquillity that come from living a life of purpose and integrity.

As we navigate the complexities of existence, let us approach life with discernment and deliberation. Let us eschew the fickleness of pursuing fleeting pleasures and instead commit ourselves to the pursuit of a singular purpose that brings us lasting joy and fulfillment. By embracing the philosophy of Epictetus, we forge a path of authenticity and wholeheartedness, living as one who is steadfast in their principles and committed to the cultivation of a meaningful and purposeful life.

30

The Relationship Tango

Duties are universally measured by relations. Is a certain man your father? In this are implied taking care of him, submitting to him in all things, patiently receiving his reproaches, his correction. But he is a bad father. Is your natural tie, then, to a good father? No, but to a father. Is a brother unjust? Well, preserve your own just relation toward him. Consider not what he does, but what you are to do to keep your own will in a state conformable to nature, for another cannot hurt you unless you please. You will then be hurt when you consent to be hurt. In this manner, therefore, if you accustom yourself to contemplate the relations of neighbour, citizen, commander, you can deduce from each the corresponding duties.

The venture through the undulating landscape of relationships is a journey fraught with unpredictability, reminiscent of an exhilarating wild safari, awash with a verdant outgrowth of emotions and expectations. These connections, especially the bonds we cultivate with our vivid, and frequently offbeat, family members, play out like an enigmatic treasure hunt. The treasures are concealed within intricate layers of unspoken duties and covert standards of behaviour, infusing a sense of mystery and intrigue into our familial ties. This complexity is further amplified when we examine relationships through the lens of Stoicism, as proposed by Epictetus, revealing a tapestry of mutual responsibilities and relational intricacies.

One of the most profound examples of these complexities is the eternal parent-child relationship. It's akin to being drafted into an unseen fellowship, where many sons and daughters find themselves wearing the wizard's hat, commandeering the unpredictable realm of modern technology. Like a seasoned wizard commanding a technomancy realm, you transform into the family's default tech guru, a role stemming from your uncanny knack to negotiate cooperation from recalcitrant gadgets. Your duties may span from setting up email accounts, akin to a master locksmith fashioning intricate keys, to decoding the enigmatic digital hieroglyphs of smartphone glitches, and even unravelling the mystic domain of hashtags and emojis to the elders. This role, although demanding, engenders a feeling of victory similar to the triumphant protagonist in an exhilarating tech-centric adventure novel.

Furthermore, the parent-child relationship often unfolds like a captivating odyssey through time's labyrinthine corridors. It includes settling into nostalgia's warm embrace as your parent regales you with chronicles from their "golden era". These narratives, aglow with memories from an epoch when smartphones were merely abstract ideas within speculative fiction and social media's influence extended only to the local gossip over a neighbour's fence, form invaluable time capsules. Despite their repetitive nature, they serve as portals to the past, helping to stitch together a magical tapestry of shared experiences that bridge the generational divide.

However, like any grand tale told through the ages, the story of the parent-child relationship isn't without its conflicts. Dragons of disapproval often rear their heads, leading to classic battles between youthful rebellion and age-old wisdom. It's crucial to recognise that beneath these confrontations, often lies a deep-seated love and concern. These disagreements are typically the result of a wellspring of protective instincts and expectations that simply want the best for the child.

Navigating the intricate dynamics of the parent-child relationship is not about masquerading as the 'model child'. It's about honouring your authentic self as your parents' irreplaceable offspring, possessing your unique strengths, weaknesses, and eccentricities. The objective isn't to emulate a paradigm but to embrace the relationship with all its beautifully flawed nuances, reminiscent of appreciating a piece of abstract artwork.

Transitioning our focus to the bustling circus of sibling relationships, the ensuing drama could indeed rival any Shakespearean play. These bonds often mimic high-stakes wrestling bouts, charged with favouritism, conflicting personalities, and perceived inequities. Yet, as Epictetus sagely advised, the theatrics belong to them - their circus, their monkeys. While you may sometimes feel entrapped within the audience, your moral compass remains steadfastly within your jurisdiction. They can only ruffle your feathers if you hand them the reins. Upholding this Stoic outlook can help you traverse the turbulent waters of sibling relationships with the finesse of an adept mariner, safeguarding your sense of self-worth.

In the grand opera of existence, each relationship script presents its unique ensemble of characters, dialogues, and narrative arcs. The ballet of relationships may periodically mirror a whimsical, off-beat performance, but it's this rhythmic oscillation, the crescendos, and diminuendos, that infuse our existence with vibrant hues. Comprehending and embracing our roles within these relationships empowers us to sway rhythmically to the symphony of human connections, contributing our distinctive beats and melodies. Thus, let's revel in the grand ballroom of relationships, finding harmony amidst their glorious unpredictability, and ensuring our smiles remain our faithful dance partners, every step of the way.

It's that juncture again when philosophy translates into life. We've listened to Epictetus' wisdom, and now it's time to let this melody resonate in our lives. The following exercises are your instruments, helping us turn the harmony of thought into the symphony of action. Shall we play? Let's transition from listening to performing, composing our own *Theory of Happiness*.

Let's begin our journey with an activity we'll call "Role Reversal". This game requires you to team up with a close friend or family member for an evening of mutual exploration. The challenge? You're going to switch roles, copying each other's behaviours, attitudes, and perspectives. If your chosen partner is your sibling, let your personality take on the thrills and spills of a rollercoaster ride operator, mirroring the unpredictable nature of sibling relationships. If you're role-playing with your parent, you might want to channel your inner traditionalist, preserving the old-world order amidst the storm of modern transformations, assuming that reflects their typical demeanour. Pay close attention to the emotions that surface within you, the instinctive reactions that pop up, and the new thought patterns that come alive as you dive headfirst into this role-play adventure. Don't be surprised if bouts of laughter punctuate your experience. However, this activity serves a purpose beyond mere amusement. It's a tool for cultivating understanding and empathy, fostering a deeper appreciation for how our actions impact others. As we try to see the world through someone else's perspective, we become more aware of our own behaviour. This newfound mindfulness helps us to navigate our relationships more effectively, armed with a more finely tuned sense of compassion.

Our journey continues with the "Monkeys in the Circus" challenge. Here, you're the ringleader, assembling a troupe of friends or family members for an improvisational theatre of life. Each participant embodies a character with idiosyncrasies mirroring those adorably chaotic circus monkeys that we all find so captivating. Encourage creativity, champion your quirks, and let the laughter become your symphony. This frolicsome exercise nudges us to detach ourselves from the personal effects of others' behaviour, finding amusement in the delightful circus that life often mirrors. It's a heartening reminder not to take ourselves or others too seriously, allowing us to celebrate the unexpected mirth and spontaneity that punctuate our relationships.

Finally, we introduce the whimsical "The Feather Resistance Challenge". Begin by selecting a feather or another light object that's easy to carry around. As you move through your day, anytime someone's actions threaten to rustle your emotional calm, grip your feather firmly. As you do this, mentally echo the phrase, "No one can ruffle my feathers without my permission." This charming exercise serves as a tactile reminder of the control we have over our reactions and emotions. It propels us towards maintaining a light-hearted perspective, empowering us to refrain from allowing others' words or actions to disrupt our inner harmony. Through consciously choosing our responses and cherishing a sense of humour, we can gracefully navigate the intricacies of relationships while embracing the comedic side of human interactions.

As we close these exercises, remember that each effort aligned with Epictetus' teachings brings us closer to a life led by wisdom. Philosophy isn't just a mental activity; it's a framework for action. The true depth of these teachings lies not just in comprehending them but in living them. Consider these exercises as your guide, directing you towards a life filled with wisdom. As you continue your journey, you'll find that philosophy isn't just intellectual; it's practical.

In essence, Epictetus teaches us that the measure of our duties lies in the web of relationships that intertwine our lives. Whether it be our parent, sibling, neighbour, or boss, our responsibilities are not dictated by the actions or qualities of others, but by the inherent ties that bind us together. We are called to uphold our end of the relational bargain, regardless of the virtues or vices displayed by those around us.

Epictetus invites us to shift our focus from the faults and shortcomings of others to our own actions and attitudes. Instead of dwelling on the perceived injustices or imperfections of our relationships, we are encouraged to examine our own responses and conduct. By cultivating a state of mind that remains true to our own nature and values, we become less susceptible to external influences and more resilient in navigating the complexities of human interactions.

In adopting this perspective, we liberate ourselves from the shackles of expectations and resentments. We learn to accept that we cannot control the actions or choices of others, but we have the power to shape our own responses and attitudes. We realise that our well-being and inner harmony are not contingent on the behaviour of others, but on our own willingness to fulfil our duties and obligations with integrity and compassion.

Epictetus's philosophy calls us to rise above the fray of interpersonal conflicts and to approach our relationships with wisdom and understanding. Rather than being consumed by judgment and resentment, we strive to cultivate empathy, patience, and acceptance. We recognise that true fulfillment and happiness lie in aligning our own actions with the principles of nature and fulfilling our duties to the best of our abilities.

As we embrace the teachings of Epictetus, we embark on a journey of self-reflection and growth, understanding that the quality of our relationships is ultimately determined by our own choices and actions. By focusing on our responsibilities rather than the perceived faults of others, we create an environment of harmony, respect, and mutual understanding.

Let us, then, embrace the philosophy of Epictetus as we navigate the intricate tapestry of our relationships. May we strive to honour our duties, treat others with kindness and compassion, and nurture a spirit of harmony and cooperation. By doing so, we contribute to the creation of a world where genuine connections are forged, and the richness of human experience is realised.

31

The Universal Rhythm

Be assured that the essence of piety toward the gods lies in this—to form right opinions concerning them, as existing and as governing the universe justly and well. And fix yourself in this resolution, to obey them, and yield to them, and willingly follow them amidst all events, as being ruled by the most perfect wisdom. For thus you will never find fault with the gods, nor accuse them of neglecting you. And it is not possible for this to be affected in any other way than by withdrawing yourself from things which are not within our own power, and by making good or evil to consist only in those which are. For if you suppose any other things to be either good or evil, it is inevitable that, when you are disappointed of what you wish or incur what you would avoid, you should reproach and blame their authors. For every creature is naturally formed to flee and abhor things that appear hurtful and that which causes them; and to pursue and admire those which appear beneficial and that which causes them. It is impracticable, then, that one who supposes himself to be hurt should rejoice in the person who, as he thinks, hurts him, just as it is impossible to rejoice in the hurt itself. Hence, also, a father is reviled by his son when he does not impart the things which seem to be good; and this made Polynices and Eteocles mutually enemies—that empire seemed good to both. On this account the husbandman reviles the gods; [and so do] the sailor, the merchant, or those who have lost wife or child. For where our interest is, there, too, is piety directed. So that whoever is careful to regulate his desires and aversions as he ought is thus made careful of piety likewise. But it also becomes incumbent on everyone to offer libations and sacrifices and first fruits, according to the customs of his country, purely, and not heedlessly nor negligently; not avariciously, nor yet extravagantly.

In the mesmerising performance that is life, we find ourselves playing various roles on an ever-changing stage, swept along by the rhythm of unseen forces. These enigmatic entities, variously referred to as destiny, karma, or simply the universe, form an integral part of our grand orchestration of existence. Just as dancers trust the choreographer's vision and the orchestra's harmony, we're called upon to perceive these cosmic directors as benign, fair-minded, and insightful guides in the narrative of our lives. Our resident philosopher, Epictetus, suggests this perspective can be a tool of empowerment, preventing us from feeling forsaken or victimised when our expectations and reality perform a less-than-perfect pas de deux.

In mastering this graceful art of cosmic understanding, we're called upon to perfect our pirouettes around the concept of control. Imagine, if you will, two boxes. One box is labelled 'Within My Control', into which you'll place your thoughts, decisions, and responses. The second box, labelled 'Beyond My Control', houses external variables such as the day's weather, the stock market's fluctuating temperament, or the unexpected cancellation of your cherished Netflix series. By allocating these events to their rightful boxes, we honour the separation between our personal sphere and the grand domain of the cosmic directors, who operate independently and unaffected by our emotional outbursts or silent pleas.

Epictetus cautions against the folly of appraising occurrences from the second box as either 'good' or 'bad'. This evaluative dance, he suggests, only leads us to stumble into a cyclical tango of frustration and resentment. Consider the disgruntled farmer, bemoaning the drought-ridden sky, or the agitated sailor, berating Poseidon for every tempestuous wave that disrupts his journey. Each of these individuals has inadvertently shifted focus to circumstances outside their control. The reality, however, is these events are part of the cosmic choreography, and our reactions to them determine whether we glide with grace or falter with frustration.

To better illustrate this, let's consider the scenario of a persistent cosmic complainer: someone who blames external circumstances for their unending dissatisfaction. Their perspective is not unlike that of a disappointed toddler who, denied unlimited candy, is convinced their benevolent father has transformed into the villainous Darth Vader. The father, in his wisdom, attempts to circumvent a sugar-fuelled meltdown and acts in the child's best interest. Similarly, a cosmic complainer expends precious energy, souring their perspective and limiting their capacity to appreciate the multifaceted marvels that life invariably presents.

In any thriving relationship, whether interpersonal or cosmic, appreciation is fundamental. It nurtures and solidifies the bonds that interlink us. This appreciation towards cosmic forces may manifest in a variety of ways: silent reflections, acts of kindness, or expressions of genuine gratitude. The true magic, though, lies in ensuring our appreciation is sincere and respectful, devoid of attempts to coax the universe into favouring our ambitions. This isn't about charming the universe into a cosmic waltz but about acknowledging our interconnected role within the grand cosmic tapestry.

Therefore, for the benefit of humanity and our personal tranquillity, let's strive to operate harmoniously within our sphere of cosmic influence. As we adeptly surf life's waves, sending out our cosmic 'thank you' notes into the vast universe, we contribute to the grand dance of existence. These expressions of gratitude, though seemingly insignificant, echo through the cosmos, symbolising our recognition of and respect for the intricate and awe-inspiring processes that govern our universe. Consequently, we are imbued with a serene realisation that we are not mere spectators, but rather integral contributors to this cosmic performance.

We are back at the threshold where ideas translate into action. We've warmed ourselves with Epictetus' wisdom, now it's time to let this heat forge our actions. The exercises to follow are your furnace, shaping the raw ore of philosophy into the tools of daily life. Ready to forge? Let's move from contemplation to creation, forging our unique *Theory of Happiness*.

Let's start by unveiling the "Celestial Shout-out", an exercise that encourages us to begin each day with a heartening expression of gratitude directed towards the universe, or our preferred cosmic director. Imagine stepping out onto your front porch, the first light of dawn spilling across the horizon. The aroma of your morning coffee wafts through the crisp air, blending with the harmonious melody of birds welcoming the new day. Amidst this picturesque scene, you pause and truly appreciate these ordinary yet beautiful moments—the rejuvenating morning air filling your lungs, the soft whispers of the breeze that gently caress your skin, or even the lively chatter of your neighbours preparing for the day. Such acts of gratitude not only infuse our day with positivity and appreciation but also resonate with the universe itself. It's akin to a cosmic handshake—an exchange of energy that solidifies our connection with the universe and its omnipresent forces.

Next on our philosophical agenda is the "Cosmic Comedy" challenge, designed to help us find humour in situations entirely beyond our control. Take, for instance, an unexpected downpour during your lunchtime walk. You might, initially, feel a surge of frustration. But imagine, instead, the comic sight of you, caught mid-bite of your sandwich, suddenly morphing into a rain-soaked wanderer. Or, picture yourself stuck in an unpredictable traffic jam, a situation usually greeted with sighs of annoyance. Instead, you seize this opportunity to indulge in a thrilling true-crime podcast that's been sitting on your playlist. Finding amusement in such unpredictable scenarios transforms life's random dance into a cosmic comedy show, where the most unanticipated events might leave you chuckling to yourself.

Following this, we encounter the practice of "Divine Acceptance". This philosophy encourages us to accept life's curveballs without the urge to categorise them into 'good' or 'bad' boxes. It's about observing life's phenomena with curiosity, much like a scientist who witnesses an unexpected reaction in a petri dish. Instead of attempting to control the outcome, we simply observe, unjudging and open. This shift in perspective, though subtle, can be a transformative force in our lives, guiding us to navigate through obstacles with grace and equanimity. By accepting life's inherent uncertainties, we unshackle ourselves from unnecessary stress and resistance, often discovering tranquillity within chaos.

Finally, let's explore the "Universal Diary" exercise. For one week, document instances when you successfully focused on what's within your sphere of control. Reflect on your emotional responses, any changes in your mood or outlook, and the overall impact on your well-being. Keeping such a record serves as a tangible testimony to Epictetus's wisdom, highlighting the benefits of concentrating our energies on the aspects of life that truly matter. This exercise also provides a personal archive of growth and empowerment, a reminder of the strides we've made in harmonising our lives with the cosmic rhythm.

At the completion of these exercises, keep in mind that each decision influenced by Epictetus brings us closer to a life shaped by wisdom. Philosophy isn't just an academic pursuit; it's a guide for everyday living. The true essence of these teachings isn't just in understanding them but in embodying them. See these exercises as your beacon, lighting your way towards a life filled with wisdom. As you move forward, you'll realise that philosophy isn't just studied, but lived.

In essence, Epictetus's philosophy implores us to cultivate a correct understanding about the immutable laws and principles that govern the universe. It's within this comprehension that we discover the key to developing a deep sense of respect and compliance towards these laws. By resolving to align our actions with the universal order and willingly accepting the events and circumstances that emerge as part of this order, we liberate ourselves from the inclination to harbour resentment or frustration when faced with adversity.

This harmonious coexistence with the universe can only be achieved by directing our focus away from external matters that are beyond our control and recognising that the true nature of good and evil resides solely within our own choices and actions. If we assign these labels to anything else, we unavoidably fall into the pitfall of attributing our disappointments or misfortunes to external factors.

Conflicts and tensions amongst humans often stem from the divergent perceptions and attributions of good and evil. Such a scenario prompts us to criticise others when our desires aren't fulfilled or when we undergo losses. However, by aligning our desires and aversions in accordance with reason, we not only cultivate healthier relationships with others, but also with the universe itself.

Epictetus's philosophy further underscores the importance of rituals and traditions, which can be understood as practices that encourage mindfulness, discipline, and a sense of connection to our community and the world around us. These practices serve as reminders of our place within the broader spectrum of existence, emphasising the importance of attentiveness and care in our actions.

In the vast canvas of existence, Epictetus nudges us to perceive ourselves not just as bystanders or victims of the universe's mechanism, but as active participants. By fostering a deep respect for the natural order and synchronising our actions with it, we can achieve a state of harmonious integration with the universe. This opens the gateway to the limitless beauty and wisdom surrounding us, providing solace, tranquillity, and fulfilment in our journey through life.

32

The Voyage of Wisdom

When you have recourse to divination, remember that you know not what the event will be, and you come to learn it of the diviner; but of what nature it is you knew before coming; at least, if you are of philosophic mind. For if it is among the things not within our own power, it can by no means be either good or evil. Do not, therefore, bring with you to the diviner either desire or aversion—else you will approach him trembling—but first clearly understand that every event is indifferent and nothing to you, of whatever sort it may be; for it will be in your power to make a right use of it, and this no one can hinder. Then come with confidence to the gods as your counsellors; and afterwards, when any counsel is given you, remember what counsellors you have assumed, and whose advice you will neglect if you disobey. Come to divination as Socrates prescribed, in cases of which the whole consideration relates to the event, and in which no opportunities are afforded by reason or any other art to discover the matter in view. When, therefore, it is our duty to share the danger of a friend or of our country, we ought not to consult the oracle as to whether we shall share it with them or not. For though the diviner should forewarn you that the auspices are unfavourable, this means no more than that either death or mutilation or exile is portended. But we have reason within us; and it directs us, even with these hazards, to stand by our friend and our country. Attend, therefore, to the greater diviner, the Pythian God, who once cast out of the temple him who neglected to save his friend.

Our odyssey through existence resembles a voyage on a capricious sea. Sometimes, the water's surface is as serene as a still pond, the path ahead brilliantly clear. Yet, there come instances when the towering waves of uncertainty emerge from the deep, transforming our journey into a dance with chaos. We find ourselves at a tumultuous crossroads, where a myriad of paths stretch out before us, each leading towards an opaque, unknown future. The signposts, bearing no discernible message, leave us in a quandary: which path should we choose? In such periods of tumult and confusion, our hearts crave guidance, a luminous beacon that can dispel the darkness and illuminate the route forward. We yearn for solace, for a semblance of certainty about the future.

On this quest for guidance, some of us might venture into the realm of fortune tellers, stepping into a dimly lit, incense-infused tent, hanging onto their every cryptic utterance. Others may turn to the convenience of technology, unlocking their mobile devices to access a plethora of astrology apps, scrolling through lines of divinely ordained forecasts, hoping to find an insight that chimes with their current predicament. Some of us may even reach out to that intuitive friend who, over countless cups of tea and meaningful heart-to-heart discussions, appears to have an uncanny knack for predicting outcomes. Although these external sources can indeed offer a comforting blanket of reassurance and, at times, boast eerily accurate foresights, they are not the only reservoirs of wisdom at our disposal.

Before we hurl ourselves headlong into these beckoning fountains of prophecy, let's pause for a moment. Let's explore a timeless source of wisdom that has been respected and delved into for centuries – the teachings of the revered Stoic philosopher, Epictetus.

Picture yourself balanced on the brink of the mysterious unknown, standing at the entrance of a fortune teller's incense-laden sanctuary or your finger poised above an enticing astrology app. The air crackles with palpable anticipation and the mystery of what's to come. However, before you succumb to the allure of these mystical sources, there's a significant point that warrants your attention: you're seeking guidance because the future, with its plethora of potential outcomes, is hidden from your sight. Yet, there's one element that you're entirely conscious of: whether the situation you're grappling with falls within the sphere of your control, or if it dwells in the domain of external influences beyond your manipulation.

Understanding this dichotomy of control forms the crux of Epictetus's philosophy. He consistently underscored the importance of discerning between these two realms – the elements that are within our purview (our actions, intentions, and desires), and those that lie beyond our control (external events, circumstances, other people's actions). Recognising this vital distinction can radically recalibrate our perspective, furnishing us with the wisdom and tranquillity needed to adeptly navigate the tumultuous seas of life.

Now, let's delve deeper into an enlightening nugget of wisdom from Epictetus. Suppose you're grappling with a situation that falls into the 'not my circus, not my monkeys' category. In other words, it's beyond your control. Epictetus maintains that this scenario cannot inherently be good or bad for you. This proposition might seem paradoxical at first. We are, after all, conditioned to categorise external events as beneficial or detrimental based on their impact on us. However, Epictetus challenges this conventional wisdom. He posits that the essence of being beneficial or harmful does not reside in the uncontrollable external events but in our responses and how we choose to react to them.

Therefore, as you venture into the mystical dominions of fortune tellers or astrology apps, resist the seduction to become overly invested in desiring or avoiding a specific outcome. An intense desire for a particular result might sow the seeds of disappointment if things don't unfold as envisioned, and conversely, persistently avoiding certain outcomes can trap you in a cycle of fear or anxiety. As tantalising as this emotional rollercoaster might seem (unless you have a peculiar affection for stress-induced migraines), it would be prudent to approach the situation with a different mindset.

Instead, arm yourself with the understanding that, regardless of the outcome, you possess the capacity to navigate it. Why is this so? Because you, dear reader, have been blessed with an extraordinary superpower – the ability to control your reactions and make the most of any given circumstance. This is your inner superhero, your source of strength and resilience. This power is so intrinsic and personal that no force in the universe, not even the mightiest of superheroes, can rob you of it.

By all means, solicit advice from the cosmos, the deities, the oracles, or even that eerily accurate Magic 8 Ball that's been languishing in your attic. These sources can yield valuable insights, alternative perspectives, and at times, astonishingly precise predictions. However, in your pursuit of external advice, remember Epictetus's poignant counsel: if you're seeking advice, be prepared to act upon it. If not, you're merely going through the motions, squandering your time and that of your sources of wisdom – including the precious time of your neglected Magic 8 Ball.

It's crucial to remember that not every decision requires external counsel. There are instances when the morally right course of action shines with such clarity, it stands out like a beacon guiding ships through the night, even if the path might seem daunting or strenuous at the outset. For instance, if a friend is in distress and you can offer support, or if an opportunity arises to contribute meaningfully to your community or country, don't hesitate or seek external validation. These moments call for the heed of your inner moral compass and demand immediate action. After all, this is a testament to fundamental decency and the inherent goodness within you.

And so, we arrive at the heart of our discourse. Listen to your internal guide, the serene and rational voice of wisdom residing deep within you. This internal guide is your personal fortune teller, your inner oracle, or as the ancients referred to it, the "Pythian God". History brims with tales of individuals who disregarded this internal counsel, only to face dire consequences. Recount the misfortune of the individual who was expelled from a temple for failing to assist a friend in need. By attuning ourselves to the wisdom within and embracing its guidance, we can tap into a profound source of insight capable of illuminating our path in remarkable ways. So, next time you find yourself at a crossroads, remember to consult your inner Pythian God and have faith in the wisdom it imparts.

It's that time again to shift from musing to doing. We've bathed in Epictetus' wisdom, and now it's time to let this wisdom cleanse our actions. The exercises that follow are your soap, washing away the dirt of ignorance with the lather of wisdom. Ready to cleanse? Let's transition from bathing in wisdom to cleansing actions, purifying our *Theory of Happiness*.

The first exercise we introduce on this philosophical journey is the whimsically named "Magic 8 Ball Musings". Much akin to consulting a fortune teller, this activity nudges you to use a Magic 8 Ball or toss a coin to decide on trivial matters in your daily life—like choosing between tea or coffee, or deciding whether to take an umbrella on a cloudy day. The intent isn't to seed decision-making power to chance but to practise acceptance of any given outcome, similar to embracing advice from the universe itself. This exercise helps you cultivate a sense of detachment from specific outcomes, nurturing acceptance of the present moment as it unfurls, embodying the very spirit of Epictetus's teachings.

Next in our toolkit is the "Universal Advice Journal". Keeping a journal has long been recognised as a potent tool for self-reflection and personal growth. This exercise encourages you to record the decisions you make throughout the day, how you manoeuvred through them, and their subsequent outcomes. As your journal brims with daily entries, you craft a dedicated space for introspection. This process opens a window to your inner workings, shedding light on your decision-making process and offering valuable insights that can catalyse self-improvement.

Stepping forward, we encounter the "Ask The Pythian God" exercise. The Pythian God here symbolises your inner voice, your personal oracle. Before seeking advice from others or scanning a horoscope, this exercise invites you to consult this inner sage. It nudges you to foster a connection with your instinctive wisdom, developing an unshakeable trust in it over time. As this trust blossoms, you'll find it increasingly easier to lean on this intuitive wisdom for more significant, life-altering decisions.

Our final stop on this exercise tour is the "Bucket Exercise". As each day melts into dusk, this exercise prompts you to reflect on the day's events, placing them into two metaphorical buckets: 'Things I Can Control' and 'Not My Circus, Not My Monkeys'. This activity echoes the core of Epictetus's teachings, underscoring the essential distinction between what is within our control and what lies beyond it. It's an effective exercise to ground ourselves amidst the whirlwind of life's events, helping us recognise the limits of our control and thereby fostering serenity.

As we finish these exercises, recall that every step taken with Epictetus' wisdom brings us closer to a life steeped in philosophy. Philosophy isn't a mere intellectual journey; it's a path for living. The true beauty of these teachings lies not just in understanding them but in incorporating them into our lives. Use these exercises as your roadmap, leading you to a life imbued with wisdom. As you navigate this path, you'll discover that philosophy isn't just about theory, but about practice.

In conclusion, Epictetus's philosophy provides us with valuable tools for seeking guidance and making decisions in our lives. He reminds us that when we turn to divination, we should approach it with a mindset of detachment, recognising that we do not know the specific outcome and that the event itself is indifferent to us. Whether it is considered good or bad is determined by our own interpretation and the choices we make in response to it.

Epictetus advises us not to bring desires or aversions to the diviner, as this would only cloud our judgment and make us vulnerable to fear and anxiety. Instead, we should approach divination with the understanding that every event is neutral and that we have the power to make the best use of it. With this mindset, we can confidently seek counsel from the gods and consider their advice in light of our own reasoning and wisdom.

However, there are situations in which divination is not necessary. When our duty calls us to stand by a friend or our country in times of danger, we should not consult the oracle for permission. Even if the diviner warns us of unfavourable omens, our own reason guides us to fulfill our obligations and support those in need, regardless of the potential risks involved. Epictetus reminds us of the story of the man who neglected to save his friend and was cast out of the temple by the Pythian God. We must rely on our own internal compass, recognising the greater diviner within us, which directs us to act with integrity and loyalty.

By embracing the teachings of Epictetus, we gain the wisdom to navigate life's uncertainties with a clear and calm mind. We learn to trust our own judgment and seek guidance from within, using divination and external advice as supplemental tools rather than absolute authorities. With a blend of philosophical insight and practical humour, we can approach life's challenges with resilience, adaptability, and a deep understanding of our own power to shape our destinies.

Let us venture forth with Epictetus as our guide, ready to face the unknown with courage, clarity, and a touch of light-heartedness. As we embark on this journey, may we continually cultivate our inner wisdom, making the most of every situation that life presents to us. With Epictetus's philosophy as our compass, we can navigate the unpredictable currents of existence, realising our potential for growth, fulfillment, and lasting happiness.

33

Sailing the Social Seas

Begin by prescribing to yourself some character and demeanour, such as you may preserve both alone and in company.

Be mostly silent, or speak merely what is needful, and in few words. We may, however, enter sparingly into discourse sometimes, when occasion calls for it; but let it not run on any of the common subjects, as gladiators, or horse races, or athletic champions, or food, or drink—the vulgar topics of conversation—and especially not on men, so as either to blame, or praise, or make comparisons. If you are able, then, by your own conversation, bring over that of your company to proper subjects; but if you happen to find yourself among strangers, be silent.

Let not your laughter be loud, frequent, or abundant.

Avoid taking oaths, if possible, altogether; at any rate, so far as you are able.

Avoid public and vulgar entertainments; but if ever an occasion calls you to them, keep your attention upon the stretch, that you may not imperceptibly slide into vulgarity. For be assured that if a person be ever so pure himself, yet, if his companion be corrupted, he who converses with him will be corrupted likewise.

Provide things relating to the body no further than absolute need requires, as meat, drink, clothing, house, retinue. But cut off everything that looks toward show and luxury.

Before marriage guard yourself with all your ability from unlawful intercourse with women; yet be not uncharitable or severe to those who are led into this, nor boast frequently that you yourself do otherwise.

If anyone tells you that a certain person speaks ill of you, do not make excuses about what is said of you, but answer: "He was ignorant of my other faults, else he would not have mentioned these alone."

It is not necessary for you to appear often at public spectacles; but if ever there is a proper occasion for you to be there, do not appear more solicitous for any other than for yourself—that is, wish things to be only just as they are, and only the best man to win; for thus nothing will go against you. But abstain entirely from acclamations and derision and violent emotions. And when you come away, do not discourse a great deal on what has passed and what contributes nothing to your own amendment. For it would appear by such discourse that you were dazzled by the show.

Be not prompt or ready to attend private recitations; but if you do attend, preserve your gravity and dignity, and yet avoid making yourself disagreeable.

When you are going to confer with anyone, and especially with one who seems your superior, represent to yourself how

Socrates or Zeno[6] would behave in such a case, and you will not be at a loss to meet properly whatever may occur.

When you are going before anyone in power, fancy to yourself that you may not find him at home, that you may be shut out, that the doors may not be opened to you, that he may not notice you. If, with all this, it be your duty to go, bear what happens and never say to yourself, "It was not worth so much"; for this is vulgar, and like a man bewildered by externals.

In company, avoid a frequent and excessive mention of your own actions and dangers. For however agreeable it may be to yourself to allude to the risks you have run, it is not equally agreeable to others to hear your adventures. Avoid likewise an endeavour to excite laughter, for this may readily slide you into vulgarity, and, besides, may be apt to lower you in the esteem of your acquaintance. Approaches to indecent discourse are likewise dangerous. Therefore, when anything of this sort happens, use the first fit opportunity to rebuke him who makes advances that way, or, at least, by silence and blushing and a serious look show yourself to be displeased by such talk.

Visualise life as a majestic voyage aboard a noble vessel, with each social interaction symbolising an important port of call. These stops might include the tranquillity of Birthday Celebrations, the gentle waves of Informal Gatherings, or the turbulent tides of Formal Business Encounters. To guide us through these often unpredictable waters, let's draw from the wisdom-filled logbook of our respected ancient philosopher, Epictetus.

Epictetus initially advises us to select the appropriate attire for the journey. Not a flashy dinner suit or an extravagant boa —unless that suits your personal taste—but rather a consistent character. This character, like a ship's steady course, should remain constant whether in the solitude of your quarters or in the midst of a crowded deck. By maintaining your moral compass and not veering off course with every gust of opinion or change of company, your journey will be secure and steadfast.

When addressing the ebb and flow of conversation, Epictetus counsels us to circumvent the traps of trivial chatter. While discussing transient topics such as weather or fleeting fashion trends might seem convenient, they often lead us towards the shoals of superficial conversation. Instead, guide your discourse towards the deeper currents of meaningful dialogue. Discuss the significance of a recently enjoyed book or muse about the strangely compelling allure of cat videos. Such conversations steer us towards meaningful connections and make us a desirable companion during social gatherings.

Humour, according to Epictetus, should serve as a soft breeze, not a storm. Avoid being the sailor who laughs louder than the ship's horn, causing a disturbance and attracting undue attention. Instead, let your laughter be like the gentle lapping of the waves against the hull, harmonious and complementary to the rhythm of the social seas.

Epictetus offers firm advice on boisterous behaviour and coarse language. If your fellow voyagers begin to act out of turn at a refined gathering, it's an indication that your association may need reassessment. After all, even if you behave appropriately, their indiscretions could risk sinking your reputation.

On the subject of possessions, it's tempting to fill your quarters with glittering trinkets and exotic curiosities. However, Epictetus cautions that such ostentatious displays will not protect you in times of storm or controversy. He suggests focusing on the essentials—qualities such as compassion, honesty, and moral integrity. These are the true possessions that will keep your ship steady in the tumultuous social sea.

For those navigating the seas solo, Epictetus offered advice on selecting companions. While it may be exciting to journey with a group of colourful characters for a time, their unruly behaviour could lead you into trouble. Conversely, one must avoid becoming overly judgemental or moralistic. Show understanding, offer help to those who are lost, and, most importantly, lead by example.

In the face of gossip or controversy, Epictetus advises us not to rush to defend every criticism or to guard your reputation overly zealously. Handle the situation like a seasoned seafarer confronting a squall—dismiss it calmly and continue to chart your course. Your calm and confident handling of the situation will demonstrate your steadfast character and command respect among your peers.

Epictetus's wisdom reminds us that our vessel will not always be able to dock in the crowded harbour of popularity. There will be solitary nights under the expansive starlit sky and challenging waves to navigate. But remember, a true seafarer isn't one who has only known tranquil seas, but one who has weathered storms and remained resolute in their course.

Whether you're a seasoned mariner or a novice still gaining your sea legs, Epictetus's wisdom serves as a reliable maritime map for navigating the ocean of social interaction. Stay true to your course, captain, and embrace the journey with wisdom and grace.

We're back at the crossroads, where philosophy matures into action. We've tasted Epictetus' wisdom, now it's time to let this flavour season our lives. The exercises to follow are your spice rack, adding the zest of philosophy into the dish of daily living. Ready to season? Let's move from tasting wisdom to living it, spicing up our *Theory of Happiness.*

Let's dive right in with our first exercise— a whimsical yet profound activity aptly titled the "Sock Mix-up". This exercise is a cheeky challenge to your regular adherence to social conventions. It's quite simple: for one week, proudly sport mismatched socks. Yes, you read that right—mismatched socks! This conspicuous deviation from the norm is bound to turn a few heads and raise a few eyebrows. The real test, however, lies in your reaction to these reactions. When inevitably someone playfully teases you about your quirky fashion choice, let a hearty laugh be your response. Follow this up with a jovial retort and carry on. The essence of this seemingly frivolous exercise lies in making you comfortable with the idea of not being swayed by others' opinions. Remember, the merit of your character is not gauged by your sock pairing abilities. Epictetus would surely agree!

The second exercise we've termed the "Silent Observer". Now, this doesn't entail you morphing into a shadowy wallflower at your next social gathering. Rather, it is an encouragement to pay more attention to listening than speaking. Challenge yourself to weigh in on the conversation only when you can add substance and eschew idle chatter or frivolous gossip. This exercise is less about promoting silence and more about fostering mindful listening and intentional conversation. By actively choosing your words and devoting attention to the spoken words of others, you nurture deeper relationships and contribute more significantly to the social milieu.

Next, let's venture into the realm of financial decisions with the "Purse String Prudence" exercise. Your next purchase, whether online or in a brick-and-mortar store, becomes the perfect opportunity to engage with Epictetus' teachings on restraint and simplicity. As you're about to make a purchase, pause and ask yourself, "Do I truly need this, or do I merely want this?" Here, the goal is to discern between necessity and luxury, to resist the shiny lure of impulsive buys. This exercise requires you to navigate the tricky terrain of desire versus need, placing a mirror to your consumption habits. Each decision to forego a non-essential item strengthens your self-control and brings you closer to mastering the art of contentment. This direct application of Epictetus's teachings encourages us to live in harmony with our means, avoiding unnecessary extravagance. The world of consumerism then transforms into an arena for cultivating simplicity and financial prudence.

Lastly, engage in the "Character Constancy" exercise. The goal here is to maintain unwavering consistency in your persona, regardless of your setting or company. Whether you're in solitude, amidst close friends, or navigating a bustling social setting, strive to uphold your authentic self. Resist the inclination to alter your character to conform to the expectations of others. Observe and reflect on how this steady authenticity impacts your interactions with others and your self-perception. You may find a newfound self-confidence and self-assuredness surfacing from this constancy.

Upon wrapping up these exercises, remember that each action guided by Epictetus' teachings is a stride towards a life enriched with wisdom. Philosophy isn't simply about thought; it's about action. The real value of these teachings isn't just in grasping them but in implementing them. Consider these exercises as your compass, guiding you towards a life enlightened by wisdom. As you advance, you'll come to realise that philosophy isn't just learned, but lived.

Steered by the teachings of Epictetus, we've charted a course through the turbulent waters of social interaction. Epictetus urges us to hold a steadfast character, engaging in meaningful discourse and laughter that's mirthful, not raucous. He warns against swearing oaths lightly and advises caution in our choice of companions, understanding that even virtuous sailors can be led off course by the wrong crew.

With a warning against ostentation, Epictetus encourages a frugal approach to life's necessities. His teachings counsel us to seek contentment in simplicity and avoid the siren call of material extravagance. Relationships, too, should be navigated with lawfulness and compassion, finding strength in our own virtue rather than seeking external validation.

Epictetus suggests responding to criticism with dignified silence, confident in our true character. He advises moderation and composure at public gatherings, keeping our attention on personal growth rather than outward spectacle. Encounters with those of higher status should be met with humility, taking cues from the wisdom of philosophical greats.

Our philosopher guide cautions against being swayed by the actions of the powerful, reminding us to keep our sense of self-worth anchored within. Excessive self-promotion and inappropriate conversations should be avoided, instead maintaining a humble demeanour and expressing disapproval of indecency subtly yet firmly.

Epictetus's teachings act as our steadfast compass, leading us through the expansive seas of social interactions. They inspire us to navigate with wisdom, authenticity, and grace, always remaining true to our principles, yet respectful of others' perspectives.

On this voyage of self-development, we strive to master social engagement and form genuine connections with our fellow travellers. These relationships, like the sturdy strands of a ship's rope, add strength and resilience to our journey, providing support, insight, and shared purpose.

So, fellow Stoics, let's hoist the sails of self-mastery, guiding our vessel towards rewarding relationships and lasting contentment. With our compass set on the principles of Stoic philosophy, we sail forth with courage and conviction.

This journey isn't solely a physical voyage, but also a profound inner journey towards self-discovery and self-realisation. As we chart our course, we do so in anticipation of unearthing deeper understanding and living in harmony with the world around us.

Bon Voyage, fellow Stoics! May the winds of wisdom and courage guide your voyage towards enlightenment and enduring contentment. Let Epictetus's teachings steer us through life's seas.

34

Savouring Self-Control

If you are dazzled by the semblance of any promised pleasure, guard yourself against being bewildered by it; but let the affair wait your leisure and procure yourself some delay. Then bring to your mind both points of time—that in which you shall enjoy the pleasure, and that in which you will repent and reproach yourself, after you have enjoyed it—and set before you, in opposition to these, how you will rejoice and applaud yourself if you abstain. And even though it should appear to you a seasonable gratification, take heed that its enticements and allurements and seductions may not subdue you, but set in opposition to this how much better it is to be conscious of having gained so great a victory.

Who amongst us can resist the siren call of an all-you-can-consume ice cream buffet? The sensory spectacle of it all: the rows of vibrantly colourful, sumptuously creamy offerings; the sweet, irresistible aromas that subtly invade your senses; the tantalising sight of chocolate swirls and sprinkles glistening beneath soft lighting. All the world's troubles could fade into the background when confronted with the sheer delight of such a cornucopia. Yet, before we give in to the temptation and dive spoon-first into a tub of Rocky Road, we ought to pause, breathe, and press the metaphorical pause button on our unrestrained desires—a pause, we must emphasise, guided by the wisdom of Epictetus.

Now, let's engage in a little mental gymnastics, conducting a thought experiment to illuminate the potential repercussions of our hedonistic indulgences. Picture two starkly different scenarios: In the first, you surrender completely to the seductive whisper of the ice cream wonderland, eventually finding yourself sinking blissfully into a third tub of Rocky Road. Each mouthful delivers a fleeting satisfaction, but as you scrape the bottom of the container, regret elbows its way past the initial pleasure. The gnawing realisation of overindulgence births guilt, which nestles uncomfortably in your conscience.

Contrast this with a second scenario, where you call upon your inner strength, exercising self-restraint and choosing a healthier option—a light, refreshing salad. The crispness of fresh greens, the colourful confetti of vegetables, the burst of flavours—these invite you to a different kind of indulgence, one devoid of guilt. A profound sense of contentment washes over you as you savour each bite, assured that you've made a wise decision aligned with your long-term well-being.

Now, let's counterpose these visions against the sweet triumph that awaits upon successfully resisting the beguiling siren call of ice cream. It may be easy to convince ourselves that the vibrant array of frozen treats is the perfect remedy after a taxing day. But we must beware—the enticing scoops are nothing more than sugar-laden sirens, waiting to whisk you away to the regret-filled cliffs of 'I-wish-I-hadn't' Island. Their lure is immediate pleasure, but the aftermath is often an unexpected burden of regret.

Instead of succumbing to such transient allure, consider the exhilarating triumph of winning this seemingly minor, yet personally significant battle of willpower. By choosing the healthier alternative, you assert control over your desires, prioritising long-term goals over short-term gratification. The victory in this small skirmish translates to success in the grand battlefield of life.

Imagine, for instance, a situation where you're working on a project with an impending deadline, and the allure of procrastination whispers sweet nothings in your ear. Here, you can apply the same principles of self-control you exercised at the ice cream buffet. By focusing on the task at hand, you silence the siren call of immediate gratification and steer towards the rewarding shore of accomplishment and success.

Consider another example, where you're saving for a cherished future goal—say, a dream vacation or a deposit on a house. Confronted with the temptation of impulsive purchases or extravagant experiences, you can tap into the same reservoir of inner strength that helped you resist the ice cream.

Keeping your financial aspirations at the forefront, you can align your decisions with your long-term objectives, staving off the ephemeral satisfaction that could disrupt your progress.

Exercising self-control is about becoming the master of your own choices, acknowledging that immediate gratification often exacts a steep price on long-term fulfilment. Each victory against the luring call of instant pleasure reinforces your capacity to make thoughtful, purposeful decisions, moulding your life in accordance with your deepest values and aspirations.

So, when the tempting allure of instant gratification beckons, remember the sweet victory that awaits you. Harness the power of your will, making choices that inch you closer to your long-term goals and authentic happiness. Each triumph will fortify your self-discipline, gradually empowering you to become the architect of your destiny.

It's that moment again when understanding shifts into application. We've flown with Epictetus' wisdom, and now it's time to let this wisdom guide our flight path. The exercises that follow are your flight plan, charting the course from the cloud of philosophy to the ground of daily life. Ready to fly? Let's transition from flying in thought to landing in action, navigating our unique *Theory of Happiness*.

Our first endeavour is an exercise cheekily named "The Great Ice Cream Stand-off". Picture your favourite flavour of ice cream sitting tantalisingly in the freezer, its siren song whispering in your ear each time you swing open the fridge door. It promises momentary bliss, a creamy respite from life's pressures. However, there's another side to the story: the potential guilt that accompanies breaking your nutritional resolutions. This scenario initiates an internal dialogue, where you find yourself weighing immediate pleasure against long-term aspirations. Challenge yourself to resist this seductive call. Each successful resistance strengthens your willpower, enhancing your awareness of the power inherent in choice and building your capacity to decline when necessary.

Next up is an exercise we call "The Salad Counter-attack". During your next meal, consciously choose to swap one of your favourite high-calorie indulgences with a nutritious salad. Initially, you might feel a twinge of discontent, perhaps even a sense of loss. But, as you crunch on the fresh greens and veggies, redirect your focus from immediate gratification to the long-term health benefits this dietary change can bring. Embrace the understanding that the path to sustained well-being isn't about satisfying every fleeting desire but nourishing your body with wholesome foods. This shift aligns well with Epictetus's philosophy, underscoring the importance of decisions that prioritise long-term welfare over momentary pleasure.

Following this, we delve into an exercise dubbed "Mindful Munching". Before you munch on any snack, pause. Consider whether you're reaching for that chocolate bar or bag of crisps out of genuine hunger, or if you're merely seeking temporary comfort from boredom or stress. By reflecting on your motivations, you shine a light on the often-overlooked factors that influence your eating habits. You may discover that mindful consideration often nudges you towards healthier alternatives, empowering you to make decisions that benefit your overall well-being.

Our final endeavour is "The Supermarket Challenge". During your next grocery run, transform the mundane task of shopping into an engaging hide-and-seek game with unhealthy cravings. Each time you successfully bypass a tempting item and opt for healthier options, you score a point against instant gratification, thereby reinforcing your commitment to well-being. Each such triumph is a step forward on your journey towards mastering self-control.

As we conclude these exercises, keep in mind that every choice driven by Epictetus' teachings is a step towards a life informed by wisdom. Philosophy isn't merely intellectual gymnastics; it's a roadmap for living. The true power of these teachings doesn't lie just in their understanding but in their application. Treat these exercises as your guiding light, leading you towards a life filled with wisdom. As you journey onward, you'll recognise that philosophy isn't just a concept, but a way of life.

To distil Epictetus's teachings on self-control, it is important to grasp the essence of his philosophy. It is not about denying ourselves all pleasures in life, but rather about exercising discernment and cultivating the strength to resist immediate gratification in pursuit of greater long-term happiness.

Epictetus urges us to guard against being dazzled and beguiled by the allure of promised pleasures. When faced with the temptation of immediate gratification, he advises us to take a step back and introduce a sense of delay. By creating space for reflection, we can bring to mind both the anticipated pleasure and the inevitable remorse and self-reproach that follows its indulgence. We are then able to juxtapose these future scenarios with the immense satisfaction and self-approval we will experience if we choose to abstain.

Even if the pleasure seems tempting and seemingly opportune, Epictetus warns us not to succumb to its enticements and seductions. Instead, we should remind ourselves of the greater joy and fulfilment that comes from exercising self-control and the sense of triumph that accompanies making virtuous choices. By embracing this perspective, we empower ourselves to resist immediate gratification and to make choices that align with our long-term well-being and happiness.

Epictetus's teachings on self-control do not advocate for asceticism or complete renunciation of pleasures. Rather, they encourage us to be intentional in our actions and decisions, considering the long-term consequences of our choices. It is through the cultivation of self-control and the ability to resist instant gratification that we attain true freedom and joy. We become the masters of our desires and the architects of our own happiness.

By incorporating these principles into our lives, we gain the capacity to make choices that are congruent with our values and aspirations. We develop the resilience to resist the temporary allure of instant pleasures and instead focus on the enduring satisfaction and contentment that arise from aligning our actions with our higher goals. In this way, self-control becomes a source of empowerment and a pathway to a more meaningful and fulfilling existence.

Let us embark on the journey of self-mastery, embracing the wisdom of Epictetus and cultivating the strength to make choices that bring us lasting happiness. Through self-control, we discover the power to transcend fleeting pleasures and to shape our lives in accordance with our truest values and aspirations. May we find joy in the victory of self-control and revel in the richness of a life well-lived.

35

Wearing Authenticity

When you do anything from a clear judgment that it ought to be done, never shrink from being seen to do it, even though the world should misunderstand it; for if you are not acting rightly, shun the action itself; if you are, why fear those who wrongly censure you?

What could be more delightful and liberating than dancing to the rhythm of our own convictions, celebrating our individuality with a touch of light-heartedness? Epictetus, the wise philosopher from yonder shores, understood the sheer joy and freedom that comes from staying true to ourselves, even when faced with the pressures of society. His teachings, like a compass guiding us through the vast sea of conformity, encourage us to anchor ourselves in the strength of our inner compass and embrace the unique path that unfolds before us.

Let me paint a vivid picture to illustrate this point. Imagine you're an artist, an imaginative soul who finds beauty and inspiration in the most unconventional materials. Your creativity knows no bounds as you transform discarded items and recycled treasures into breathtaking works of art. As you proudly display your masterpieces, onlookers raise an eyebrow and question your choice of materials, unable to fathom the beauty that lies within the unexpected. But Epictetus, the whimsical philosopher, would offer you a mischievous grin and a playful remark: "Oh, let them wonder! Who needs their approval when you're turning the forgotten into something extraordinary? Embrace your artistic adventure and let your creativity fly".

However, Epictetus is not suggesting that we rebel against societal norms simply for the sake of rebellion. His wisdom, sprinkled with a dose of mirth, invites us to explore the intent behind our actions and distinguish between genuine nonconformity and superficial provocations. Take, for instance, the infamous fashion faux pas of wearing socks with sandals. If your intention is to genuinely express your personal style and find comfort in this unconventional pairing, Epictetus would applaud your audacity with a twinkle in his eye. But if you're simply seeking attention or trying to shock others, he might gently remind you to seek authenticity in your choices, emphasising that true self-expression emerges from a genuine place within, rather than mere fashion statements.

This sentiment, drenched in the mirthful air of self-discovery, echoes the importance of aligning our actions with our values and intentions. It calls us to examine our motives and ensure that our decisions reflect our authentic beliefs, rather than seeking external validation or conforming to societal expectations. Yes, we should embrace our individuality and resist the pressure to conform, but we should also consider the impact and intention behind our choices. By doing so, we maintain our integrity and cultivate a sense of authenticity that radiates from within, like a whimsical glow.

Epictetus, through his teachings, emphasises the significance of embracing our inner convictions and exuding confidence, even in the face of judgment. He playfully challenges us to question why we allow the opinions of others to dictate our choices when we have a clear understanding of our own truth. By aligning our actions with our personal values, we nurture a profound sense of self-worth and peace. Epictetus might playfully add, "If you're wearing socks with sandals because it brings you joy and comfort, let your feet dance freely. But if you're aiming for shock value, perhaps consider channelling your unique self-expression through art, music, or an eclectic collection of whimsical hats! The world is your canvas, my friend".

This unwavering commitment to our beliefs and values, coupled with a light-hearted approach, cultivates a deep sense of self-worth and authenticity. By embracing Epictetus's wisdom with a playful twinkle in our eyes, we confidently march to the beat of our own drum, unswayed by the judgments of the world. In doing so, we celebrate our individuality, infuse our lives with joyous laughter, and lay the foundation for personal growth, fulfillment, and an unapologetically authentic existence. Therefore, let's turn up the volume, my fellow free-spirited souls, and dance to our own rhythm, savouring the vibrant melody of life with each step we take. With Epictetus as our dance partner, let's waltz through the tapestry of existence, twirling in the joy of being true to ourselves and casting our unique light upon the world.

Once more, we're at that tipping point where philosophy converts into practice. We've climbed Epictetus' wisdom, now it's time to let this wisdom guide our ascent in life. The upcoming exercises is your climbing gear, helping you scale the mountain of philosophy to reach the peak of everyday living. Ready to climb? Let's move from contemplation to ascension, scaling our unique *Theory of Happiness*.

Our journey begins with the "Dress to Express" exercise. Imagine shaking up your wardrobe for a day, dressing in a manner entirely unlike your usual style. You might don a vibrant colour you've always shied away from, experiment with a daring pattern, or perhaps even stride out in the much-debated combo of socks and sandals. The goal here is to celebrate your uniqueness, shrug off judgment, and stand firm in your personal choices. By dressing to express, you'll metaphorically embody Epictetus's teaching, inviting a stronger sense of self-assurance and authenticity into your life.

Next, we venture into the tantalising territory of the "Ice Cream Standoff". Picture yourself standing before an ice cream parlour, hypnotised by the cavalcade of flavours peering at you from behind the glass. Now, give yourself a full three minutes to wrestle with your inner cravings. Will you yield to the siren call of the pistachio gelato or the sweet whispers of the almond crunch? Remember, the choice is yours. This exercise reinforces your ability to make conscious decisions, showing you that power is nestled in your ability to resist or yield to temptation.

Continuing our journey, we meet the "Rumours Relay" exercise. Suppose a friend tells you about someone who has been disparaging you behind your back. Rather than launching into defensive rebuttals or explanations, you respond with something utterly unrelated and amusing. You might cheekily retort, "Did they also mention my enviable knack for peeling bananas with my toes?" This exercise is about cultivating a light-hearted outlook and maintaining your composure amidst gossip. It's a reminder that your self-worth does not hinge on others' judgments.

Finally, we arrive at the "Authentic Engagement" exercise. Imagine receiving an invitation to a social event that doesn't resonate with you. Your task is to politely decline, but instead of creating a fanciful excuse, you'll exercise authenticity. Communicate your reason for not attending with sincerity and respect, such as, "I appreciate your invitation, but at this time, I've chosen to focus on other activities that align more closely with my interests". This exercise encourages you to honour your preferences and ensures that your commitments align with your personal values and interests, all while embracing authenticity and clarity in communication.

At the end of these exercises, it's important to remember that each action rooted in Epictetus' philosophy brings us closer to a life illuminated by wisdom. Philosophy isn't just an intellectual pastime; it's a toolkit for life. The true value of these teachings is discovered not just in understanding them but in practicing them. View these exercises as your guideposts, marking your way towards a life of wisdom. As you press forward, you'll discover that philosophy is not just a subject, but a way of life.

In conclusion, our exploration of Epictetus's teachings has unveiled the extraordinary power of embracing authenticity, resilience, and personal empowerment. Like a refreshing breeze on a sunny day, his wisdom invites us to transcend the confines of societal expectations and discover the freedom that comes from staying true to ourselves. Through the lens of a lighthearted perspective, we learn that it is not the circumstances we face, but our reactions to them, that shape our happiness and well-being.

Epictetus's philosophy encourages us to navigate life's complexities with grace, self-assurance, and a sprinkle of humour. By aligning our actions with our personal values and convictions, we unleash a profound sense of self-worth and inner peace. So, let us boldly lace up those socks and sandals, be they literal or metaphorical, and embark on a transformative journey filled with laughter and wisdom, as we strive for an authentically joyous existence.

With Epictetus as our guide, we stride confidently along the path of self-discovery, unafraid of the misconceptions or judgments of the world. His teachings embolden us to embrace our individuality, celebrating the quirks and idiosyncrasies that make us uniquely ourselves. We revel in the knowledge that it is our genuine essence, not the opinions of others, that defines our worth and purpose.

As we dance to the rhythm of our own drumbeat, unburdened by the expectations of conformity, we infuse our lives with joyous laughter and cultivate a deep sense of fulfillment. Like a whimsical waltz through the tapestry of existence, we twirl with abandon, savouring each step and casting our vibrant light upon the world. Epictetus, our dance partner in this cosmic symphony, smiles mischievously, encouraging us to embrace the richness of life with unyielding enthusiasm.

Therefore, my fellow free-spirited souls, let us turn up the volume of our laughter, celebrate our uniqueness, and revel in the symphony of authenticity. With Epictetus as our eternal companion, we navigate the twists and turns of life's dance floor, finding solace in our unwavering commitment to our beliefs and values. Together, we forge a path of personal growth, fulfillment, and an unapologetically authentic existence that leaves a lasting impression on the world around us.

In the grand choreography of life, let us remember that the spotlight is ours to claim, and the dance is ours to create. Let's kick up our heels, twirl with abandon, and immerse ourselves in the joy of being true to ourselves. With Epictetus as our ever-present partner, we can embrace life's delightful rhythm, celebrating the beauty of our individuality and weaving our own unique tapestry of happiness and fulfillment.

36

Choices and Connections

As the proposition, "either it is day or it is night", has much force in a disjunctive argument, but none at all in a conjunctive one, so, at a feast, to choose the largest share is very suitable to the bodily appetite, but utterly inconsistent with the social spirit of the entertainment. Remember, then, when you eat with another, not only the value to the body of those things which are set before you, but also the value of proper courtesy toward your host.

Epictetus offers us a delightfully insightful perspective on buffet-iquette. This seemingly light-hearted metaphor, on closer examination, reveals the profound complexity of choices we grapple with in our lives, akin to a smorgasbord of options at a buffet table. Each selection carries its implications, mirroring the labyrinth of life's decisions. Here, Epictetus's wisdom emerges as our reliable compass.

Envision yourself stepping into a buffet. An array of dishes, each with its unique culinary melody, fills the tables. Amidst the tantalising aromas and visual feast before your eyes, Epictetus's philosophy unfolds. He nudges us to see the buffet experience extending beyond a sensory indulgence. It transforms into a social ballet, where fostering genuine connections and engaging in stimulating conversations become as satisfying as the pleasure derived from the food.

Now, let's imagine a buffet-style wedding reception. Here, the enticing fare is outshone by the ambience and the guests' narratives. Guided by Epictetus's wisdom, you shift your focus from the gastronomic allure to the individuals surrounding you. You weave through the crowd, initiating conversations, and expressing genuine interest in their experiences. Consequently, the buffet experience elevates from mere culinary pleasure to a vibrant tableau, painting memorable connections that transcend the temporal confines of the event.

Epictetus, with his discerning lens, urges us to consistently consider the broader implications of our actions. The grand buffet of life presents a ripple effect, where every decision and interaction influences not just our journey, but those of others around us. Social gatherings become more than venues for indulgence; they transform into golden opportunities for personal growth. Here, virtues like empathy, kindness, and restraint are not only exercised but also cultivated. By striking a balance between gastronomical desires and the nurturing of relationships, we transform everyday buffets into experiences that nourish our souls.

So, the next time you find yourself at a buffet, recall Epictetus's teachings. The experience extends beyond a tête-à-tête between you and the enticing variety of dishes on offer. It is an open invitation to embark on a journey that weaves together sensory satisfaction, interpersonal bonding, and shared experiences. Buffet-iquette, as per Epictetus, is not merely about filling your plate; it is an intricate dance of connection, personal development, and the harmonious coexistence of self-indulgence and altruism. By demonstrating moderation and respect for our fellow diners, we transform into enlightened individuals. We understand the genuine worth of shared connections and the joy of shared meals, embracing life's banquet not as gluttonous consumers, but as participants in the communal tapestry of existence. Epictetus's philosophy, therefore, extends from the buffet table to the fabric of our lives.

We're back at that intersection where thought evolves into action. We've breathed in Epictetus' wisdom, now it's time to let this wisdom oxygenate our actions. The exercises that follow are your lungs, breathing the oxygen of philosophy into the blood of daily living. Ready to breathe? Let's transition from inhaling wisdom to exhaling action, breathing life into our *Theory of Happiness*.

Starting off our journey into the practical exploration of Epictetus' buffet-iquette, we introduce the "Food Fiesta Challenge". Picture yourself in front of a tantalising buffet that offers delicacies from around the globe. The aroma of exotic spices and freshly cooked dishes wafts towards you, making your stomach rumble in anticipation. But here's the twist: you must limit your selection to only three types of food. This constraint, while seemingly restrictive, actually invites you to practise restraint and discernment. It mirrors life's plethora of choices, reminding us that even when options abound, wisdom lies in making judicious selections. In doing so, we not only manage our consumption, but also engage our creativity as we strive to curate the most diverse plate possible with just three types of food.

We now move on to the "Mingling Muncher". In this exercise, you're tasked with initiating a conversation with a different person for every new food item you try. Much like the diversity of dishes at a buffet, life too presents us with a colourful array of people. By engaging with various individuals, you gain the opportunity to savour the richness of human experience and perspectives, akin to the unique flavours each dish offers. This exercise nudges you out of your comfort zone, encouraging the formation of diverse relationships, and promoting understanding and empathy.

Our next offering is the "Self-Control Shuffle". Here, we add a dash of spontaneity into the mix. Partner up with a friend and traverse the buffet line together, with each person taking turns to select dishes for the other. This exercise presents a test of trust and adaptability. As you yield control over your food choices, allowing your friend's preferences to influence the selection, you learn to embrace uncertainty, much like the unpredictable buffet that is life. This exercise enhances your capacity for flexibility, encouraging open-mindedness and a willingness to savour unexpected delights.

Rounding off our buffet-iquette exercises, we have the "Plate Picasso". This activity inspires you to channel your creativity into the arrangement of your plate. Using the buffet as your palette, you're tasked with balancing colours, textures, and flavours to create a visually appealing meal. Much like life, where presentation often plays a crucial role, the aesthetics of your plate can significantly enhance the overall dining experience. A beautifully arranged plate can make each bite more enjoyable, turning an ordinary meal into a memorable feast for the senses.

Having completed these exercises, bear in mind that every endeavour influenced by Epictetus is a step towards a life steeped in wisdom. Philosophy isn't simply a mental exercise; it's a compass for life. The real worth of these teachings lies not just in their understanding but in their actualisation. See these exercises as your roadmap, directing you towards a life shaped by wisdom. As you continue, you'll recognise that philosophy isn't just about thinking, but about living.

In summarising our exploration of Epictetus' philosophy, known herein as buffet-iquette, we unearth wisdom of profound depth that aids us in navigating the complexities of social gatherings. When stepping into the banquet of life, we're reminded that it's not simply about satiating our physical appetites, but equally about embracing the spirit of community, harmony, and respectfulness.

Epictetus implores us to look past the immediate appeal of the largest portion, and instead concentrate on the value of proper etiquette and consideration towards our hosts and fellow diners. It's a call to reflect on how our actions reverberate through the social fabric of the gathering, balancing our personal desires with the interconnectedness and collective nature of the event.

By embracing this perspective, we undertake a transformative journey, shifting our mindset from self-centered indulgence to a broader consideration for others. We learn to value the joy of sharing, the art of conversation, and the charm of authentic connection. Consequently, our own experiences are enriched, and we contribute positively to those of our fellow participants.

Adopting Epictetus' teachings on buffet-iquette necessitates patience, resilience, and a willingness to cultivate a social spirit transcending mere self-gratification. It invites us to transcend our individual appetites and embrace the collective joy of the feast. Through considerate choices and respectful interactions, we can foster an atmosphere brimming with warmth, camaraderie, and shared merriment.

Let's raise our glasses to the banquet of life, savouring each moment with gratitude and mindfulness. Guided by Epictetus' wisdom on our journey, we uncover that the essence of the feast lies less in the quantity of food we partake in, and more in the quality of our interactions and the depth of our connections.

Bon appétit, my fellow travellers on the road to happiness! May our lives be filled with delightful dialogues, cherished memories, and a genuine appreciation for the company of others. As we taste the diverse flavours of existence, let us uphold the significance of courtesy, kindness, and the harmonious ballet of social interaction. Here's to a life well-lived, wherein the feast of happiness is shared and savoured by all.

37

Being True to Oneself

If you have assumed any character beyond your strength, you have both demeaned yourself ill in that and quitted one which you might have supported.

We often find ourselves at various crossroads of life, drawn towards the tantalising temptation to step into another person's shoes. This longing may manifest in the form of dreams and fantasies, where we envisage ourselves donning the capes and masks of superheroes, equipped with extraordinary powers that ignite admiration and awe. Picture yourself standing atop a stage, just like a rockstar, commanding a symphony of emotions that enthrals an enthusiastic audience. The applause reverberates in your ears, resonating like a harmonious melody. These illusions are captivating, almost impossible to resist, for who hasn't yearned to be the life of the party, the triumphant entrepreneur, or the trendsetter setting the fashion world ablaze?

Yet, Epictetus alerts us to the dangers lurking beneath these beguiling illusions. He proposes that pretending to be a persona far removed from our true selves is like a child trying to perform a magic trick without understanding its mechanics. In our efforts to project ourselves, for instance, as the 'High Flyer', we not only falter but also run the risk of obscuring our genuine self. Our authentic strengths, deep-seated values, and sincere aspirations, which form the bedrock of our identity, become concealed in this charade.

Consider it like attending a masquerade, where your true self is hidden behind a mask and costume. On the surface, you dazzle, and yet you feel the poignant chasm between your façade and your true identity. Imagine attending a glamorous social gathering, where you're surrounded by seemingly successful, impressive personalities. The pressure to adapt, conform, and meet the expectations of the social circle weighs heavily on your shoulders, pushing you into a relentless spotlight. It seems as though you're coerced to don a persona that feels foreign and awkward.

This might be akin to a shy, introverted individual feeling pressured to act as the life of a party, attempting to tell jokes or draw attention. It might not only feel uncomfortable, but it may also fail to genuinely engage others, as the authenticity is missing. As you endeavour to blend in, you may erect a disguise, crafting a persona that doesn't align with your authentic self. The confidence and success you project may deceive the crowd, but internally, you may wage a war against feelings of disconnection, unease, and dissatisfaction. It's like wearing a pair of shoes that are a size too small; they pinch and constrain, and yet you force yourself to walk with grace, grimacing with each painful step.

However, Epictetus, in his infinite wisdom, offers a different perspective—a beacon of guidance towards authentic fulfilment. He suggests that true happiness emerges not from impressing others with a mask, but from honouring and accepting our authentic selves. When we acknowledge and appreciate our unique qualities, strengths, and values, we align ourselves with the unique role we were destined to play in the world's grand theatre.

Reflect on people like Albert Einstein, who didn't succumb to the pressure to be like others but rather embraced his unique intellectual abilities, or artists like Frida Kahlo, who expressed her unique experiences and emotions through her artwork. These figures embody Epictetus' philosophy—instead of attempting to emulate others, they focused their energy on honing their unique talents, fostering personal growth, and making their own unique imprint on the world.

In embracing and expressing our authentic selves, we inspire others and forge deep connections that are genuine and meaningful. We become the real heroes of our stories, each with our unique superpowers and a tailor-made cape.

Therefore, as we navigate the maze of life, let's heed Epictetus' wisdom. Resist the allure to be someone else. By succumbing to this lure, we forfeit the chance to shine in our own authenticity. Instead, let's honour our unique attributes, follow our passions, and remain true to our values. By doing so, we lay the groundwork for a life rich in purpose, fulfilment, and genuine happiness. As Epictetus sagely stated, "First, know who you are, then adorn yourself accordingly". And if your true self involves a dash of whimsy, well, that's the icing on your life's cake!

Once again, we're at that turning point where philosophy finds its expression in action. We've been bathing in the light of Epictetus' wisdom, now it's time to let this wisdom illuminate our actions. The exercises that follow are your torch, lighting the path from understanding to practice. Ready to carry the light? Let's move from enlightenment to enactment, illuminating our unique *Theory of Happiness*.

The first dance step of our journey is the "Mirror, Mirror Exercise". Imagine starting each day standing in front of a mirror, staring into your eyes—the windows to your soul. Take a moment to affirm your unique strengths, virtues, and values, and reflect upon them. This isn't about donning the mask of pretence; it's about discovering and accepting the person beneath it, imperfections and all. It's akin to having a personal cheerleader, conveniently housed in your mirror, ready to kick-start your day with positivity and self-love. The dance with your reflection is not a stiff waltz, it's a spontaneous freestyle.

Add a dash of amusement with a few dance moves or silly faces —it's your mirror party, after all!

Next on our dance card is the "Reality Check Challenge". It's a reflective tango that requires you to identify five instances where you might have donned a mask, all to blend in, to impress, or perhaps gain approval. Picture each situation, recall the emotions it stirred, and ask yourself: How might it have been different if I'd danced to my own rhythm instead? This dance of contemplation is like a magnifying glass probing moments of pretence, illuminating the heightened sense of fulfillment, connection, and joy authenticity could bring. Add a touch of comedy—envision yourself wearing a literal clown mask or a feathered masquerade mask—because in life's grand dance, it's essential to have a sense of humour!

The third dance, the "Costume Party Game", takes the waltz of self-discovery to a whimsical level. Imagine attending a fancy-dress party, where the theme is—you! What costume would best embody your authentic self? Maybe you'd choose a superhero cape, symbolising your inner strength, or perhaps a hat festooned with trinkets representing your passions and interests. Whatever your choice, it's about celebrating the individual rhythm you bring to the grand dance of life. This imaginative jig allows us to creatively showcase our authenticity, while also reminding us that our most compelling role is being ourselves. It's like a cha-cha with our true selves, where revealing our unique quirks can inspire others to join the dance.

We wrap up the dance party with the "Honesty Hour"—a day dedicated to being utterly and unapologetically yourself, irrespective of circumstances. Just like a dancer who forgets the audience and loses themselves in the rhythm of the music, observe the shift in your thoughts, emotions, and interactions when you embrace your true self. Take note of the newfound confidence that stem from this unfiltered expression of self. If your dance with honesty leads to bouts of laughter, as you navigate through the sometimes awkward but always genuine moments, savour it—laughter is the best dance partner, after all.

As we finish these tasks, keep in mind that each choice rooted in Epictetus' teachings brings us closer to a life filled with wisdom. Philosophy isn't just a cerebral activity; it's a practical guide for living. The true significance of these teachings lies not just in comprehending them but in embodying them. View these exercises as your lighthouse, illuminating the path towards wisdom-filled living. As you forge ahead, you'll discover that philosophy isn't just a matter of discussion, but of action.

In conclusion, Epictetus's teachings on embracing our authentic selves resonate with a light-heartedness that invites us to shed the weight of pretence and embrace the joy of being true to who we are. He warns against assuming a character that exceeds our capabilities, as it not only diminishes our self-worth but also deprives us of the opportunity to fully embody a character that aligns with our strengths.

With a playful twinkle in his eye, Epictetus reminds us that we are the creators of our own dance, and the choice of our dance partners—our chosen character—should be a reflection of our true selves. He encourages us to embrace our unique qualities, quirks, and idiosyncrasies, knowing that it is in these authentic expressions that we find true happiness and fulfillment.

Imagine stepping onto the dance floor of life, adorned in a cape that perfectly embodies your strengths and values. As you twirl and sway to the rhythm of your own music, you radiate confidence and joy, captivating those around you with your genuine presence. Epictetus's wisdom reminds us that we have the power to choose a character that not only suits us but also allows us to shine brightly and inspire others.

In this dance of self-discovery, growth, and self-expression, Epictetus invites us to laugh at our missteps and celebrate our triumphs. He encourages us to embrace the dance floor as a playground for self-discovery, where we can explore different characters, learn from our experiences, and gracefully pivot when we find a character that aligns better with our true selves.

By heeding Epictetus's teachings, we liberate ourselves from the pressure to conform to societal expectations and discover the freedom of embracing our authentic selves. It is through this journey of self-acceptance and self-expression that we find true contentment, as we realise that the most fulfilling dance is the one that reflects our unique essence.

My fellow dancers of life, let us step onto the dance floor with confidence, humour, and a touch of whimsy. Let us embrace our true selves, knowing that in our authenticity lies the key to genuine happiness and the power to create a dance that is uniquely our own. With Epictetus as our guide, let us dance through life with a lightness of spirit, celebrating the beauty of our individuality and joyously twirling to the rhythm of our own hearts.

38

The Mind's Lego Maze

As in walking you take care not to tread upon a nail, or turn your foot, so likewise take care not to hurt the ruling faculty of your mind. And if we were to guard against this in every action, we should enter upon action more safely.

Embark with me on a delightful journey into the maze of our minds. Imagine navigating through a room, strewn with Lego bricks, the aftermath of playful gremlins' fervent playtime. Each colourful block, strewn haphazardly, awaits the unsuspecting soles of your feet, ready to unleash their surprising and agonising impact. This navigation requires the finesse and vigilance similar to manoeuvring through a minefield where, instead of perilous explosives, we're artfully avoiding a carpet of vibrant plastic bricks. If we take this analogy a step further, it wonderfully mirrors the careful vigilance needed to traverse the complex landscape of our minds. Welcome to the philosophical world of Epictetus, where mental mindfulness becomes your personalised superpower.

Epictetus championed the preservation of our mental sharpness. He advocated treating our cognitive clarity with the same conscientious care we use to protect our feet from Lego booby traps. This mindfulness, a heightened form of mental vigilance, requires us to be consciously watchful of our actions and recurrent thought patterns that have the potential to cloud our judgment. Think of it as fashioning a suit of mental armour, sturdy and resilient, designed to deflect any stray Lego bricks—or negative thoughts—that may disrupt our steady stride towards self-improvement and fulfilment.

In the complex, ever-changing labyrinth of life, this mindful vigilance becomes an indispensable tool. Consider arming yourself with a sturdy mental hard hat, paired with a toolbox brimming with an array of tools designed to help navigate life's unpredictable twists and turns. By maintaining an acute awareness of our thought processes and the diverse external influences shaping them, we prepare ourselves to avoid the snares of detrimental psychological patterns. Envision possessing a mental radar, an invaluable instrument to swiftly dodge the imposing walls of self-doubt, the hazardous landmines of negative thinking, and the concealed pitfalls of impulsive decisions.

By embracing the discipline of mental vigilance, we equip ourselves with the ability to avoid blunders and obstacles that could potentially impede our daily pursuits. It's as though we've uncovered a hidden ability that enables us to leap over daunting hurdles of self-defeat and sidestep the pitfalls of impulsive decision-making. Epictetus would likely agree that there's a profound elegance and strength in navigating life's path with mindfulness and attentiveness. It's akin to becoming the agile master of your own mind, expertly evading mental obstacles with grace, style, and a steadfast sense of self-confidence.

As we practice mental vigilance, we foster an enhanced sense of self-awareness and become adept at recognising the powerful sway our thoughts exert over our actions and emotions. We develop the reflexes to catch ourselves before we plunge into the quagmire of negative thinking or slide on the slippery slope of unchecked ego or arrogance. This mental discipline bestows upon us the freedom to consciously and mindfully respond to life's varied challenges, rather than being carried away by the unpredictable currents of our fluctuating emotions.

Through the dynamic potency of mindful self-awareness, we not only enhance our decision-making capabilities but also cultivate a deeper understanding of ourselves. Imagine having a backstage pass to our own mental theatre, offering a front-row view to the intricate interplay between our thoughts, emotions, and actions. This level of self-awareness enables us to make conscious, purposeful choices that align with our core values, steering us towards lives full of purpose, fulfillment, and, yes, the occasional hearty laugh.

Epictetus's teachings on mental vigilance provide us with the toolkit to traverse life's vast expanse of challenges with unwavering clarity, a resolute sense of purpose, and undeterred dedication to our authentic selves. As you step onto your journey of self-discovery and personal growth, remain watchful for those rogue Lego pieces—symbolic of negative thoughts and harmful patterns—that may lurk in your path. Remember to incorporate a playful hop, skip, and jump as you skilfully dodge these obstacles. Embrace the whimsy and absurdity that often accompany life's journey, and let your mindful strides guide you to a realm where clarity, joy, and self-discovery rule.

It's that time again to shift from the realm of ideas to the world of deeds. We've dwelt in Epictetus' wisdom, and now it's time to build this wisdom into our lives. The exercises to follow are your blueprints, shaping the edifice of philosophy into a home of daily living. Ready to build? Let's transition from dwelling in thought to construction in action, building our unique *Theory of Happiness*.

Our first exercise, aptly titled the "Mindful Walking Exercise", invites us on an imagined meander through a serene park or a bustling city street. As you navigate this mental landscape, endeavour to infuse mindfulness into your stroll. Picturing physical hurdles such as water puddles, pebbles, and cracks in the pavement as symbolic representations of negative thoughts can be a revealing exercise. Perhaps the puddle signifies pessimism, the rock embodies anger, and the crack reflects self-doubt. By consciously manoeuvring around these obstacles, you are essentially training your mind to recognise and sidestep potential hindrances, infusing mindfulness into the tapestry of your everyday experiences.

Secondly, we encounter the "Thought Replacement Challenge". This mental exercise encourages a heightened awareness of your thoughts and emotions throughout the day. When a negative thought flutters into your mind, practice consciously substituting it with an uplifting counter-thought. Should you catch yourself in a loop of self-doubt, thinking, "I can't do this", consciously switch it with, "I am capable and resilient", You might be pleasantly surprised at how this practice can gradually rewire your thinking patterns, fostering a more positive and empowering mindset.

Next, we delve into the "Legos of the Mind Game". Envision your mind as a room scattered with Lego pieces, each one representing a distinct thought. Some pieces are vibrant and enticing, while others appear dull and negative. In this mental playground, you must consciously choose which Lego pieces you engage with, signifying the thoughts you decide to entertain, and which ones to avoid, representing thoughts that may be detrimental to your well-being. This practice hones your discernment skills, empowering you to be the active selector of thoughts that shape your experiences and overall mental health.

Lastly, we introduce the "Mindful Journaling Exercise". This exercise urges you to set aside a little time each day for reflection, documenting instances when your thoughts swayed your emotions or clouded your decision-making. This practice invites introspection, enabling you to identify patterns and garner valuable insights from your own thought processes. Through mindful journaling, you cultivate a deeper self-understanding and gain the ability to consciously adjust your thoughts and actions, aligning them with your desired outcomes.

Upon completion of these exercises, remember that every step taken in accordance with Epictetus' wisdom leads us towards a life defined by philosophical insight. Philosophy isn't merely theoretical; it's a manual for action. The true strength of these teachings lies not just in their comprehension but in their application. Treat these exercises as your signposts, guiding you on your journey towards a life of wisdom. As you progress, you'll find that philosophy isn't just thought-provoking, but life-altering.

In essence, Epictetus's philosophy calls us to tread carefully in the dance of life, not only watching our physical steps but also guarding the precious faculty of our minds. With a touch of whimsy, we can imagine navigating a room strewn with Lego pieces, each representing a potential distraction or obstacle to our clarity of thought. Just as we carefully avoid stepping on those sharp Legos, we must exercise the same level of caution to protect the ruling faculty of our minds.

By embracing this mindful approach, we embark on a path of greater safety and wisdom. Mindfulness becomes our guiding principle, allowing us to navigate the complexities of life with a clearer perspective. We become attuned to the subtleties of our thoughts and emotions, gently guiding them towards greater harmony and tranquillity. In this dance of mindfulness, we gain the ability to make wiser choices and respond to life's challenges with resilience and grace.

Epictetus's teachings remind us that our mental well-being is just as important as our physical safety. It is not enough to avoid physical hazards; we must also safeguard our minds from negative influences, distorted thinking, and unhealthy patterns of behaviour. Through mindfulness, we develop the capacity to discern what is beneficial and align our actions with our values, thus nurturing our mental well-being and inner harmony.

As we embrace mindfulness and cultivate a light-hearted approach to life, we begin to realise that the dance of existence is enriched by our ability to stay present, attentive, and attuned to our inner selves. The dance floor becomes a sanctuary where we can fully experience the beauty of each moment, appreciating the intricate steps and gentle rhythms that weave together the fabric of our lives.

Let us pick up our Lego bricks and construct a path illuminated by mindfulness and light-heartedness. With Epictetus as our building mentor, we skilfully navigate the intricate landscape of existence, avoiding the Lego traps that threaten to undermine our mental well-being. Through our mindful construction, we unlock the gateway to greater wisdom, resilience, and a profound sense of inner peace. As we build our Lego-inspired journey, let us revel in the joy of creation, knowing that with each brick, we are shaping our own happiness and flourishing in the vibrant world of possibilities.

39

Shallow Splendour

The body is to everyone the proper measure of its possessions, as the foot is of the shoe. If, therefore, you stop at this, you will keep the measure; but if you move beyond it, you must necessarily be carried forward, as down a precipice; as in the case of a shoe, if you go beyond its fitness to the foot, it comes first to be gilded, then purple, and then studded with jewels. For to that which once exceeds the fit measure there is no bound.

Epictetus' guidance on maintaining our 'proper measure' is an enlightened philosophy that invites us to scrutinise our lives, making sense of the cacophony of choices and influences vying for our attention. As we navigate the ebb and flow of modern life, it serves as a beacon, illuminating the path towards authenticity and discernment.

Imagine your body as a sage style consultant, an entity inherently attuned to your authentic self. The body, much like a discerning connoisseur, doesn't just select anything that's presented to it. It keenly identifies what complements its stature, enhances its grace, and resonates with its inherent personality. Sherlock Holmes, for instance, would never be caught donning a garish, oversized deerstalker hat. He would select the one that enhances his silhouette and aids in his sleuthing, rather than overwhelming him.

The principle of 'proper measure', however, is an ideal that is constantly put to the test in today's consumerist society. We are immersed in a deluge of temptations, all dressed in the glamorous veneer of desirability – the latest smartphone model with an array of features we may never use, the trendiest designer wear that might restrict our comfort, the flashy sports car that may never quite suit our driveway. Amidst this swirling vortex of choices, Epictetus advises us to dance to the rhythm of our own music.

Consider the example of an individual passionately dedicated to sustainable living. The allure of a fast-fashion garment might be powerful, with its intricate designs and runway-worthy appearance. However, she recognises that this piece, no matter how appealing, transgresses her 'proper measure' as it is fundamentally at odds with her values of sustainability and mindful consumption. Wearing it would be as uncomfortable and unfulfilling as attempting to spend an entire evening dancing in stilettos two sizes too small.

Moreover, Epictetus's wisdom prompts us to honour and recognise our inherent worth. Overindulging ourselves in the trappings of materialism can create an unhealthy divergence from our true selves, akin to overestimating our appetites at a sumptuous all-you-can-eat buffet, only to find that our eyes have written cheques our stomachs cannot cash.

This philosophy, though expressed through the lens of fashion, is applicable to all facets of life. Be it choosing a career, forging relationships, or even decisions related to our health and wellbeing. For instance, accepting a high-profile job that offers prestige but severely compromises your work-life balance is comparable to showing up to a black-tie event in a neon suit. It just doesn't feel right. Similarly, persisting in a relationship that fails to fulfil you emotionally can be as unsatisfying as trying to quench your thirst with salty seawater.

Therefore, as we traverse through life's labyrinth, it's essential to uphold our 'proper measure', which becomes our guiding lighthouse. It leads us towards authenticity and safeguards us from being engulfed by the illusory charms of superficiality. The pursuit of genuine happiness and contentment lies in comprehending our unique needs and desires, prioritising comfort, our values, and authenticity over all else. After all, continuously wearing a mask that doesn't fit will only strain the face beneath it. Epictetus's wisdom prompts us to don the life that fits us just as perfectly as a suit tailored to our precise measurements. Through this lens, the pursuit of a life well-lived is both a personal journey and an art, requiring a discerning eye, a robust sense of self, and the courage to resist the lure of one-size-fits-all solutions.

We are back at the fork in the road where thought paths converge with action trails. We've been swimming in Epictetus' wisdom, and now it's time to channel these currents into our lives. The exercises to follow are your channels, guiding the flow of philosophy into the riverbed of practice. Shall we navigate? Let's move from swimming in wisdom to channelling it into action, shaping our own *Theory of Happiness*.

Begin your journey with an exercise titled "Reflective Style Appraisal". Each day, set aside a few moments to stand before the mirror, acknowledging and celebrating your individual style and the traits that truly make you unique. Consider this your personal platform to experiment with various fashion choices, always keeping in mind that these should align with who you truly are, rather than impersonating others or following trends mindlessly. Recognise and embrace what you might see as 'imperfections' or quirks, acknowledging them as integral facets of your distinctive style. This exercise encourages self-love and acceptance, reminding you to let your innate charm and genuine self inform your fashion choices. In other words, understand your 'proper measure', and adorn yourself accordingly.

Next, rise to the challenge of the "Trend Evasion Endeavour". For a full month, steer clear of the lure to blindly follow the latest fashion fads. Instead, pour your energy into nurturing a personal style that is a faithful reflection of your genuine essence. This exercise liberates you from societal pressures to comply with fleeting trends, serving as a reminder that while trends may fade, your unique style remains timeless.

The third exercise, "Stylish Discourse", proves particularly beneficial in social settings where the implicit pressure to impress others with showy attire exists. Instead of letting your clothes do the talking, initiate engaging conversations with those around you. This shift from an emphasis on external appearances to fostering sincere connections underlines the fact that your fashion choices should be a reflection of your inner values and beauty, not mere tokens of wealth or societal status.

Lastly, embark on the "Wardrobe Audit Meditation" exercise. Set aside some time to thoroughly review your closet and isolate pieces that no longer resonate with your authentic style. As you sort through your apparel, pay attention to what aligns with your current style and what seems to be in discord. This exercise provides insights into your evolving fashion inclinations, setting the stage for exciting style experiments and a more thoughtfully curated, intentional wardrobe.

As we close these exercises, remember that every endeavour aligned with Epictetus' teachings brings us closer to a life guided by wisdom. Philosophy isn't a mere intellectual challenge; it's a roadmap for meaningful living. The true power of these teachings is not just in understanding them but in living them. See these exercises as your compass, directing your path towards a life filled with wisdom. As you continue to move forward, you'll discover that philosophy isn't just a topic for discussion, but a guide for action.

To encapsulate, Epictetus imparts an invaluable lesson, impressing upon us the need for harmony between our inward essence and outward presentation, whilst cautioning against the perilous charm of superficial glamour. As we reflect upon his wisdom in the context of our stylistic choices, we're inspired to honour our distinct personal flair, stay true to our authentic requirements, resist the magnetic pull of hollow glitter, and focus on projecting our most authentic selves.

Epictetus's philosophical perspective incites us to reconsider fashion, not merely as an instrument to blend in with societal norms, but as a vibrant canvas for expressing our unique individuality and inner brilliance. Yet, his philosophy is far from being restricted to the tangible sphere of style and attire. His teachings prompt us to appreciate our authentic selves, devoid of needless embellishments. He advocates for a harmonious alignment of our possessions and desires with our personal 'measure', our inherent characteristics and capacities. This parallels the harmony between a shoe and its foot.

Venturing further into his philosophy, we discern that the route to genuine happiness is not paved with ostentatious display or outshining others, but with understanding and respecting our distinct nature and requirements. Indeed, a shoe may be encrusted with jewels and seem captivating, but it forsakes its fundamental purpose if it does not provide comfort to the foot. Similarly, a life resplendent with excessive, luxurious possessions may provoke envy but is bereft of authentic satisfaction if it doesn't truly resonate with the one leading it.

Epictetus counsels us that exceeding our 'proper measure' propels us towards a cliff edge of insatiable desires and ambitions, for the realm of human longing and aspiration knows no bounds. Much like a shoe that ceases to serve its primary function when adorned beyond necessity, the focus shifts away from its original purpose.

In life's grand tapestry, Epictetus's philosophy prompts us to value authenticity over pretentiousness, simplicity over complication, and seek balance and poise in our existence. Here, fashion emerges as a metaphor for life itself - a chance to reject transient trends and societal pressures in favour of deeper, intrinsic self-expression that echoes our true individuality. Thus, Epictetus's philosophy extends beyond just informing a refined sartorial sense; it provides a profound framework for attaining a balanced, fulfilling life, replete with happiness and contentment.

40

Inner Awesomeness

Women from fourteen years old are flattered by men with the title of mistresses. Therefore, perceiving that they are regarded only as qualified to give men pleasure, they begin to adorn themselves, and in that to place all their hopes. It is worthwhile, therefore, to try that they may perceive themselves honoured only so far as they appear beautiful in their demeanour and modestly virtuous.

As the stage curtains draw apart to unveil the vibrant yet turbulent spectacle of our teenage years, we find ourselves thrust into the limelight by a societal mantra that is both disconcerting and prevalent. This dictum, represented through the symbolic metaphor of a proverbial branding iron, imprints onto our young minds a troublesome notion: "Your worth is directly proportional to the quality of your latest duck-faced selfie!" In this digital epoch where filters and follower counts hold sway, we often find ourselves transforming into splendid, attention-seeking peacocks, parading our vibrant plumage in the relentless and often harsh beauty pageant that is online popularity.

Yet, amidst this frenzy of clamour and ostentation, we turn our attention to the timeless wisdom of Epictetus. His teachings offer a grounding contrast to this tumultuous climate, reminding us that true respect is not gauged by the number of 'likes' garnered or the glittering spectacle of our painstakingly fashioned social media avatars. It is not about portraying an immaculate image through a filtered sunset selfie or accumulating a multitude of followers to marvel at our virtual façade.

Epictetus propounds that genuine respect is rooted in something far more profound. It is found in exhibiting a natural grace without resorting to attention-seeking antics, in embodying humility devoid of any trace of deceit, and in radiating an aura of authenticity that stems from the very core of our being. It is about nurturing an inner glow that outshines any external spotlight, much akin to the way a firefly's subtle luminescence outclasses the garish neon signs of a Las Vegas strip.

In a world spinning on the axis of online popularity and digital validation, Epictetus invites us to pause and reassess our values. He instructs us that true respect emanates from character cultivation, establishing sincere relationships, and positively influencing others' lives. It's about embodying kindness, empathy, and compassion — virtues that are beyond the reach of any photo editing tool.

Envisage this: an individual with a perfectly curated Instagram profile amassing thousands of followers, yet their offline demeanour bears as much authenticity as a spray tan. Contrast this with someone who might not have a vast online following but consistently exhibits integrity, kindness, and meaningful human interactions. Who would you truly respect and admire? The answer is as clear as a well-crafted selfie filter.

Epictetus encourages us to divert our focus from the superficial realm of external validation to the substantive sphere of intrinsic worth. He prompts us to foster virtues such as honesty, humility, and compassion, thus allowing our inherent brilliance to shine forth. It's akin to becoming a human beacon of authentic awesomeness, casting a captivating glow that surpasses the digital boundaries of social media.

In a society where self-worth is often equated with online popularity, Epictetus reminds us to prioritise substance over spectacle. It's not about pursuing the ephemeral approval of others or seeking validation through an array of emojis and 'likes'. True respect is won through our authentic actions, the robustness of our character, and the positive imprint we leave in the tangible world. So, let's channel our inner firefly, illuminate our genuine brilliance, and leave an enduring impression that extends beyond the virtual sphere. After all, there's nothing more 'likable' than being authentically awesome.

We have reached the doorway where wisdom turns into deeds. We've been nurtured by Epictetus' philosophy, now it's time to grow these insights into our lives. The following exercises are your gardener, cultivating the seeds of philosophy into the fruits of everyday living. Ready to grow? Let's transition from nurturing wisdom to growing actions, cultivating our *Theory of Happiness*.

First on our agenda, let's dive into the "Inner Gaze Challenge". For an entire week, place your selfie stick on the shelf and cease your selfie routine. Shocking? Indeed, but in its stead, invest your time in introspective activities that nourish your soul. Engage in self-dialogue, let your thoughts flow onto the pages of a journal, expressing your innermost emotions and experiences. Use this period to deepen your understanding of yourself, beyond your physical appearances, nurturing the beauty of your demeanour and modest virtues. By shifting from external validation to internal reflection, you may find a revolution in your perception of self-worth.

Next, we're rolling out the "Beneath the Surface Compliment". Each day, challenge yourself to offer five sincere compliments that appreciate virtues beyond physical appearances. Celebrate someone's kindness, resilience, determination, or their positivity that illuminates any room. In recognising and appreciating these qualities in others, you simultaneously underscore their importance in yourself.

Proceeding further, let's engage with the "Hidden Kindness Experiment". For a week, engage in a discreet act of kindness each day without seeking recognition or a platform to showcase your benevolence. This could involve small deeds such as tidying up a public space, paying for a stranger's coffee, or anonymously leaving a thank-you note for someone. These silent acts of kindness not only help enhance your self-respect but also inject your day with joy.

Lastly, we're introducing the "Reflection of Character" exercise. Dedicate moments each day to dive into deep self-reflection. Assess your character traits honestly, acknowledging your strengths and identifying areas for growth. Document these insights and create a personal growth plan that focuses on nurturing your virtues and improving your demeanour. After a week, reflect on your self-discovery journey and the growth you've made.

At the end of these exercises, it's crucial to remember that every choice guided by Epictetus' teachings is a step closer to a life enriched by wisdom. Philosophy isn't simply an academic subject; it's a compass for mindful living. The real value of these teachings lies not in understanding them but in incorporating them into our lives. Treat these exercises as your guideposts, leading you towards a conscious, wisdom-driven life. As you carry on, you'll realise that philosophy isn't just learned, but lived.

To summarise, Epictetus bestows upon us profound insight into the concepts of self-worth, authenticity, and inner fortitude. He urges us to harmonise our values and aspirations with what is truly substantial, alerting us to the treacherous path of excess and superficiality. Epictetus advocates for earning authentic respect through the embodiment of refined elegance without ostentatiousness, the preservation of modesty without contrived humility, and the projection of an allure that originates from the very core of our existence.

Epictetus, with his timeless wisdom, elucidates that the source of genuine happiness and influence doesn't lie in the transient nature of social media popularity or the relentless pursuit of external validation. Instead, it emerges from the authenticity and strength inherent in our inner selves. In his view, our worth is not defined by external accolades or titles, but by our demeanour, our modest virtue, and our inner essence.

In his philosophical teachings, Epictetus noted the societal pressures that often lead individuals, from an early age, to place disproportionate value on their physical attractiveness and the approval of others. He observed that these pressures might prompt people to hinge their hopes and self-worth on outward adornments and the capacity to give pleasure. In a contemporary context, Epictetus encourages us to challenge this perspective, emphasising that true esteem should be associated not with transient, superficial factors, but with the enduring qualities of refined grace and modest virtue. His philosophy promotes the idea that the true worth of individuals lies not in their ability to attract or please others, but in the strength of their character and their commitment to personal growth and integrity.

Embracing this wisdom allows us to see that true honour and happiness do not come from the ephemeral world of physical allure and societal flattery, but from our character, virtue, and the elegance of our demeanour. Our authenticity, resilience, and modest virtue are the true sources of respect and self-worth. Epictetus' philosophy invites us to find our happiness and self-esteem in these genuine, substantive attributes.

Moving forward, it's time to embrace these teachings wholeheartedly, to rejoice in our individuality, and to let the radiance of our character shine through as we traverse the extraordinary journey of life. Remember, it's not about meeting societal standards or expectations. It's about honouring and being true to ourselves, cultivating our inner virtues and letting them guide us to a life of authenticity, resilience, and happiness.

41

Brains vs Brawn

It is a mark of want of intellect to spend much time in things relating to the body, as to be immoderate in exercises, in eating and drinking, and in the discharge of other animal functions. These things should be done incidentally, and our main strength be applied to our reason.

There exists a secret in life, so universally acknowledged yet so frequently overlooked, that its revelation may initially strike us as a perplexing paradox. We are, as creatures of the modern world, frequently immersed in the ceaseless pursuit of bodily upkeep, so much so that we may entirely overlook the existence of an intricate labyrinth within our minds—a labyrinth that necessitates equal, if not more, exploration and nurturing. This disproportionate focus on the physical over the intellectual is akin to aimlessly wandering in a complex maze without the aid of a map or compass, devoid of any coherent direction or purpose. Epictetus will help us unravel this convoluted tapestry woven with muscles, meals, relentless fitness regimens, and the all too familiar and tantalising obsession with bodily perfection.

Now, close your eyes for a moment and imagine this: you're in the middle of a back-breaking workout. Every muscle in your body strains as you heave another monstrous iron weight, sweat trickles down your face, your biceps bulge—almost as if you're a contestant in Mr. Universe. It's tempting, isn't it, to become absorbed solely in your physical prowess? However, let me pose a little question: when your days transform into relentless marathons aimed at reaching the finish line of a chiselled body or mastering the splits, don't you reckon something vital is being left in the dust—perhaps your intellectual development?

Epictetus nudges us towards a profound truth: balance is the key to it all. While it's undeniable that our bodies warrant care and attention, should they be the sole stars around which our lives revolve? A life dominated by physical pursuits might result in a physique to make Hercules green with envy, but it could also lead to intellectual stagnation. Imagine living in a world where dumbbells and protein shakes overshadow pursuits of the mind like reading an engrossing novel, learning a new language, or solving a particularly tricky Sudoku. A hulking bicep or a toned abdomen is undoubtedly a commendable accomplishment, but it pales in comparison to the fireworks of a well-nurtured mind.

That said, let's not swing the pendulum too far in the other direction and demonise our occasional indulgences. There's nothing wrong with savouring a scrumptious cheeseburger or a refreshing pint now and again. But when these pleasures start stealing the show in our lives, it might be a good idea to give our priorities a little shake-up. It would be akin to going to a circus, but being so engrossed in your popcorn that you miss the daring acrobatics happening right in front of you.

So, what's the solution? Here's a little food for thought: it might be time to nudge our bodily pursuits to the supporting roles, rather than the lead characters, in the grand opera of life. By all means, continue to challenge your body at the gym, but don't let that overshadow the untapped potential of your intellect. Stir up a debate at your next dinner party, lose yourself in a riveting book, explore new fields of interest, or simply sit and ponder upon the mysteries of the universe.

In a world that often places physical appearances on a gilded pedestal, Epictetus' wisdom provides a refreshing counter-narrative. He prompts us to find the sweet spot—the golden mean—between caring for our bodies and nurturing our minds. It's much like being a superhero, where your physical strength and agility are undoubtedly important, but your most potent superpower is your intellectual prowess—the ability to reason, think critically, and make a positive impact on the world.

The significance of intellectual growth, paired with physical well-being, cannot be overstated. It's like a finely tuned guitar that requires both the right chords and a good strum to produce enchanting melodies. We must strive to cultivate our bodies and minds in tandem, to reach our maximum potential. This isn't about favouring the brain over the brawn, but about orchestrating them into a harmonious symphony of personal growth.

Engaging in intellectual pursuits equips us with essential tools to navigate life's complexities and make sound decisions. By actively nurturing our intellect, we widen our horizons, deepen our reservoir of knowledge, and hone our critical thinking skills. Pair this with a physically healthy body, and we become a force to be reckoned with, ready to leave our mark on the world.

So, let's take Epictetus' advice to heart and embark on a journey of balanced growth. Let's challenge ourselves both physically and intellectually, relishing the rewards of both domains without letting one overshadow the other. After all, it's through this harmonious fusion of physicality and intellect that we can truly unlock our potential and lead lives brimming with fulfilment, purpose, and satisfaction.

Here we are again, at the crossroads where profound knowledge morphs into practical action. We've been inspired by Epictetus' wisdom, and now it's time to bring this inspiration into our day-to-day actions. The exercises up next are your muse, guiding you from the abstract realm of philosophy to the concrete world of practice. Ready to be inspired? Let's move from inspiration to action, creating our unique *Theory of Happiness*.

Our first exercise on this journey is the "Mind Flex Challenge". Just as the name suggests, it is an opportunity to put your physical workouts on pause, allowing your mind to seize the spotlight. This challenge prompts you to wrestle with a thought-provoking puzzle, an intricate riddle, or an elaborate brain-teaser. Make this a social occasion by inviting friends to join you in this cerebral adventure, or go solo for a deeper, more introspective experience. The ultimate goal is to solve the problem at hand, but along the way, prepare for stimulating brainstorming sessions, captivating deductions, wild guesses, and, of course, those electrifying "aha!" moments that shine a light on the unfathomable potential of your intellect. This challenge, aside from being delightful fun, serves as a potent reminder that the mind's prowess extends well beyond the realm of mere physical strength.

Next on our journey, we introduce the "Mind Body Scavenger Hunt". This exercise tests not only your mental agility and creativity but also puts your physical prowess to the test. Your task is to design a scavenger hunt, combining physical and intellectual challenges in an entertaining blend. Craft elusive clues that lead participants through a maze of different locations, where each challenge demands a fusion of physical effort and mental ingenuity. For instance, deciphering a riddle could lead to a secret cache of dumbbells, or a challenge might require participants to perform an impromptu dance whilst reciting a profound quote from our favourite philosopher,

Epictetus. Be prepared for a day teeming with laughter, camaraderie, unforeseen twists and delightful surprises!

Finally, we introduce the "Mind Buffet Book Club". This is an opportunity to assemble a group of like-minded friends or ignite an engaging online conversation, establishing a unique literary gathering. The aim is to delve into a variety of books that offer intellectual stimulation, spanning diverse genres from philosophy to psychology, and including deeply thoughtful fiction that explores profound philosophical themes. To infuse some fun into your intellectual journey, we recommend encouraging participants to share humorous anecdotes or notable quotes from the books. Perhaps even consider dramatising particularly captivating scenes to add a touch of theatrical flair to your discussions. By combining intellectual pursuit with humour, not only will your mind be continuously challenged, but your meetings will be permeated with hearty laughter, ensuring an enjoyable and enlightening experience for all.

Having completed these exercises, bear in mind that every action inspired by Epictetus brings us closer to a life imbued with wisdom. Philosophy isn't just a scholarly pursuit; it's a practical guide for life. The real potency of these teachings lies not just in comprehending them but in actualising them. Consider these exercises as your milestones, leading you towards a life influenced by wisdom. As you press on, you'll understand that philosophy isn't just a concept, but a way of life.

As we conclude, we reflect once more on Epictetus's philosophy, which offers a timely reminder: while safeguarding our physical health is undeniably crucial, it should not eclipse our pursuit of intellectual growth. He beckons us towards equilibrium, urging us to nurture our minds even as we tend to our corporeal needs. According to him, this harmonious interplay between mind and body forms the bedrock of a truly enriched life.

Epictetus does not ask us to renounce physical gratifications. On the contrary, he champions mindful enjoyment of life's pleasures, ensuring that such activities do not encroach upon the precious time and energy we should dedicate to cultivating our intellect. In his eyes, the body and mind are not isolated entities but rather an integral team, collaboratively steering us through life's remarkable journey.

This Stoic philosopher invites us to regard our bodies not merely as physical vessels but as co-travellers in our pursuit of intellectual advancement. He argues that investing excessive time and energy in bodily affairs, such as immoderate exercises, indulgent eating and drinking, or other primal functions, might denote a lack of intellectual engagement. Instead, these bodily activities should be managed sensibly, allowing our primary focus to be invested in nurturing our reasoning capabilities.

Epictetus's philosophy is not a call for asceticism but a manifesto for balance - an ethos that champions the temperate indulgence in physical activities, ensuring they serve as a means to support our intellectual growth rather than become an end in themselves.

As we navigate through life's complexities, let's honour this extraordinary collaboration between our body and mind. Let's strive to ensure that our muscles and minds are both in prime condition, ready to embrace the exciting challenges life throws our way. By achieving this equilibrium, we can lead a life that truly embodies the wisdom of Epictetus – one filled with both intellectual richness and physical vitality, contributing to a complete and fulfilling human existence.

42

Criticism into Comedy

When any person does ill by you, or speaks ill of you, remember that he acts or speaks from an impression that it is right for him to do so. Now it is not possible that he should follow what appears right to you, but only what appears so to himself. Therefore, if he judges from false appearances, he is the person hurt, since he, too, is the person deceived. For if anyone takes a true proposition to be false, the proposition is not hurt, but only the man is deceived. Setting out, then, from these principles, you will meekly bear with a person who reviles you, for you will say upon every occasion, "It seemed so to him."

Life often feels akin to navigating an unpredictably vast ocean. Like intrepid sailors, we occasionally encounter the looming shadows of criticism or malicious gossip. These distressing elements can resemble stormy clouds on our horizons, threatening to pour down and dampen our spirits, thereby putting our resilience to the sternest of tests. However, in such moments, the ancient wisdom of Epictetus can act as our guiding star. He advises us to reinterpret these 'attacks' from a unique perspective. According to Epictetus, those who engage in criticism or gossip are merely operating based on their interpretation of what they perceive to be right. This concept might initially strike us as puzzling, but upon contemplative immersion, it unfolds its profound depth.

To better understand this, let's consider a scenario. Imagine you're traversing the convoluted journey of life, filled with confidence and vigour, when you're abruptly swamped by a barrage of unkind words and slanderous remarks. It might feel as though you've wandered into a tempest without an umbrella, getting drenched by the downpour of harsh words. But here's where the idea comes into play: the individuals who instigate this uproar aren't voyagers on your mental landscape. Instead, they're trapped in their labyrinths of misunderstanding and skewed perceptions of righteousness.

Seeing things from this viewpoint offers an intriguing insight: if these individuals' moral compasses are misaligned, it is they who are ambling through life's maze like wayfarers lost in an unfamiliar city. They may believe they're helping by pointing out your perceived flaws, but their criticisms and judgements do not devalue your inherent worth or the unyielding resilience of truth. Instead, their misguided attempts highlight their flawed judgments, unwittingly casting them as the lead actors in their tragicomedy of errors.

Let's picture another scenario: you find yourself caught in the swirling eye of a gossip storm. Barbed words and wild rumours whirl around you like debris in a tornado. Instead of taking shelter or retaliating, you stand tall, armed with a serene smile and a calm, thoughtful rebuttal that leaves them scrambling for a comeback.

In such situations, it is beneficial to distance yourself from the negativity or avoid a futile tit-for-tat exchange. Instead, seek solace in the unusual aspects of their behaviour. Give yourself permission to have a light-hearted chuckle at the absurdity of the situation. By doing so, you're essentially saying, 'Well, their antics add a dash of unexpected drama to my day!' Maintaining your emotional balance and self-assurance allows you to transform their misguided criticisms into a catalyst for personal growth and introspection.

Suppose someone spreads a groundless rumour about your singing abilities, drawing an unflattering parallel between your melodic voice and the discordant screeching of a stray cat. Instead of letting their false accusations stifle your song, respond with a dash of wit wrapped in harmless sarcasm. Meet their derogatory jibes with a grin and a playful retort like, "Indeed, my unique vocal range is an acquired taste. I've been told I'm a shoo-in for 'The Voice: Feline Edition' – it's quite a niche market, don't you think?" A response like this not only deflects their intended offence but also throws a spotlight on the ludicrousness of their assertions.

In the grand narrative of life, it's essential to remember that you're the protagonist of your unique tale. When faced with criticism or gossip, maintain your composure and reframe their negative words as opportunities for self-reflection and personal development. And why not add a dash of humour to lighten the situation?

So, gear up to skilfully manoeuvre through life's curveballs, demonstrating to the world that no amount of negativity can eclipse your glowing spirit or dampen your unwavering resilience. The stage of life is yours to command, and every challenge you overcome serves as a stepping-stone towards personal growth, contributing to your continuous evolution. In this way, you transform life's trials into unforgettable chapters that celebrate your journey with grace, wisdom, and a generous sprinkling of humour.

Once again, we're at the junction where philosophy and action intertwine. We've been fuelled by Epictetus' wisdom, and now it's time to drive these insights into our daily routine. The following exercises are your GPS, directing you from the fuel station of philosophy to the highway of action. Shall we hit the road? Let's transition from fuelling wisdom to driving actions, steering our unique *Theory of Happiness*.

Our first exercise, the "Role-Playing Rumble", invites you to step into a theatrical sphere where life scenarios serve as the script. Picture a group of friends, each taking turns to tread the boards of this makeshift stage, embodying various characters and predicaments. Here, the aim is not merely to endure these encounters, but to sail through them with grace, composure, and a dash of humour, truly embodying the Stoic principles championed by Epictetus. Imagine the room filling with roars of laughter and valuable insights when a friend attempts to emulate Epictetus while dealing with a simulation of workplace gossip or an exaggerated parking dispute! It's a unique blend of improv theatre and philosophy class, topped off with a generous helping of laughter therapy.

Next, we journey to the realm of written expression with the "Gossipy Gibberish Journal". Here, your personal journal serves as the canvas for documenting anecdotes and experiences where you've found yourself under the harsh spotlight of negative chatter. Instead of allowing this chatter to ruffle your feathers, you transform it into an opportunity for introspection and growth. As you chronicle these instances, you realise that you are the master of your emotions, and no external event or comment can wield power over you unless you permit it. This therapeutic exercise functions as a mirror, reflecting the negativity back onto its origin and helping you cultivate a mindset fortified against such harmful comments.

Our third exercise is the exhilarating "Stoic Stand-up". This exercise channels your inner comedian, encouraging you to extract humour from the sour grapes of unpleasant encounters and press them into the fine wine of comedy. Imagine taking the stage and delivering a comic monologue that transforms the petty annoyances of everyday life into a source of hilarity. It's a cathartic exercise that reshapes your experiences and lightens your emotional load, enabling you to find humour in even the most unlikely places.

Our final exercise, "Mindful Meditations", offers a tranquil retreat for your mind. During these daily sessions, you are encouraged to mentally rehearse your reactions to harsh criticism or unkind words. Envision yourself responding with tranquillity, serenity, and a touch of humour, transforming the potential sting of harsh words into a soft tickle of amusement. To enhance the experience, consider creating a humorous mantra to repeat during the meditation—something along the lines of, "I'm a serene lotus, you're just muddy water..." or "I'm a sturdy oak, you're but a gust of wind..."

As we wrap up these exercises, remember that every endeavour guided by Epictetus' wisdom is a step towards a life governed by philosophical insight. Philosophy isn't merely an intellectual endeavour; it's a roadmap for action. The true essence of these teachings lies not just in grasping them but in implementing them. Use these exercises as your navigational stars, guiding your path towards a life of wisdom. As you continue your journey, you'll find that philosophy isn't just about cognition, but about living.

In summary, we find Epictetus championing the virtues of emotional resilience and the power of humour when faced with challenges. He urges us to maintain our equilibrium and envisage life as a theatrical performance, in which we have been cast as the lead.

Epictetus emphasises that it's not the events themselves that shape our emotional reactions, but rather our interpretation of these occurrences. It is here that his philosophy dovetails beautifully with a light-hearted perspective: if we choose to interpret life's situations with an element of humour and levity, we empower ourselves to navigate them with grace, resilience, and laughter.

When someone speaks ill of us or treats us poorly, Epictetus asks us to remember that they are acting based on their perception of what's right, not ours. If their perception is skewed, they are the ones at a loss, for they are the ones deceived. This mindset encourages tolerance and understanding, letting us bear criticism or negativity with a certain lightness, viewing it more as a source of amusement rather than a personal attack.

Through his teachings, we are better equipped to transmute criticism and negativity into humorous reflections and opportunities for personal evolution. This shift in perspective, this ability to laugh in the face of adversity, makes us emotionally robust and, ultimately, more content. We learn to shrug off negativity with a smile and a light-hearted remark, echoing Epictetus: "It seemed so to them."

In essence, Epictetus invites us to a transformative journey where emotional resilience, a sense of humour, and personal growth become our loyal companions. This paves the path to authentic happiness, allowing us to navigate the ebb and flow of life with a heart brimming with joy and a mind armed with fortitude. Life, according to Epictetus, is less a battlefield and more a stage for our performance - a performance best played with laughter, resilience, and understanding. So, let the curtains rise on your show, and remember, even when the critics abound, to take it all in stride, with a smile and a cheerful quip.

43

The Serene Suitcase

Everything has two handles: one by which it may be borne, another by which it cannot. If your brother acts unjustly, do not lay hold on the affair by the handle of his injustice, for by that it cannot be borne, but rather by the opposite—that he is your brother, that he was brought up with you; and thus you will lay hold on it as it is to be borne.

Embarking on the voyage of understanding life through Epictetus' philosophy, we find ourselves facing a suitcase. Not your everyday suitcase but a peculiar one that carries a profound message symbolised by its two handles. Each one represents a different emotional response to life's challenges.

One handle is rugged and jagged, much like a treacherous mountain terrain. This signifies our instinctive emotional reactions when faced with unexpected adversities—responses often fuelled by anger, frustration, and resentment. It's as if in the face of a sudden, unsettling incident, we instinctively reach out to this spiky handle, reacting with wrath or bitterness. This reflexive action is equivalent to holding onto the metaphorical suitcase's jagged handle—an act that's inherently uncomfortable, painful, and unpleasant.

On the other hand, the suitcase's other handle is smooth and polished, akin to a beautifully rounded pebble. This handle symbolises a mindful, measured approach to life's hurdles—an attitude steeped in patience, understanding, and empathy. Choosing this handle means navigating tricky situations with grace and composure instead of impulsively surrendering to reactive behaviour. It's about consciously deciding to respond with tranquillity, even amidst the tumult of the situation.

To illuminate these concepts, let's delve into a variety of everyday situations. Consider a typical workplace scenario: an ambitious colleague unceremoniously claims your diligent work on a project to impress your manager. The easy, instinctive reaction is to grab the spiky handle, leading to a confrontational showdown. But Epictetus encourages a different approach. He recommends choosing the smooth handle—pausing, reflecting, and addressing the issue tactfully with your colleague or, if necessary, a supervisor.

Moving from the professional realm to a personal scenario, imagine a close friend betraying your trust by disclosing a secret you've confided in them. Instead of clutching the spiky handle of resentment, Epictetus urges you to grasp the smooth handle of understanding. This might mean initiating an open conversation about trust and respect, instead of harbouring resentment or abruptly severing ties.

Bringing this philosophy closer to home, let's consider a common family situation. Your sibling, in a fit of theatrical melodrama, parades around in your favourite shirt they've borrowed without permission or reveals your most embarrassing childhood secrets to your friends. You could reach for the spiky handle, snap back in anger or humiliate them in revenge. But Epictetus, with his enduring wisdom, encourages a different perspective. He prompts us to grasp the smooth handle, to act from a place of patience and understanding. Instead of being infuriated by your sibling's antics, you might instead take a moment to laugh, to remember that despite their current bout of melodrama, you share a unique bond, a history filled with shared experiences and laughter.

The philosophy of Epictetus not only guides us in handling conflicts, but also encourages us to inject humour to lighten the emotional burden. Consider these trying situations not as catastrophic crises, but as amusing anecdotes in the grand narrative of life. Perhaps your colleague is left stammering when asked to elaborate on the project they've claimed as their own, or your friend's clumsy attempt at apology provides a chance for mutual laughter. Maybe your sibling's over-the-top melodrama can be seen as a comedic scene in the sitcom of life.

This approach doesn't advocate suppressing initial feelings of annoyance or anger. Instead, it's about consciously choosing a response that nurtures personal peace, growth, and positive relationships. Infusing humour into reactions can diffuse tension and foster an atmosphere of shared amusement and camaraderie, even amidst conflicts.

When navigating life's challenges. remember this suitcase analogy. Visualise its two handles—one prickly, one smooth. Consciously choose to respond with patience, understanding, and empathy, over anger and frustration. With practice, this mindful response can become second nature, transforming potential conflicts into opportunities for growth and deeper connections.

Epictetus presents us with a strategy to navigate life's turbulent seas. By consciously selecting our emotional response—choosing the smooth handle—we can transform conflicts into opportunities for growth, understanding, and shared laughter. Life's journey then evolves from a relentless storm into a voyage marked by personal growth, understanding, shared smiles, and moments of humour.

We're back at the point where contemplation matures into action. We've been powered by Epictetus' wisdom, and now it's time to energise our daily lives with these insights. The exercises to follow are your power plant, transforming the potential energy of philosophy into kinetic action. Ready to power up? Let's move from contemplating wisdom to energising actions, powering our *Theory of Happiness*.

Our first exercise, coined the "Handle Handle Revolution", presents a peculiar yet intriguing name. The activity itself is a brain-teaser, designed to stimulate your thinking faculties. It invites you and a friend to brainstorm diverse life scenarios. Each scenario is visualised as a metaphorical suitcase with two distinct handles—one uncomfortably jagged, the other soothingly smooth. Your mission, should you choose to accept it, is to dissect each scenario and craft a strategy for choosing the 'smooth handle'. In other words, you are tasked with figuring out how to respond to each situation with patience, understanding, and empathy. Engaging in this exercise illuminates the potent Stoic principle of choosing our reactions, turning potential prickly situations into manageable, even enjoyable, ones.

For those with an artistic streak, the "Sibling Saga Comic Strip" offers an appealing twist. This creative exercise requires you to sketch a comic strip that vividly portrays a dramatic sibling incident. However, the crux lies in depicting that pivotal moment where you consciously choose the 'smooth handle', steering the narrative towards a more positive, harmonious outcome. This practice goes beyond mere artistic expression—it underlines the transformative power of making mindful choices amidst emotionally charged situations.

Following this artistic endeavour, we step onto the stage of the "Role Reversal Theatre". This exercise is a journey of empathy that can be both entertaining and enlightening. It requires you and a partner—a friend, family member, or even a co-worker—to swap roles for an entire day. The idea of experiencing life from another person's perspective, as whimsical as it might seem, provides an invaluable opportunity to understand their outlook. Walking a mile in their shoes for a day might seem challenging, but it can offer a deeper insight into their actions and reactions, fostering empathy and mutual respect. As you navigate through their typical day, you get a chance to truly appreciate the struggles they face, the decisions they make, and the unique circumstances that shape their life. This exercise, though draped in humour, offers an essential lesson in empathy and perspective-taking. It's an opportunity to step out of your shoes and into another's, shedding light on the power of understanding and respect in building stronger, more empathetic relationships.

Finally, we embark on a nostalgic journey through "Memory Lane Meander". This introspective exercise invites you and your relationship partner—be it a friend, family member, or colleague—to reminisce about the shared experiences that have contributed to the strength of your bond over time. Recalling these common moments of joy, laughter, challenge, or triumph can fortify the bond you share, making it easier to maintain perspective during future disagreements. Instead of immediately resorting to the 'spiky handle' of resentment and anger, you're reminded of the value of this relationship, fostering a broader perspective that can help you navigate beyond temporary conflicts. Though reflective, this exercise brings to light the power of shared experiences and memories in building stronger relationships. It encourages you to lean into your shared history, using it as a compass for empathy, patience, and mutual understanding, especially during times of conflict.

Upon finishing these exercises, remember that every choice made with Epictetus' wisdom brings us closer to a life enlightened by philosophy. Philosophy isn't just about abstract thinking; it's a guide for meaningful living. The real power of these teachings lies not just in understanding them but in bringing them to life. Treat these exercises as your compass, leading your way towards a life rich in wisdom. As you proceed, you'll discover that philosophy isn't just a field of study, but a way of life.

As we bring this to a close, we reflect on the crux of Epictetus' wisdom, which shines a light on our personal perception of events. He illuminates the idea that it's not the events themselves that unsettle us, but rather our reactions to them. As such, judicious selection of our responses can metamorphose our familial relationships from potential minefields of tension into abundant fountains of delight and harmony.

Epictetus employs a simple yet powerful metaphor: he views every situation as having two handles—one that is difficult to bear and another that can be held comfortably. If a person in your life—be it a partner, sibling, friend, or co-worker—acts in a way you perceive as unfair, Epictetus' philosophy encourages you to grasp the situation by its 'bearable handle'. In essence, Epictetus' philosophy guides us to approach situations infused with perceived unfairness not with a knee-jerk reaction of anger or frustration, but with understanding and empathy.

This strategy entails acknowledging the individual's role and shared history in your life, as opposed to fixating solely on the perceived injustice. Simply put, Epictetus advocates navigating the complexities of relationships by fostering an attitude of understanding, patience, and empathy.

By immersing ourselves in Epictetus' teachings, we can augment our understanding of our own reactions, fine-tune our emotional responses, and foster a familial atmosphere that thrives on laughter, understanding, and mutual respect. By doing so, we can transform the very essence of our interactions with others, evolving from a reactive approach to one that is more mindful and harmonious.

Following the wisdom of Epictetus, we are empowered to cultivate an environment within our relationships that is rooted not in tension and conflict, but in genuine respect, hearty laughter, and empathetic understanding. We learn to view disagreements not as insurmountable hurdles, but as opportunities for growth and deeper understanding. This fosters a sense of unity and positivity across all our interactions, whether in our personal relationships, workplace dynamics, or broader social interactions.

In essence, Epictetus teaches us that in the grand theatre of life, the ability to laugh, to forgive, and to empathise with those around us is not just the path to harmonious relationships, but also a pivotal element in our journey towards personal happiness and contentment. As we continue on this journey, let us remember to grasp the right handle of every situation. In this way, we confront challenges with a smile, a sprinkle of wisdom, and an abundance of laughter, promoting harmony in all our interactions and relationships.

44

Interweaving Self-Worth

These reasonings have no logical connection: "I am richer than you, therefore I am your superior." "I am more eloquent than you, therefore I am your superior". The true logical connection is rather this: "I am richer than you, therefore my possessions must exceed yours". "I am more eloquent than you, therefore my style must surpass yours". But you, after all, consist neither in property nor in style.

The concept of self-worth can be a bit of a slippery eel. We're all susceptible to the occasional blunder of equating our worth to our wealth or our skills, especially in comparison to others. We've probably all caught ourselves thinking, "I've got more in the bank, I must be better", or "I could talk the hind legs off a donkey, therefore, I'm superior". It's a tempting perspective, particularly when society often gives a standing ovation to those with fuller wallets or extraordinary talents. However, when we sit down and really chew on it, we realise this thinking is as misguided as comparing the crunch of an apple with the zest of an orange - an exercise as pointless as a chocolate teapot and entirely neglectful of the inherent qualities that make each fruit special.

Imagine you and a friend have found yourselves in the middle of a bountiful orchard. You're drawn to the apples, enchanted by their red blush and smooth skin. Your friend, on the other hand, can't resist the allure of the oranges with their zingy fragrance and bumpy skin. You both start picking your favourite fruit, and as your basket brims over with apples while your friend's oranges are a little fewer, a thought pops up: "Am I better because I have more apples?" The silliness of this question is apparent when you remember that apples and oranges, while both fruits, are not the same, each boasting unique qualities and charms. Comparing oneself to others based on wealth or skills is just as absurd as claiming superiority over your friend based on the number or type of fruit in your basket.

Shifting our gaze a tad, we find more sensible ground if we stick to factual observations like, "I've saved up more, so I have more toys in the attic", or "I've spent years perfecting my speech delivery, so I could probably outspeak you". These statements don't equate the riches or talents to personal worth; they simply outline particular achievements or levels of proficiency. However, it's crucial to keep in mind that our worth isn't something you can count in pounds or rate by a skill level.

Our friend Epictetus chips in with some sage advice at this point, nudging us to grasp that our self-worth outshines our bank balance or the list of our talents. He points out that we're not paper-thin, one-trick ponies defined by a single characteristic or achievement. We're wonderfully complex jigsaws, with pieces made up of various traits, values, and life experiences that complete our unique picture. Our worth isn't a number on a spreadsheet or a tally of accomplishments; it's our unique, irreplaceable imprint on the world.

When we start comparing bank balances or talents to gauge superiority, we tread on thin ice. It risks diminishing human worth to mere numbers or abilities, while ignoring the beautiful mosaic of traits and experiences that make us who we are. Epictetus nudges us to untie our self-worth from these external measures and to cherish the depth and uniqueness of our own individuality. Our worth is not something that can be counted or clocked; it lies in our intrinsic qualities - our capacity for empathy, our ability to love, and our potential to bring about positive change.

So, the next time you're drawn into a game of comparisons, remember the apples and oranges. Just like each fruit has its unique taste and character, so does every person have a unique blend of traits that can't be quantified or measured. Enjoy the uniqueness of your individuality and remember, true worth is far more intricate and nuanced than any external success meter can show.

By doing this, we float above the confines of comparison and appreciate the magic of our own existence. We shake off the shackles of seeking external validation and set sail on the exciting voyage of self-discovery. This voyage nurtures self-acceptance and self-love, steering us towards a profound sense of contentment and joy. When we acknowledge and appreciate our individuality, we discover the key to happiness. Recognising our irreplaceable uniqueness and value is the foundation of authentic self-worth and the doorway to a fulfilled existence. Therefore, remember, your worth isn't in your wallet or on a certificate. It's in the mirror, beaming right back at you.

It's that time again to switch from understanding to implementing. We've been stirred by Epictetus' philosophy, and now it's time to mix these insights into our daily lives. The exercises up next are your blender, mixing the ingredients of philosophy into the smoothie of practice. Ready to blend? Let's transition from stirring wisdom to mixing actions, blending our unique *Theory of Happiness*.

First, let us set sail on the "Fruit Salad Chronicles". Picture a vibrant marketplace bustling with energy, a smorgasbord of colours, aromas, and sounds. Amidst the chaos, fruits of all kinds dance in a beautiful symphony of shapes, colours, and flavours. Now, envisage yourself as a bright, succulent apple, basking in the glory of your unique virtues, experiences, and strengths. Amongst the crowd, others express their essence through the guise of oranges, cherries, or bananas. An exercise of imagination and introspection, this requires you to jot down instances when you've compared your worth to others. The goal here is not to fuel self-doubt, but to kindle self-awareness and celebrate the diversity of this metaphorical fruit salad. Every apple, orange, or cherry contributes a distinctive flavour to the salad, making it a delightful medley. Likewise, it's our unique attributes that make us indispensable threads in the rich tapestry of humanity.

Then comes the "Speech and Wealth Improv", a lively and spirited interaction. Picture an improvisation scenario wherein one character exudes arrogance about their amassed wealth or command over language. Another character, donning the cloak of Epictetus' wisdom, humbly reframes the narrative to emphasise the inherent worth that lies beyond these superficial attributes. This light-hearted exchange serves as a gentle nudge, reminding us to look beyond the shiny veneer of material wealth or eloquence, to acknowledge the deeper value within each person. Real worth isn't quantifiable by worldly possessions or abilities, but is defined by the empathy we extend, the kindness we share, and the meaningful impact we create in others' lives.

Next, we delve into the heart-warming "Positively You Collage" exercise. Here, you're asked to gather pictures, quotes, symbols - anything that can visually capture the different facets of your personality, values, passions, and experiences. Arrange these eclectic pieces into a collage that serves as a visual testament to your unique identity. This vibrant mosaic reminds us of the multitude of qualities and experiences that shape our individuality, extending our worth far beyond the realm of material possessions or skills. It's a celebration of your existence, a snapshot of the radiant blend of qualities that make you uniquely, wonderfully you.

Lastly, the "Quirky Algebra Quiz" challenges our flawed reasoning with a pinch of humour. Here, you're encouraged to craft a quirky quiz for your friends and family, with real-life scenarios that underscore the absurdity of our often-irrational comparisons. It could be contrasting career paths, contrasting hobbies, or a variety of life experiences. The aim is to spotlight the fact that these comparisons frequently neglect the richness of individual experiences and characteristics. This light-hearted exercise helps us question the validity of our comparisons and embrace the unique path each person traverses.

As we conclude these exercises, bear in mind that every step in line with Epictetus' teachings brings us closer to a life guided by wisdom. Philosophy isn't just a cerebral pursuit; it's a blueprint for action. The true essence of these teachings lies not just in knowing them but in living them. Use these exercises as your roadmap, steering your path towards a wisdom-filled life. As you venture forward, you'll come to understand that philosophy isn't just a subject, but a lifestyle.

In conclusion, it is paramount to recognise that we often, almost inadvertently, may tumble into the trap of measuring our worth and that of others through a lens of comparison. This simplistic method risks reducing the vibrant, nuanced tapestry of human beings into mere cogs in a machine, transforming individuality into simplistic variables for comparison.

Epictetus, however, invites us to view this trend with gentle humour and critical introspection. He encourages us to realise that we're significantly more than the mere tally of our possessions or the finesse of our skills. Each of us is spectacularly, marvellously unique—an individual unlike any other.

In his teachings, Epictetus carefully untangles the misguided conflation of wealth, eloquence, or any other external attribute with intrinsic human worth. He emphasises that being richer or more eloquent than another merely denotes the superiority of one's possessions or articulation skills and not the overall worth of an individual.

Moreover, he prompts us to acknowledge that our real essence lies not in transient worldly possessions or skills, but in our unique combination of experiences, values, character, and perspectives. The value of this personal uniqueness is immeasurable and irreplaceable. The wisdom of Epictetus teaches us that while external traits might differentiate us, they certainly do not define us.

In the grand arithmetic of life, Epictetus encourages us to assign the highest value not to our comparative attributes, but rather to the celebration of our individuality. He underscores the joy of acknowledging and cherishing our irreplaceable selves.

As we journey through life, it is essential that we warmly and unapologetically embrace our unique selves. We should express our individuality with humour and pride, celebrating the quirks and passions that make us who we are. Our personal narrative isn't just a tally of external attributes; it's a unique mosaic shaped by our thoughts, dreams, values, and experiences.

Epictetus reminds us that we are more than the sum of our external attributes. The true essence of our identity lies in our individuality—our own distinct stories that contribute to the grand tapestry of human existence. It is this realisation that should guide us as we navigate life, encouraging us to cherish our personal journeys and embrace the infinite value of our unique selves.

45

Beyond Quick Judgments

Does anyone bathe hastily? Do not say that he does it ill, but hastily. Does anyone drink much wine? Do not say that he does ill, but that he drinks a great deal. For unless you perfectly understand his motives, how should you know if he acts ill? Thus, you will not risk yielding to any appearances but such as you fully comprehend.

You are now invited to explore an approach to perceiving the world that is steeped in understanding, empathy, and a keen sense of restraint from rushing to conclusions. Drawing from Epictetus's philosophy, we'll venture into the realm of hasty judgments and learn to tread more carefully, shifting our focus to uncover the motivations and experiences underlying people's actions.

Consider the scenario where you witness someone savouring their meal with the intensity of a competitive eater. The temptation might be to label them as a glutton swiftly. However, Epictetus urges us to pause and reconsider. Could this person be an enthusiast of quick consumption? Their eating style might appear excessive, but have we taken the time to understand the potential motives driving their behaviour? They might regard mealtime as an exercise in mindfulness, a period where they focus on experiencing the act of eating fully. Their apparent haste could be an attempt to savour every morsel and remain wholly present in that moment. Through this lens, the quick eater is no longer a 'glutton' but an individual practising their unique form of mindfulness.

Similarly, suppose you encounter a person partaking in wine with an intensity that suggests a race against time. It might be easy to hastily deduce they are struggling with alcohol. However, could it be that they are merely a wine connoisseur, revelling in the subtle nuances each vintage offers? Their love for wine might stem from a profound understanding and respect for the craft of winemaking, and their rapid consumption might reflect their deep reverence for the beverage. Epictetus would advise us to refrain from such quick judgments until we fully grasp the context. It would be as imprudent to formulate an opinion about a film after watching only half of it as it is to judge a person without understanding their full story.

Adopting this practice of mindful restraint allows us to steer clear of hasty conclusions that often stem from biases or a lack of understanding. It's akin to cleaning a dirty windowpane

—only once the grime is removed can we genuinely appreciate the view beyond. As we navigate the often-labyrinthine paths of social interactions, it's essential to remember that each person is like an iceberg, with most of their personality concealed beneath the surface. Applying Epictetus's teachings not only nurtures empathy and understanding but also enhances our worldview.

When we exercise such mindful restraint, we foster a culture of empathy and open-mindedness. This understanding of the multitude of factors that influence individuals' actions encourages us to approach each person with curiosity, poised to delve into their unique perspectives and experiences. This mindset liberates us from the constraints of hasty judgments and offers us a clearer lens through which to view the world.

Epictetus enlightens us to the fact that our perceptions aren't absolute truths, but interpretations sculpted by our limited perspective. By suspending judgment and seeking to comprehend the entire context, we deepen our appreciation of human complexity. We begin to understand that each person's story, motivations, and challenges influence their behaviour. This newfound understanding fosters compassion, paving the way for a more harmonious society.

In integrating Epictetus's teachings into our daily lives, we cultivate the ability to handle social interactions with greater sensitivity and wisdom. We become more observant, alert to the subtleties of human behaviour, and approach each interaction with an open mind, eager to embrace the full context and appreciate the individual's unique attributes. Through this mindful restraint, we contribute to both our personal growth and a more empathetic, enlightened society.

Let's embody Epictetus's teachings and practice mindful restraint in our daily interactions. By deferring judgment and striving to gain a deeper understanding of others, we nurture empathy and open-mindedness, leading to a more nuanced worldview. Let's endeavour to look beneath the surface, to appreciate the complex narratives that unfold beneath. With these principles as our compass, we can foster a society that values compassion, understanding, and the wisdom of careful judgment.

Once again, we're at the junction where philosophy graduates into action. We've been electrified by Epictetus' wisdom, and now it's time to light up our actions with these insights. The following exercises are your lightbulb, illuminating the path from the power source of philosophy to the light of practice. Ready to light up? Let's move from electrifying wisdom to lighting actions, brightening our own *Theory of Happiness*.

Our first exercise, rather cheekily named "Gusto vs. Gluttony", transports us to the bustling atmosphere of a dinner party or a family feast. Picture this, you're seated at the head of the table, your task being akin to a food critic, but with a slight twist. Instead of sampling the delicacies, you are observing the varied eating styles of your fellow diners. Be it Auntie May, who is cherishing each bite as if it were her last, or young cousin Jack, who is devouring his pudding with a zealous intensity. Even if Uncle Bob is shovelling pasta into his mouth with such efficiency that would put a competitive eater to shame, our task isn't to label him as 'gluttonous'. We're here to exercise restraint, opting for less judgmental descriptors like 'efficient' or 'energetic'. This first exercise allows us to embody Epictetus's philosophy by suspending our initial judgments and appreciating each diner's unique approach to their meal, bearing in mind cultural norms, personal preferences, and appetites vary widely among individuals.

Next in line, we have the "Slow Sip Challenge", an exercise steeped in mindfulness. Here, everyone is to savour their drink at a leisurely pace, turning the otherwise mundane act of drinking into a grand ceremony. The aim isn't to guzzle the drink hurriedly but to be the last one to savour the final sip. By consciously slowing down, we are enhancing our sensory experience of the act of drinking. This exercise encourages mindful consumption and further provides a platform to share and discuss individual experiences. It's about deepening our observation skills and consciously resisting the temptation to rush to conclusions.

Venturing into a more introspective terrain, we introduce the "Inner Workings Journal". This exercise encourages you to keep a diary for a week, documenting your daily interactions. The goal here isn't just to record but also to reflect. Each day, select one individual you interacted with and dive deep into the nuances of their behaviour. The challenge is to concentrate on instances where you succeeded in refraining from making hasty judgments about their motivations or actions. Through this practice, we challenge our ingrained preconceptions and biases, learning to approach others with curiosity and openness, reminiscent of Epictetus' teachings.

Last, but by no means least, is the "Reality Check Debate", where we gather our friends for a discussion about a recent act by a celebrity. However, this isn't your typical tittle-tattle. The rules are clear—it's an observation-only debate, judgments and assumptions are strictly forbidden. The aim here is to dissect the act objectively, without being swayed by preconceived notions, even if the celebrity's actions may appear puzzling or unconventional. This exercise encourages us to suspend our pre-existing beliefs and engage in thoughtful dialogue, cultivating empathy and broadening our understanding of diverse perspectives.

At the completion of these exercises, keep in mind that every decision influenced by Epictetus' wisdom brings us closer to a life illuminated by philosophy. Philosophy isn't merely an intellectual activity; it's a manual for mindful living. The true power of these teachings isn't just in understanding them but in living them out. See these exercises as your guiding light, illuminating your path towards a life of wisdom. As you advance, you'll recognise that philosophy isn't just thought-provoking, but life-altering.

As we draw the curtains on this discussion, let's reiterate the essence of Epictetus' teachings on the criticality of resisting immediate judgements and striving to grasp the full context behind each individual's actions. Epictetus prompts us to view actions not in a moral vacuum but within the rich tapestry of motives, experiences, and circumstances that lead to them.

By wholeheartedly absorbing and applying this philosophy, we can begin to appreciate the complexity and richness inherent in each individual's story. Our interactions become less a case of stark black and white judgements and more a dance of curiosity, empathy, and understanding. In doing so, we encourage a society that values understanding over condemnation, empathy over bias.

Epictetus' wisdom impels us not to classify someone's action as 'bad' or 'ill' based on our limited observations. Instead, he invites us to observe the action as it is, shorn of moral judgement, such as noting that a person is bathing hastily or drinking much wine, without presuming to judge the morality of these actions without comprehending their motives fully.

So, let's step forward on this enlightening path, observing and appreciating the beauty of each person's unique narrative. Let's learn to suspend our judgements and revel in the profundity that comes from understanding and empathising with others' experiences.

As we continue to apply Epictetus' philosophy to our everyday lives, we find ourselves in a world of richer, more nuanced interpersonal relationships. In this world, individuals are understood and respected for their unique stories, rather than summarily judged for perceived transgressions. This serves as a crucial foundation for the *Theory of Happiness*, as envisioned by Epictetus.

46

Epictetus at the Dinner Table

Never proclaim yourself a philosopher, nor make much talk among the ignorant about your principles, but show them by actions. Thus, at an entertainment, do not discourse how people ought to eat, but eat as you ought. For remember that thus Socrates also universally avoided all ostentation. And when persons came to him and desired to be introduced by him to philosophers, he took them and introduced them; so well did he bear being overlooked. So, if ever there should be among the ignorant any discussion of principles, be for the most part silent. For there is great danger in hastily throwing out what is undigested. And if anyone tells you that you know nothing, and you are not nettled at it, then you may be sure that you have really entered on your work. For sheep do not hastily throw up the grass to show the shepherds how much they have eaten, but, inwardly digesting their food, they produce it outwardly in wool and milk. Thus, therefore, do you not make an exhibition before the ignorant of your principles, but of the actions to which their digestion gives rise.

Epictetus's teachings highlight a beautiful principle: actions make a stronger statement than words. Picture yourself at a construction site, the incessant hammering echoing in your ears, almost as tiresome as a prolonged, dense philosophical debate. But Epictetus suggests a more appealing route. Rather than broadcasting our beliefs in heavy words, we should let our actions illustrate our principles. It's akin to offering someone a taste of a fine wine, allowing them to appreciate its nuances without submerging them in the entire barrel.

Now, transport yourself to a dinner party, surrounded by friends and familiar faces. The good news is, there's no need to transform into an etiquette-obsessed social butterfly or an overly conscious eater, worrying about every crumb you put into your mouth. Instead, just be yourself and live your truth. The way you treat others can speak volumes about your character and values, just as a flourishing garden tells us about the green-fingered gardener's dedication and love for plants. Think of Socrates, the heavyweight champion of philosophy, who, despite his vast knowledge, didn't feel the need to flash his intellectual muscles at every opportunity. His humble, genuine approach encourages us to do the same, leading to more meaningful conversations and heartfelt connections.

Sometimes, it's wiser to stay quiet, particularly if our understanding of certain ideas is still simmering on the back burner of our minds. Epictetus emphasises the value of knowing when to listen and learn. Responding to criticism with grace and composure, much like a tree standing firm amidst a storm, is a sign of our commitment to the quest for wisdom, growth, and understanding. It's a quiet yet powerful demonstration of our philosophical resilience.

Take a lesson from our fluffy friends, the sheep. They don't show off by regurgitating their food (thank goodness for that!) to prove how much they've eaten. Instead, they quietly digest it and produce wool and milk, giving back to the world without a single baa about their process. Likewise, there's no need for us to parade our philosophical insights before those who may not be quite ready to grasp them. Our actions can paint a beautiful picture of our values, much like a skilled artist expresses their talent through their artwork. By aligning our actions with our principles, we become a living, breathing representation of our philosophy, making it relatable and easy to understand.

Epictetus nudges us to be philosophical artists, using our actions as the brush to paint our principles onto the canvas of life. This echoes Harry S. Truman's thought, "Actions are the seed of fate. Deeds grow into destiny". While it's a simple idea, it can be as challenging to execute as nailing the perfect TikTok dance routine. However, guided by Epictetus, we can let our deeds become the spokesperson for our thoughts and philosophies. It's about showing our ethos rather than just telling it, making philosophy a part of our daily lives. So, like the modest sheep, let's strive to create value and make a positive impact with our actions, allowing them to sing a beautiful song of our values.

Here we are again, at the turning point where knowledge evolves into action. We've been quenched by Epictetus' philosophy, and now it's time to irrigate our actions with these insights. The exercises up next are your irrigation system, channelling the water of wisdom to the fields of practice. Ready to irrigate? Let's transition from quenching wisdom to irrigating actions, nurturing our *Theory of Happiness*.

Our first step in this experiential journey is an activity named the "Silent Dinner". Imagine your next family reunion or friendly get-together, typically filled with the boisterous hum of chatter and laughter. But this time, let's introduce an intriguing twist to the scenario: a challenge to communicate solely through actions, as if you're participating in an extended, real-life game of charades. This isn't merely a quirky amusement but a thought-provoking exploration of non-verbal communication. It amplifies the potency of actions as conveyors of emotions, intentions, and concepts - often more eloquently than words. Picture yourself in darkness, where your senses are heightened and perception keen, unveiling unexplored avenues of comprehension. In the absence of verbal conversation, we become increasingly aware of each other's body language, facial expressions, and gestures, fostering a deeper level of connection and mutual understanding. It reveals the transformative power of our actions as effective communicators, bridging gaps where words might stumble or misrepresent.

Next, we traverse to the realm of the "Socratic Soirée". Picture yourself hosting a themed party, where each guest arrives dressed as their favourite philosopher. However, the intrigue doesn't stop at costumes. The guests must also embody the doctrines of their chosen philosopher through their conduct and actions, without directly declaring them. This philosophical masquerade nudges us to vivify abstract concepts, to step into the shoes of historical figures and traipse along their philosophical roads. It's a journey of the imagination that encourages us to emulate the virtues we admire, thus facilitating a deeper understanding of diverse philosophical doctrines. It also promotes empathy as we perceive the world through the lens of different philosophies, appreciating the variety of perspectives.

Following the philosophical soirée, we delve into the practice of "Reaction Reflection". When confronted with criticism or adversity, it's natural for our knee-jerk reaction to be defensive. Instead, take a moment to breathe and acknowledge your emotions. Picture your composure as a serene lake disturbed by a thrown pebble. This moment of reflection, akin to the silent pause before a singer belts out their first note, allows us to transition from impulsive reactions to measured responses. It's a personal exercise in emotional self-regulation, a vivid incarnation of Epictetus's essential teachings. By preserving tranquillity in the face of turbulence, we foster resilience, self-awareness, and emotional intelligence.

Finally, we introduce the "Sheepish Challenge". Identify a practical skill you're particularly adept in and perform it silently, without any verbal explanation. The intention isn't to bewilder your audience but to allow your expertise to radiate through your actions. Like the unassuming sheep quietly grazing yet producing valuable wool and milk, your proficiency becomes apparent through your actions. This silent demonstration of skill eliminates the need for ostentatious narratives or self-promotion. It resonates with the old saying, "actions speak louder than words", reinforcing that the influence created through our expertise overshadows any amount of self-praise.

Having finished these exercises, remember that every action inspired by Epictetus is a stride towards a life informed by wisdom. Philosophy isn't simply a mental activity; it's a guide for meaningful living. The real value of these teachings isn't just in grasping them but in putting them into practice. Treat these exercises as your guide, steering your course towards a life shaped by wisdom. As you press on, you'll realise that philosophy isn't just a topic for discussion, but a lived experience.

In drawing this to a close, we come full circle to the pragmatic wisdom of Epictetus. He shifts our focus away from ostentatious displays of intellectualism, steering us instead towards the authenticity of action. According to him, being a philosopher isn't about participating in lengthy, lofty debates or professing profound ideas. It's about letting our actions do the talking, becoming living testimonials of our values and principles. In his philosophy, actions command the stage and illuminate our philosophical convictions far more brightly than mere words ever could. Thus, our deeds should serve as the vibrant paintbrushes we use to depict our philosophical leanings on the canvas of life. With Epictetus as our guide, we learn that embodying philosophy isn't about the grandeur of our discourse, but rather the sincerity, coherence, and integrity of our deeds.

As we aspire to integrate Epictetus's teachings into our lives, we are called upon to be like the humble sheep, patiently chewing and digesting our philosophical principles, before translating them into tangible actions. This calls for a thoughtful, steady application of philosophy that mirrors more of a constant nourishment than a quick, flashy exhibition. As we journey through the landscape of philosophical introspection, it's crucial to remember this metaphor, focusing our energy on manifesting our beliefs into actions, instead of merely articulating them. For it is our actions that stand as the most persuasive testament of our philosophy, bearing witness to our beliefs in the most authentic and impactful way.

In the spirit of Epictetus's humility, let us pledge to keep our philosophical pursuits modest and genuine. Our goal shouldn't be to earn applause or recognition, but to truly grasp and live out our principles. This perspective is a powerful reminder that philosophy is not an intellectual exercise meant to impress, but a way of life intended to transform. To echo the words of Epictetus, the philosophy we embody isn't about the rhetoric we speak—it's about the life we choose to lead. As we conclude this chapter, let's carry forward this wisdom and aspire to be philosophers not in proclamation, but in action, shaping our destiny through our deeds, one step at a time.

47

Balancing Thrift and Discretion

When you have learned to nourish your body frugally, do not pique yourself upon it; nor, if you drink water, be saying upon every occasion, "I drink water". But first consider how much more frugal are the poor than we, and how much more patient of hardship. If at any time you would inure yourself by exercise to labour and privation, for your own sake and not for the public, do not attempt great feats; but when you are violently thirsty, just rinse your mouth with water, and tell nobody.

In a world overrun by opulence, this philosophy of Epictetus stands as a poignant counterpoint. He implores us to embrace frugality, not as a token gesture but as a profound lifestyle transformation.

Imagine a chilly evening where your kitchen pantry is about as full as the Gobi desert. However, instead of falling into the warm embrace of costly take-away food, you tap into your inner Nigella Lawson. With a few culinary strokes of genius, you transform a modest pasta packet and a motley crew of long-forgotten vegetables into a gastronomic delight. That sense of satisfaction that bubbled within you, that wasn't just about the meal, was it? It was about the triumph of resourcefulness over convenience, of creativity over waste.

Perhaps you also recall the day you decided to swap your gas-guzzling automobile for an old-fashioned bicycle. Despite the steep inclines and the bemused glances from neighbours, you persisted. You became a moving tableau of healthy, economical living, your resolute pedalling and cheerful wave becoming a part of the neighbourhood's morning scenery.

And who can forget the day you bid adieu to the fizzy temptress of carbonated drinks, opting instead to enjoy the clear elixir of life - water. Much like a wine connoisseur savouring a rare vintage, you learned to appreciate the refreshing simplicity of this common liquid.

Such milestones, however minor they may appear, are the defining landmarks on your personal map of frugality. But, in the spirit of Epictetus's teachings, remember this journey of austerity isn't for the applause of an Instagram audience or for a 'Frugality Champion' trophy. It's a voyage towards self-improvement, of consciously choosing satisfaction over abundance, need over greed.

The frugal lifestyle is not a sprint but a marathon. Embrace each moment, celebrate each achievement and recognise the profound effect of your actions. Each time you rinse your mouth with water to quench your thirst instead of mindlessly downing a glass, you aren't merely practising restraint. You are demonstrating the transformative power of mindfulness and discipline in your life.

In the pursuit of frugality, let's draw inspiration from those less fortunate, who chart life's choppy waters with far fewer resources. The grace with which they accept adversity and make the most of their scant means serves as a humbling reminder of the relative luxury of our chosen frugality.

When you infuse these principles into your daily life, it isn't an act of showmanship but a harmonious melding of your values and actions. You become a living embodiment of frugality, evolving into a conscientious individual who derives contentment not from material acquisitions, but personal growth.

Embark on your journey towards frugality, sprinkling your path with dashes of humour and light self-deprecation. Revel in the quirks of your new lifestyle, embracing them with a smile. This is not just about wearing a badge of frugality, but about displaying it with warmth and authenticity.

Remember the wisdom of Epictetus, which reminds us of the responsibility that accompanies a frugal lifestyle. It is a commitment to yourself, your financial health, and the broader world. It's about showcasing a sustainable way of life that merges personal fulfilment with sensible spending.

Step forward, holding dear the teachings of Epictetus. This journey isn't just about confronting the world but savouring it too. Stand tall as an advocate of a life that unites frugality and fulfilment, prepared to enjoy every step of the adventure.

We now find ourselves back at the crossroads where philosophy transforms into practice. We've been rejuvenated by Epictetus' wisdom, and now it's time to vitalise our actions with these insights. The following exercises are your wellness coach, guiding you from the spa of philosophy to the gym of practice. Shall we start training? Let's move from rejuvenating wisdom to vitalising actions, shaping our unique *Theory of Happiness*.

Our journey into the realm of frugality kicks off with the rather flavourful "Ramen Chef Challenge". Imagine yourself not just as a home cook, but a culinary virtuoso appearing on a riveting episode of a cooking show. Your mission? To morph an unassuming packet of economy ramen into a culinary masterpiece, using only three additional ingredients from your pantry. This challenge not only tests your thrifty prowess, but also illuminates the transformative potential of creativity. How, might you ask? Imagine the humble ramen, now brought to life with the vibrant hues and aromatic enchantment of fresh herbs, the complex depth of sesame oil, and the satisfying richness of a perfectly boiled egg. The question then isn't whether your packet of ramen can become a gourmet delight, but how you, armed with a pinch of creativity, can unveil its hidden potential.

Following our culinary expedition, we now transition into a rather tranquil pursuit as we channel our inner "H2O Whisperer". For a full day, your hydration choices are distilled to the most essential element - water. This is to be done in serene silence, devoid of explanations or justifications, much akin to a monk immersed in peaceful meditation. This modest exercise encapsulates Epictetus' teachings on discretion and leading by example. Like a seasoned actor who slips into their character effortlessly without fanfare, your frugal practice becomes a wordless influence, a testament to the power of action over discourse.

Our next venture, dubbed the "Everest of Frugality Challenge", presents a formidable test of endurance within the realm of thriftiness. The task at hand is to dedicate a day to extreme thriftiness, striving to save at every possible juncture. Herein lies the catch, though: this exercise isn't about public grandstanding or social media validation, but about savouring the intrinsic rewards of frugality. Can you relish the small victories of saving, soak in the satisfaction that comes from self-discipline, without broadcasting it for a cascade of 'likes'? If you can, you're well on your way to internalising Epictetus' teachings on humility and self-reliance, consequently gaining a deeper understanding of true contentment.

Our final adventure is the "Frugality Field Day", a day of community and celebration of simplicity. Plan a day out with friends or family, mindfully choosing activities that are free from excessive costs. Picnics in the park, a game of frisbee, a nature walk—opt for these over swanky restaurants or expensive cinema tickets. As you revel in shared laughter, creating memories within the confines of simplicity, you realise that the essence of joy lies not in expensive indulgences, but in shared moments of simplicity.

As we close these tasks, bear in mind that every endeavour inspired by Epictetus' teachings brings us closer to a life directed by wisdom. Philosophy isn't merely a field of study; it's a practical guide for life. The true essence of these teachings lies not just in studying them but in embodying them. View these exercises as your compass, guiding your journey towards a life filled with wisdom. As you continue, you'll understand that philosophy isn't just pondered, but enacted.

In conclusion, let's contemplate Epictetus' insight into the humble, yet potent, virtue of frugality. In his philosophical reflections, practicing frugality isn't about grandstanding or donning a brightly lit marquee proclaiming our frugality to the world. Rather, it's about letting our actions subtly articulate our commitment, emanating an understated assurance that's akin to a tranquil waterfall—silent yet potent, with no need for blaring announcements or grand displays.

Epictetus imparts to us that the true essence of frugality is anchored in conscious, mindful decisions that not only streamline our lives but also uncover the latent elegance in simplicity. It's a subtle dance with life, where we learn to relish the extraordinary richness concealed within the seemingly ordinary. The idea is to unearth satisfaction and joy within life's simplest offerings and view our world with a heart full of gratitude. Through the lens of frugality, what was once mundane becomes laced with magic, revealing the concealed treasures sprinkled throughout our everyday life.

Frugality, as per Epictetus' philosophy, evolves beyond a mere lifestyle choice and transforms into a conduit guiding us towards joy, fulfilment, and deeper wisdom. It stands as a vibrant beacon, gently reminding us that authentic happiness isn't always cocooned in grandeur or entangled within intricate complexities. More often than not, it sprouts from the simplest of places, from the everyday choices we make, and from our ability to appreciate the understated and overlooked aspects of life.

In embracing frugality, we echo Epictetus's wisdom, inviting simplicity and mindfulness into our lives. We leverage this philosophy to guide us towards appreciating the simple and the understated. It's not ostentatious, but a humble testament to wisdom, inspiring prudent choices and highlighting the extraordinary in our everyday lives. With this frugal approach, we illuminate our existence with a richness often overlooked.

48

From Spectator to Philosopher

The condition and characteristic of a vulgar person is that he never looks for either help or harm from himself, but only from externals. The condition and characteristic of a philosopher is that he looks to himself for all help or harm. The marks of a proficient are that he censures no one, praises no one, blames no one, accuses no one; says nothing concerning himself as being anybody or knowing anything. When he is in any instance hindered or restrained, he accuses himself; and if he is praised, he smiles to himself at the person who praises him; and if he is censured, he makes no defence. But he goes about with the caution of a convalescent, careful of interference with anything that is doing well but not yet quite secure. He restrains desire; he transfers his aversion to those things only which thwart the proper use of our own will; he employs his energies moderately in all directions; if he appears stupid or ignorant, he does not care; and, in a word, he keeps watch over himself as over an enemy and one in ambush.

In the grand spectacle that is life, we often find ourselves cast in different roles. Some of us might play the part of the bewildered spectator, watching as life unfolds before our eyes, as unpredictable and thrilling as a trapeze artist's high-flying act. This archetype, fondly known as 'Average Joe', tends to regard his life as a series of unexpected events, directed by the unseen hand of fate.

Consider the moment when 'Joe' gets an unexpected promotion. He might attribute his career upswing to the sympathetic ear of a benevolent boss, the favourable alignment of his horoscope, or even the magical properties of his lucky rabbit's foot, conveniently overlooking his own relentless efforts, those late nights at the office, the countless projects he led to success.

Similarly, when 'Joe' encounters a setback, like losing a crucial deal or facing rejection, he's quick to point fingers at everything but himself. He blames his failure on a sudden turn of market trends, the unsolicited interference of a colleague, or even the misfortune brought upon him by a black cat crossing his path earlier that day. In these moments, 'Joe' prefers to shield himself behind the comfortable curtain of external factors, avoiding the harsh spotlight of personal responsibility.

Now, let's contrast this with the Philosophers of life - the sages who realise that they're not just spectators but active participants in their own existence. For them, life is less of a random spectacle and more of a carefully choreographed ballet. Epictetus, the ancient stoic philosopher, embodies this mindset perfectly. He believed that we are not helpless leaves adrift on the wind of fate, but the wind itself, capable of steering our own course.

In his discernment, the Philosopher (for simplicity, we'll use the masculine pronoun here) recognises that he has the capacity to orchestrate the pace and rhythm of his existence. He comprehends that his life could be choreographed as an energetic jig or a dignified waltz. The choice is his: to step into the spotlight or follow another's steps, to navigate the dance floor independently or in the company of a partner. Acknowledging his autonomy, he wields it with thoughtful intent, simultaneously accepting the inherent unpredictability that punctuates the rhythmic sequence of life's dance.

As the Philosopher treads along his path, he learns to see others not as flawless performers or clumsy amateurs, but as fellow dancers, each with their own unique rhythm and style. This understanding allows him to appreciate the inherent dignity of all beings, irrespective of their dance skills. He refrains from idolising or demonising others, recognising that everyone, just like him, is striving to make their dance meaningful and enjoyable in their own unique way.

Moreover, true to his philosophical beliefs, the Philosopher doesn't feel the need to boast about his dance moves or his knowledge of different dance styles. He derives satisfaction not from the applause he receives, but from the dance itself - from the joy of movement, the feeling of the rhythm, the interplay with his partner, and the satisfaction of a step well executed. It's the same delight a skilled puppeteer derives from flawlessly controlling his marionettes, even though his hands remain unseen by the audience.

When the Philosopher stumbles or steps on his partner's toes, he doesn't rush to blame the slippery dance floor or the distracting music. Instead, he introspectively evaluates his performance, identifying areas where he might have been out of sync or off-balance. It's much like a tightrope walker who, after a fall, reflects on his balance, concentration, and technique, rather than blaming the rope or the wind.

When the Philosopher receives a standing ovation, he responds with a humble bow, not letting the applause inflate his ego. He knows that the true measure of his worth is not the number of claps he receives, but his dedication to his craft, his continuous striving for improvement, and his ability to enjoy the dance in each moment.

Similarly, when faced with criticism or ridicule, he chooses to respond not with defensiveness or resentment, but with grace and humour. He's like a street performer who, upon being heckled, weaves the heckler's remarks into his performance, turning a potentially confrontational situation into a shared moment of laughter and enjoyment.

As the Philosopher navigates his path, he does so with the caution of a person treading on a newly frozen lake, acutely aware of the risks beneath the surface. He's conscious of the lure of complacency, the temptation to take the easy path, and the danger of slipping back into old habits. Like a person recovering from an addiction, he knows he must maintain a continuous vigilance over his actions, thoughts, and choices.

Returning to 'Average Joe' and the Philosopher at the end of the day, we see two starkly different perspectives. 'Joe', in his simplicity, might attribute the day's ups and downs to chance, luck, or the actions of others. The Philosopher, however, pauses to reflect. He recognises his choices, actions, and reactions as the choreographer of his dance, understanding the significance of each step and misstep.

In welcoming philosophical wisdom into our lives, we are invited to step off the sidelines and take the centre stage in the dance of life. No longer are we mere spectators, standing passively on the fringes, but we become the choreographers of our own existence. We become the active architects of our reality, mindfully crafting a dance that reverberates with the beat of our values, aligns with the contours of our goals, and resonates with the rhythm of our hearts.

This transformation is not instantaneous but represents a continuous, unending journey. It is a process that necessitates deep introspection, fostering a heightened self-awareness, and championing personal accountability. It is a commitment to continuously tuning into the inner cadences of our beings, identifying our values, recognising our passions, and aligning our actions accordingly.

By undertaking this journey, the dance of life metamorphoses into a magnificent ballet of self-realisation and growth. Every step we take, every move we make, becomes a testament to our evolving selves. It is a dance where missteps are not failures but opportunities for learning, where every twirl and leap mirrors our growth, resilience, and adaptability.

This is the power of philosophical wisdom—it empowers us to infuse the dance of life with a sense of intentionality and purpose. We begin to dance not merely to the rhythm of external circumstances, but to the harmony of our inner symphony, creating a life that is not only successful in conventional terms but also meaningful, fulfilling, and deeply resonant with who we truly are.

Once again, we're at the point where contemplation turns into implementation. We've been energised by Epictetus' wisdom, and now it's time to charge our actions with these insights. The exercises up next are your battery, storing the energy of wisdom and releasing it in the form of action. Ready to charge? Let's transition from energising wisdom to charging actions, energising our *Theory of Happiness*.

Our first exercise, the delightful "Secret Grin", invites us to imagine ourselves at the heart of a lively gathering, with friends and acquaintances showering us with compliments and applauding our accomplishments. Many of us, whether due to habit or societal conditioning, may find ourselves either luxuriating in the praise or squirming uncomfortably, and then trying to shift the spotlight away. However, this exercise proposes an alternative. Rather than responding with words, you simply offer a knowing smile. This subtle, non-verbal signal communicates your gratitude, without falling into the trappings of long-winded speeches or overzealous self-deprecation. In effect, it's a quiet acknowledgement of your inner peace and a reminder that your value does not rely on external recognition. This exercise encourages us to cultivate humility and reinforces the idea that true worth is independent of outside validation.

We now move on to the "Stoic Sentry" exercise. Here, we visualise ourselves as watchful guards of a stronghold. Yet, our vigilance is not directed outward, but inward - towards our thoughts, feelings, and actions. Much like a watchful sentry detecting the faintest rustle in the dead of the night, we are tasked with maintaining a heightened awareness of our internal landscape. By undertaking this exercise, we uncover subtle thought processes and emotional responses that often slip under the radar amidst the commotion of our daily lives. The role of the Stoic Sentry is not just to observe, but also to understand and rectify patterns that might be hindering our growth.

Next, we enter the "No Rebuttal Zone". This exercise is about cultivating emotional resilience. Picture a scenario where you're at the receiving end of criticism. Instead of rising to the bait and jumping into a heated debate, you simply acknowledge the other person's point of view. You stand steadfast, like a sturdy tree swaying in the wind without snapping. You accept their critique, without feeling the need to defend or justify yourself. In doing so, you understand that the criticism is a reflection of their experiences and not a personal attack.

Our final exercise, the "Blame Game Reversal", pushes us to take complete responsibility for any obstacles or setbacks that come our way in a single day. Rather than pointing fingers at others or blaming external factors, we turn our gaze inward. In detective-like fashion, we carefully sift through our choices and actions, identifying any potential contributions to the unfavourable outcome. This exercise may initially seem daunting, but it cultivates a strong sense of personal accountability, making us the masters of our fate.

At the end of these exercises, remember that every step inspired by Epictetus' teachings is a step towards a life of wisdom. Philosophy isn't just an intellectual pursuit; it's a guide for conscious living. The true power of these teachings isn't merely in understanding them but in living them out. Use these exercises as your roadmap, directing your way towards a life enriched with wisdom. As you journey on, you'll realise that philosophy isn't just studied, but lived.

Drawing this to a close, let's take a moment to reflect on the wisdom of Epictetus. He implores us to grasp the notion that true enlightenment isn't primarily about changing the world around us, but rather reshaping our own perspective. It's about recognising our inherent power and embracing our responsibility as captains of our life's ship, steering it confidently across the capricious winds and unpredictable currents of life's vast ocean of experiences.

In stark contrast to the 'Average Joe', who might passively let his ship be tossed by the waves, deferring control to external circumstances, the philosophy of Epictetus offers us a compelling alternative. We learn to wield the ship's wheel and adjust our sails skilfully, matching the mercurial winds of life, seizing control of our destiny.

Epictetus places great emphasis on humility and self-awareness. He encourages us to break free from the confining shackles of others' judgments and to assert control over our own actions and reactions. As we tread this path, we find ourselves moving away from the domain of 'Average Joe', transcending the limitations of relying on external factors for our self-worth.

In absorbing Epictetus' teachings, we need to remember that we have within us an enormous reservoir of potential. This potential could be our greatest ally in shaping a life of wisdom and fulfillment, or it could transform into our most formidable adversary if we let it remain unexplored or misdirected. Recognising this truth is not a cause for disquiet, but rather a call to embark on a journey of profound growth and transformation, one illuminated by the light of our own potential.

As you embark on this enlightening voyage of self-discovery, under the guidance of Epictetus, remember to allow space for laughter and joy. Delight in those unexpected moments of hilarity when life takes you by surprise, find amusement in the incongruities and paradoxes that punctuate our existence, and cherish the delightfully odd moments that add a dash of quirkiness to your journey.

Remember the 'Average Joe', who might miss these moments of joy while he's busy attributing his circumstances to luck or fate. Contrast this with the philosophy-guided individual, who learns to find joy in every moment, knowing that life's humorous and odd moments are just as valuable as the profound ones.

Laughter is the golden thread that weaves together joy and camaraderie in the grand tapestry of our shared human experience. It's a gentle reminder not to take life too seriously, even when we're engrossed in our philosophical pursuit of wisdom. Indeed, Epictetus' teachings suggest that true enlightenment emerges not just from deep introspection and personal growth, but also from the ability to find joy and amusement amidst the undulating waves of our human journey. So, let's set sail with courage, resilience, and laughter, steering our ship towards the horizon of enlightenment.

49

Living Philosophy

When anyone shows himself vain on being able to understand and interpret the works of Chrysippus, say to yourself: "Unless Chrysippus had written obscurely, this person would have had nothing to be vain of.

But what do I desire? To understand nature, and follow her. I ask, then, who interprets her; and hearing that Chrysippus does, I have recourse to him. I do not understand his writings. I seek, therefore, one to interpret them".

So far there is nothing to value myself upon. And when I find an interpreter, what remains is to make use of his instructions. This alone is the valuable thing. But if I admire merely the interpretation, what do I become more than a grammarian, instead of a philosopher, except, indeed, that instead of Homer I interpret Chrysippus?

BEN VAN DE BELD

When anyone, therefore, desires me to read Chrysippus to him, I rather blush when I cannot exhibit actions that are harmonious and consonant with his discourse.

Epictetus offers us a unique perspective on the pursuit of knowledge. He likens it to a fox who has stumbled upon a henhouse, gleefully piling up eggs, yet failing to notice the wisdom embodied by the mother hen, busily tending to her brood. In the grand theatre of philosophy, Epictetus plays the role of this mother hen, offering a beacon of understanding amidst the convoluted works of philosophical giants. His philosophy is our lighthouse in the tempestuous sea of highfalutin ideas, keeping us from losing ourselves in the vast, and sometimes intimidating, ocean of abstract thoughts.

In Epictetus's philosophy, being a philosopher isn't about reaching an intellectual finish line. Picture philosophy instead as a never-ending dance—a waltz, a tango, a samba of thoughts. The dance of philosophy isn't choreographed to reach a perfectly poised finale but is instead an improvised dance-off. The joy isn't in nailing a flawless routine but in learning, tripping, adjusting, and dancing again. Just as an amateur dancer grows from every stumble, so do we from every philosophical misstep, ultimately becoming more attuned to the world and ourselves.

Consider the complex works of philosophers like Chrysippus as a dance form that might feel as intricate as trying to master a tango with a blindfold on. This is where a translator comes into play—acting as our dance instructor— someone who can decode these elaborate pirouettes of thought and transform them into simple two-steps we can keep pace with. As we twirl deeper into this dance of understanding, we stumble upon insights that have the power to change our very existence, shining brighter than the most dazzling disco ball on the dance floor.

But understanding the philosophy dance doesn't stop at comprehending the choreography. Imagine you've learnt all the moves of a complex ballet routine but never stepped on the stage. You'd be like a bird with a beautiful song but no urge to sing. Thus, we must let philosophy influence our moves on the stage of life, not just learn the steps. To admire Epictetus's teachings from the audience without embodying the dance in our daily lives would be like joining a dance party and not moving to the beat.

Therefore, when someone asks us about Epictetus's philosophy, it's an invitation to showcase our philosophical dance, not just recite the steps. Parroting Epictetus's teachings without their influence reflected in our daily life would be like practicing for a flamenco performance but executing a square dance instead. Living his teachings means letting them shape our dance of life—our choices, our perspectives, our actions. This calls for a metamorphosis, transforming us from passive readers to active dancers, living and breathing the wisdom of Epictetus.

Imagine our 'Average Joe' immersed in the profound works of Epictetus. This isn't about seeking intellectual showmanship or impressing others with his grasp of Stoicism. Rather, it's a process of internal transformation, where Joe integrates Epictetus's wisdom into the very fabric of his daily life. He learns to waltz through the highs and lows of life with elegance and poise, fosters a nurturing compassion amid life's trials, and dances to the rhythm of wisdom's captivating tune. Like Joe, we all possess the innate potential to engage in this philosophical dance-off, weaving the teachings of Epictetus seamlessly into our individual life scripts.

Now is the moment to dust off those dancing shoes, to loosen up, and ready ourselves for the philosophical dance that lies ahead. Epictetus's philosophy isn't akin to a rigid, uncompromising waltz; rather, it resembles a vibrant jive, a passionate tango, a lively foxtrot. It's a dance suffused with wisdom that can bring about transformative change in our lives. This wisdom fuels our intellectual growth, bolsters our happiness, and arms us with the confidence and resilience to face the dance floor of life, no matter the tempo of the music.

Epictetus's teachings form the pulsating rhythm, the enchanting melody, and the invigorating groove of our dance of life. They provide the beat that inspires us to strut with conviction, twirl with joy, and glide with resilience. This dance celebrates our strengths, acknowledges our vulnerabilities, and exalts our personal growth.

With the music poised to play, let us synchronise our steps with the rhythm of Epictetus's wisdom, readying ourselves to navigate life's dance floor with an exuberant spirit and a joy-filled heart. Prepare to embark on the most meaningful dance of your life. Dance with abandon, for this dance is about embracing our authentic selves and relishing the beauty of existence. Let's step onto the dance floor, ready to sway to the philosophical boogie.

We're back at the fork in the road where theory morphs into practice. We've been soothed by Epictetus' wisdom, and now it's time to massage these insights into our daily actions. The exercises to follow are your masseuse, kneading the wisdom into the muscles of practice. Ready for a massage? Let's move from soothing wisdom to massaging actions, shaping our unique *Theory of Happiness*.

We start this intellectual expedition with the "Crossword Conundrum" exercise. Picture this: You're faced with a crossword so puzzling it could give the Enigma code a run for its money. Now, imagine the philosophical concepts we're about to uncover as similar enigmas. Instead of getting bogged down by complexity, view it as an intriguing jigsaw. Savour the intellectual journey, relishing each puzzle piece as it clicks into place, rather than fixating solely on the final picture. For instance, when engaging with a multi-layered concept like the nature of free will, view each argument, counter-argument, and insight as pieces of a grand puzzle. Each part contributes to the overall understanding, even if they don't always neatly align. Embrace the complexity, the uncertainties, and the joy of discovery that come with it. The aim here isn't just to arrive at a solution, but to cultivate a mindset that appreciates the intricate beauty of the path leading to it.

Next, we'll morph into "Observers of Nature". In this exercise, we'll swap our reading glasses for a pair of binoculars, metaphorically speaking. Spend an entire day letting the wonders of the natural world wash over you. Feel the earth beneath your feet, the wind in your hair. Witness the vibrant dance of colours in a sunset, the rhythmic rustling of leaves, the soothing cycle of the tides. Detect the patterns etched into nature's grand canvas, from the predictability of the changing seasons to the waxing and waning of the moon. What's more, strive to align your actions with nature's profound harmony—adopt sustainable habits, conserve resources, or simply take time to appreciate its grandeur. This practice not only bolsters mindfulness but also cements our connection to the environment, highlighting the intricate web of life we're part of.

Up next is the "Practical Interpreter" challenge. Here, you're tasked with unravelling a captivating complex idea, diving deep into philosophers' musings or thought-provoking theories. Upon comprehending the concept, the challenge is to seamlessly weave this newfound knowledge into your everyday life. Say you've studied the concept of empathy. The task then becomes practising acts of kindness, understanding, and compassion in your daily interactions. By doing so, you transform philosophy from a distant, abstract concept into a lived reality—a guiding light illuminating your path.

The final leg of this journey involves the "Mirror the Master" exercise. Here, you choose a piece of wisdom from Epictetus or any philosopher that resonates with you. Ponder upon their teachings, decipher the lessons they hold, and identify a principle that strikes a chord. The ultimate challenge is to incorporate this wisdom into your character and actions—essentially embodying the philosophical nugget you've chosen. If you find Epictetus' emphasis on resilience inspiring, the challenge is to consciously cultivate habits promoting resilience, like regular reflection or nurturing a growth mindset.

Upon concluding these exercises, bear in mind that every action rooted in Epictetus' wisdom brings us closer to a life guided by philosophical insight. Philosophy isn't just a mental exercise; it's a practical blueprint for life. The real essence of these teachings lies not just in knowing them but in enacting them. Treat these exercises as your guiding stars, illuminating your path towards a life filled with wisdom. As you move forward, you'll understand that philosophy isn't just a topic of discussion, but a lifestyle.

In summing up, it's essential to appreciate that delving into the philosophical orchestra involves more than merely deciphering the notes of its composition. It's about immersing oneself in its symphony, letting its rich melody pervade your soul, influencing your actions, experiences, and very essence.

Epictetus' teachings highlight the significance of transcending a purely intellectual grasp of philosophy. It's about fully embracing its principles and entwining them into the fabric of our everyday lives. This process of incorporation transforms abstract philosophical concepts into practical compasses for sailing the often-stormy waters of life. Philosophy's true essence extends beyond comprehending complex theories; it's about permitting these teachings to seep into our existence, illuminating our paths with wisdom and insight.

As we absorb this wisdom, we undergo a metamorphosis, becoming agents of constructive transformation. We don't merely consume philosophy; we live it, we breathe it, we embody it. In doing so, we not only amplify the quality of our own lives, but we also contribute to our shared, collective journey. It's a sublime dance of integrating theory and practice, wherein we become living testimonies to the philosophies we study.

Epictetus beckons us to a grand feast of wisdom, but the invitation extends beyond mere intellectual indulgence. Instead, we are urged to allow the teachings to permeate our very core, reshaping our inner selves and transforming our approach to life.

This is not a feast where we merely digest the ideas of philosophers like Chrysippus. Rather, we contemplate their teachings deeply, allowing them to seep into our spirits, and fundamentally influencing our perceptions and experiences. We are challenged to metabolise this wisdom, to let it shape our thoughts, words, and actions.

Epictetus prompts us to go beyond an intellectual appreciation of philosophy; we are encouraged to live it. Our goal is to embody the teachings we hold dear, translating abstract thoughts into concrete actions. To be a philosopher, as per Epictetus, is to navigate life's currents using the philosophical principles as our compass.

Thus, we are invited to turn philosophy from a mere subject of contemplation to a guiding force in our lives, transforming our intellectual feast into a journey of self-growth and enlightenment. The question now is, will you accept Epictetus's invitation?

50

Your Inner Socrates

Whatever rules you have adopted, abide by them as laws, and as if you would be impious to transgress them; and do not regard what anyone says of you, for this, after all, is no concern of yours. How long, then, will you delay to demand of yourself the noblest improvements, and in no instance to transgress the judgments of reason? You have received the philosophic principles with which you ought to be conversant; and you have been conversant with them. For what other master, then, do you wait as an excuse for this delay in self-reformation? You are no longer a boy but a grown man. If, therefore, you will be negligent and slothful, and always add procrastination to procrastination, purpose to purpose, and fix day after day in which you will attend to yourself, you will insensibly continue to accomplish nothing and, living and dying, remain of vulgar mind. This instant, then, think yourself worthy of living as a man grown up and a proficient. Let whatever appears to be the best be to you an inviolable law.

And if any instance of pain or pleasure, glory or disgrace, be set before you, remember that now is the combat, now the Olympiad comes on, nor can it be put off; and that by one failure and defeat honor may be lost or—won. Thus Socrates became perfect, improving himself by everything, following reason alone. And though you are not yet a Socrates, you ought, however, to live as one seeking to be a Socrates.

Adopting Epictetus's philosophy is not about dredging through archaic textbooks—it's about forging a robust set of principles—an ethical compass—that navigates the ship of our lives. These principles aren't merely lofty ideals floating in ether; instead, they're meant to be embraced and practised with fervour akin to an athlete's tenacity. Picture yourself greeting each dawn with a renewed commitment to virtues such as honesty, compassion, or courage. These aren't just ethereal constructs; they form the bedrock of your actions, shaping your character and sketching the blueprint of your life's journey.

Now, imagine you're amidst a whirlwind of opinion exchange, similar to a lively panel discussion on the telly. It's a bit like a scene from a reality show, with everyone jostling for attention and applause. The draw to partake in this spectacle can be compelling, much like the allure of a cool refreshment on a warm day. However, Epictetus nudges us to resist this pull. He urges us to tune out the clamour of public validation, suggesting we cultivate our character and champion our personal growth, standing firm in our convictions, even in the face of criticism.

Epictetus's teachings resonate particularly when we find ourselves in a pattern of stalling our self-improvement, forever waiting for the 'perfect' mentor or 'right' moment. He encourages us to confront this habit of procrastination. Are we in a cycle of telling ourselves, "I'll start tomorrow"? As mature individuals, the responsibility for our self-growth lies squarely on our shoulders. If we continue in this pattern of delay, we risk becoming a mere backdrop in our own lives, as noticeable as an unnamed character in a cinematic spectacle. Instead, Epictetus prompts us to step forward, seize our narrative, and assume the leading roles in our life's story.

Epictetus further emphasises the importance of treating life's challenges as a personal proving ground, where delays are as welcomed as an unappetising dish. He views every moment as a unique opportunity to uphold our principles, to put our character to the test, and to showcase our strengths. This philosophy was embodied by Socrates, who leveraged every situation as a stepping stone for personal growth, adhering unwaveringly to reason's path.

Importantly, our goal is not to attain perfection at breakneck speed but to strive for consistent growth. The Socratic standard isn't a target to be hit, but more of a guiding light, helping us navigate through life's complex maze of ethical dilemmas. We're called to nurture our inner philosopher and let our wisdom radiate—not because we've donned a philosopher's toga, but because we're genuinely dedicated to learning, evolving, and polishing our character until it mirrors the sheen of our chosen principles.

Finally, Epictetus reminds us that philosophy isn't all stern expressions and thoughtful silence. He advocates for a sprinkling of light-heartedness in our philosophical pursuits. Just as Socrates was known to intersperse his wisdom with a touch of wit, we too can adopt a playful approach in our philosophical journey, crafting anecdotes and quips that could even make Plato smile!

Philosophy, as we have come to realise, is not a dormant, academic discipline languishing in the ivory towers of academia. Rather, it is a pulsating journey, a rousing adventure that prompts us to incorporate our principles into action, question established norms, and delve into the profound depths of our own wisdom. The dusty facades of ancient treatises give way to the illumination of enlightened thought, the glitter of self-discovery, and the thrill of ongoing self-awareness.

Witnessing the profound influence of Epictetus's teachings, we derive inspiration to embody philosophical doctrines in our everyday lives. This interweaving of theory and practice forms a dance of enlightenment that can't be disentangled. Such commitment represents a vow to ourselves, a pledge to harness the wisdom within us to elevate our existence. It's an affirmation of our worthiness, acknowledging that we deserve the efforts invested in carving out a life of meaning, satisfaction, and depth.

Now, prepare to embark on your journey, standing on the precipice of the next leap. Grasp the reins of life, ready to guide your path with the strength of your convictions. Embrace life's stage with courage, casting aside hesitation and fears. It is time for your philosophical brilliance to shine brightly, lighting up the world with wisdom and joy.

Let your actions resonate with your inner wisdom, and let your joy be a reflection of your authentic self. Exude an aura of enlightenment and observe as it infuses the world with hues of wisdom and authentic joy. Life is your stage, and your journey is a philosophically enriching dance. Step out, and allow the rhythm of wisdom to guide you towards a life of enlightenment and profound joy.

It's that time again to transform theory into practice. We've been balanced by Epictetus' wisdom, and now it's time to align our actions with these insights. The exercises up next are your yoga instructor, guiding your pose from the balance of philosophy to the alignment of practice. Ready to align? Let's transition from balancing wisdom to aligning actions, shaping our unique *Theory of Happiness*.

First on our agenda, we have "The Lawmaker" exercise. This exercise invites you to delve deep within, prompting a profound reflection on your values and principles. The objective is to carefully formulate a set of rules or guidelines that resonate with your authentic self, outlining who you aspire to be. Consider these rules as your moral compass, a beacon that illuminates the path to your actions and decisions. Dedicate a full week to living by these self-imposed laws, treating them as if they were the incontrovertible statutes that govern your existence. Picture yourself as the drafter of your own constitution, armed with a bespoke Bill of Rights and Responsibilities. This immersive experience serves to cultivate a heightened sense of discipline, simultaneously reinforcing the significance of actions that resonate with your deeply cherished values. For instance, if you hold honesty in high esteem, draft a rule that compels you to always uphold truth, even in the face of adversity. If you're inclined towards kindness, make a daily commitment to executing at least one act of compassion. This exercise acts as a potent reminder that our choices mould our character, and that leading a life in alignment with our values paves the way to a richly satisfying existence. So, arm yourself with your imaginary gavel and allow the philosophical laws of your own making to steer your course.

Next in line, we have "The Silent Drama". This exercise encourages you to devote a full day to liberating yourself from the iron grip of societal opinions. All too often, we find ourselves ensnared in the dramas and judgments of others, caught in an endless pursuit of validation and approval from external sources. In this task, consciously disengage yourself from the craving for external validation, choosing instead to live authentically, in harmony with your own principles. Relish the emancipating sensation that emerges when you cast off the heavy burden of others' judgments and opinions. Foster a habit of self-acceptance and self-validation, knowing that your worth and identity are independent of how others perceive you. Through nurturing this internal fortitude, you cultivate a resilience that allows you to remain true to yourself. Imagine yourself as the star of your very own silent film, where you require neither dialogue nor the applause of an audience to exude confidence and contentment.

Following this, we have "The Olympic Challenge". Pinpoint a situation in your life that you currently find challenging. It could be a demanding project at work, a personal relationship that requires tending, or a personal ambition you're endeavouring to fulfil. Envision this situation as your personal "Olympic moment," a golden opportunity for you to shine and display your best performance. Just as athletes stand at the apex of their careers, approach your challenge with focus, determination, and a burning desire to exceed your own expectations. Kindle the competitive spirit within you—not to contend against others but to conquer your own inhibitions and doubts. Compel yourself to stride that extra mile and unleash your latent champion. This exercise incites you to tap into your inner reservoir of strength, allowing you to realise your full potential. Visualise yourself atop the podium, receiving a gold medal for your exceptional display of philosophical prowess!

Lastly, we're going to tread "The Socratic Path". Each day, select a particular situation or encounter and ponder how you could utilise it as a springboard for personal development. Embody the spirit of Socrates, the celebrated philosopher, contemplating how you could apply reason and wisdom to navigate life's challenges and blossom as an individual. Pose thought-provoking questions to yourself: What lessons can I glean from this experience? How can I react in a manner that harmonises with my values? By proactively seeking growth and introspection in everyday situations, you encourage personal evolution and heighten your understanding of both yourself and the world that surrounds you. Picture having your own personal philosopher on speed dial, ready to navigate you through life's conundrums and furnish you with the wisdom necessary to surmount any impediment.

As we wrap up these exercises, keep in mind that every choice made under Epictetus' teachings brings us closer to a life enlightened by wisdom. Philosophy isn't just about thought; it's about action. The real power of these teachings isn't just in comprehending them but in applying them. Consider these exercises as your milestones, guiding your journey towards a life governed by wisdom. As you forge ahead, you'll discover that philosophy isn't just a concept, but a way of life.

As we bring this to a close, we underscore the paramount importance of unfaltering devotion to your guiding principles, remaining impervious to the criticisms and judgments of others. The teachings of Epictetus reinforce that you should strive for lofty personal ambitions and, crucially, resist the lure of procrastination that can impede your journey towards self-improvement.

Epictetus' philosophy serves as a clarion call to demand the highest version of yourself, without any delay. This internal demand for excellence shouldn't be postponed under any pretext. Indeed, our personal journey of growth is never a borrowed endeavour; it is a quest we must embark upon independently, without any excuses.

Drawing inspiration from the profound teachings of Epictetus and Socrates, we emphasise the tremendous value of leading a life that is a true reflection of your authentic self. This is not a journey towards imitation, but a journey of genuine self-realisation and enlightenment, where every action resonates with your core values.

It is crucial to grasp that you are the protagonist in your life's play. You are encouraged to command the stage, captivating your audience not just with the depth of your intellectual insight and philosophical wisdom, but by embodying these teachings in your actions and character.

Remember, each day is an opportunity for growth, a unique chance to be a better version of yourself. Whether it's a moment of joy or sorrow, success or failure, every experience is an invaluable teacher, shaping us into a fuller version of ourselves.

This is your personal Olympiad. The arena may be tough, the challenges daunting, but remember that it is through this struggle that greatness is often born. Socrates achieved his wisdom through relentless pursuit of truth, learning from every situation life presented to him. Even if you aren't a Socrates yet, it's imperative to live as one aspiring to achieve such intellectual and moral excellence.

Our journey of self-improvement and growth is not an act of one grand moment, but a series of continuous small steps, each contributing to our overall development. Let's be mindful of this and celebrate our progress, however small it may seem. Because, in the grand scheme of life, these 'small' steps often lead to the most significant transformations.

51

The Philosophy Game

The first and most necessary topic in philosophy is the practical application of principles, as, We ought not to lie; the second is that of demonstrations as, Why it is that we ought not to lie; the third, that which gives strength and logical connection to the other two, as, Why this is a demonstration. For what is demonstration? What is a consequence? What a contradiction? What truth? What falsehood? The third point is then necessary on account of the second; and the second on account of the first. But the most necessary, and that whereon we ought to rest, is the first. But we do just the contrary. For we spend all our time on the third point and employ all our diligence about that, and entirely neglect the first. Therefore, at the same time that we lie, we are very ready to show how it is demonstrated that lying is wrong.

Upon all occasions we ought to have these maxims ready at hand:

Conduct me, Zeus, and thou, O Destiny,
Wherever your decrees have fixed my lot.
I follow cheerfully; and, did I not,
Wicked and wretched, I must follow still.

Who'er yields properly to Fate is deemed
Wise among men, and knows the laws of
Heaven.

And this third:

"O Crito, if it thus pleases the gods,
thus let it be." "Anytus and
Melitus may kill me indeed; but
hurt me they cannot."

As we leaf through the final pages of this tome, we find ourselves navigating the metaphorical chessboard of philosophy. Each square symbolises a critical decision we confront in life, every move reverberating through the expansive labyrinth of existence. The first step in this complex ballet of thought and action is to transform the philosophical principles we've internalised throughout our journey into practical, tangible actions within our real world.

To illustrate, consider the age-old and potent maxim, 'Don't spin a web of lies'. This guiding light serves as an ethical satnav, helping us negotiate the tempestuous seas of moral quandaries. Suppose a friend asks your opinion about an outfit you don't particularly like. Instead of resorting to a lie to dodge discomfort, you might offer a gentle, truthful opinion, in adherence to this principle. By doing so, you evade the entangling web of deceit and the self-inflicted chaos that ensues. This practice of honesty then ripples outward, affecting your relationship and laying a foundation of trust and integrity.

Having embedded our actions with this ethical underpinning, we progress to the second phase, delving deeper into the 'why' behind these principles. We grapple with questions such as, 'Why should I value authenticity in a world that often rewards artifice and illusion?' This question might return us to our earlier example. Perhaps you ponder why honesty was the superior approach in the scenario with your friend, especially when a lie might have been the path of least resistance. Upon deeper excavation, you might realise that honesty fosters trust and respect, which are crucial for any healthy relationship. Understanding the ethical underpinnings of these principles fortifies our resolve to act with integrity, even in challenging circumstances.

Transitioning to the third phase, we embark on a scholarly quest to connect the dots between the first two phases. We strive to confirm that our ethical stance, like honesty, is not just morally admirable but also logically consistent. For instance, we might scrutinise if honesty aligns with our other values and beliefs. Does it contribute to a peaceful and harmonious society? Is it universally applicable? This phase is a philosophical detective hunt that untangles the logical connections underpinning our ethical principles.

However, as we tread this path, Epictetus cautions us against losing ourselves in this labyrinth of proofs and theoretical conjectures. He underscores the importance of grounding our philosophical insights in practical reality. Picture a chef who spends days studying recipes and techniques but never steps into the kitchen to cook. The potential for creating a culinary masterpiece remains unrealised without the practical application, just as our philosophical insights risk becoming sterile without their implementation in our day-to-day life.

To stave off this peril, Epictetus equips us with a set of philosophical touchstones:

1. 'Lead the way, Zeus and Destiny. I'll follow cheerfully, for if I resist, I'd still have to follow, albeit reluctantly'. This aphorism underlines Stoic acceptance of our circumstances, fostering resilience and adaptability. It's like being dealt a challenging hand in a game of cards and choosing to play strategically rather than bemoaning our luck.
2. 'He who flows with life's current is deemed wise, understanding the laws of the universe'. This adage, much like a sailor harnessing the winds to navigate the seas, reminds us to adapt and align with life's ever-changing tides rather than fight against them. It's an invitation to embrace life's highs and lows with equanimity.

3. 'If this is the gods' will, then so be it. People may attempt to harm me, but they cannot touch the integrity of my spirit.' This maxim serves as an impenetrable philosophical shield, a reminder to remain steadfast in our values, irrespective of external circumstances or the judgment of others. It's akin to an unshakeable mountain standing firm amidst a raging storm.

Life's grand game, akin to an epic chess match, is a dance of strategic moves, unpredictable outcomes, and invaluable lessons. We manoeuvre our pieces across the board, driven by the guiding strategies of philosophical principles. Much like a chess grandmaster anticipates several moves ahead, we strive to apply the wisdom of Epictetus, acknowledging the interconnectedness of our actions and their wider implications. So, as we continue our play in the grand game of life, let us take heart in the timeless wisdom of Epictetus, whose teachings help us navigate life's complexities with grace, resilience, and unwavering conviction.

For the last time, we're at the intersection where philosophy feeds into action. We've been nourished by Epictetus' wisdom, and now it's time to digest these insights into our daily lives. The following exercises are your dietitian, planning your diet from the nourishment of philosophy to the health of practice.

Ready to digest? Let's move from nourishing wisdom to digesting actions, shaping our unique *Theory of Happiness*.

Launching our expedition, we first encounter the intriguing "Truth Teller" exercise. Picture yourself on a mission for the day: to tell not a single lie, not even the smallest white fib that often innocuously peppers our daily chats. The objective of this exercise is to hone our ability to be truthful, thereby fostering trust and integrity within our relationships. Imagine, for instance, a mate showing you their new flashy attire, eagerly seeking your verdict. Rather than defaulting to a diplomatic, albeit insincere, compliment, venture to give an honest opinion, one that could genuinely assist them. In doing so, we understand the profound influence our words can have on relationships, promoting authenticity and sincerity. We metamorphose into a steadfast mate, offering fashion counsel with utmost honesty, earning the title of a "trustworthy fashion consultant".

Propelling forward, we arrive at the intriguing "Question Master" exercise. This task beckons us to embrace our inner philosopher, encouraging us to delve into the reasons behind the significant value we attach to honesty. Akin to a researcher on a quest, document your reflections and dissect the principle under scrutiny. Challenge yourself to uncover how honesty can spur personal development, foster constructive relationships, and contribute to a more harmonious society. Reflect, for instance, on how transparency in communication builds trust, obliterates misunderstandings, and creates space for profound connections. Through this philosophical exploration, we reinforce our commitment to embodying honesty, akin to a philosopher who persistently probes the right inquiries.

Next, we don our detective hats for the "Logic Detectives" exercise. The task is akin to a philosophical Sherlock Holmes mission, urging us to find a cogent argument supporting our belief in honesty. Through meticulous introspection and contemplation, we strive to unearth the bedrock of our conviction, questioning the ethical and practical consequences of honesty. As you develop your argument, converse with a confidante to gauge the solidity of your points and spark meaningful discussions about honesty's significance. This exercise nurtures a robust understanding and gifts us with a logical foundation to uphold honesty as a guiding beacon. It's as if we've become the philosophical barrister, presenting an unassailable case for honesty.

Finally, we step into the captain's shoes for the "Life Sailor" challenge. Imagine yourself at the helm of a ship for an entire week, practising acceptance and flowing with life's unpredictable tides. Embrace the unforeseen challenges that cross your path and jot down your experiences and lessons in a journal, mirroring a captain's logbook. Say, for instance, a sudden detour in plans or a hiccup at work catches you off guard; instead of resisting or yielding to frustration, approach the circumstance with acceptance and adaptability. Examine how this mental pivot empowers you to navigate obstacles more effectively, transforming them into opportunities for growth. By sailing life's turbulent waters with a spirit of acceptance, we garner invaluable insights about ourselves and our surroundings, paving the way for personal evolution and resilience. We shape-shift into the philosophical captain, steering life's ship with fortitude amidst tempestuous seas.

Having navigated through these final exercises, it's essential to recall that every action guided by Epictetus' wisdom brings us closer to a life enriched by philosophy. Philosophy isn't just a mental activity; it's a guide for meaningful living. The true power of these teachings lies not just in grasping them but in embodying them. Consider these exercises as your signposts, leading you on the path towards a life filled with wisdom. As you carry on, you'll discover that philosophy isn't just a field of study, but a lifestyle.

As we draw the curtain on this book, I hope it has become evident that the true allure of philosophy lies not in the ceaseless analysis of intricate proofs or impenetrable theoretical constructs. Rather, it is found in the heartfelt adoption and manifestation of philosophical principles in the theatre of our daily lives.

The wisdom of Epictetus invites us to delve beyond intellectual understanding and theoretical knowledge. His teachings urge us to step out of the realm of abstract contemplation, inspiring us to translate philosophical principles into tangible actions that can profoundly shape our existence. By integrating these principles, we tap into the transformative power of philosophy, enabling us to fashion a life replete with purpose, meaning, and contentment.

This journey into the heart of Epictetus' philosophy should not be seen as a strenuous task but rather a delightful exploration that adds depth and richness to our existence. The profound maxims proposed by the sage serve as guiding lights to help us navigate life's intricate maze. Whether the path is strewn with roses or brambles, we are reminded to embrace every moment with an open heart and a tranquil mind.

As we progress on this philosophical voyage, we're encouraged to remember the fundamental virtues of honesty and introspection. These virtues become our compass, guiding us as we sculpt a life of substance and authenticity. By adhering firmly to these principles, we begin to discern the contours of a fulfilling existence carved out through wisdom and moral fortitude.

This exploration of philosophy, however, does not end with the closing of this book. Indeed, it's merely the starting point for a lifetime of learning, understanding, and personal growth. As we tread this path, let us remember the words of Epictetus, entrusting our fate to the cosmos, accepting what comes our way, and knowing that true wisdom lies in aligning ourselves with the natural laws of the universe.

And so, as we imbibe the wisdom of Epictetus and stride forth in our quest for enlightenment, let us keep in mind his final maxim: "O Crito, if it thus pleases the gods, thus let it be." By adopting this stance, we yield to the greater wisdom of the cosmos, unafraid of the obstacles we may encounter. We recognise that our fate might be influenced by external forces, yet we understand that no one can rob us of our inner peace and tranquillity.

As we continue our journey through the rich landscape of philosophy, let's stay anchored in the wisdom of Epictetus, maintaining our resolve to cultivate a life imbued with joy, virtue, and an unyielding quest for wisdom.

REFLECTING AFTER THE
MIND MARATHON

Well done! You've navigated through the compelling journey of the "Enchiridion", guided by the wisdom of Epictetus. As you are about to close this book, take a pause to absorb the profound wisdom that has illuminated your path.

In our modern era, swamped by ceaseless noise and a flood of information, the stoic perspective offered by Epictetus becomes a timely reminder. Wisdom need not be grave and remote; rather, it often surfaces in unexpected corners— amidst life's absurdities, within the laughter that echoes through chaos, and through the meaningful bonds we form with others.

Epictetus, through his insightful narratives, has demonstrated that Stoicism extends beyond ancient texts and dusty volumes. It's a practical compass guiding us through the complexities of contemporary life, urging us to harness the power of choice, confront our fears boldly, and unearth contentment within ourselves amid countless distractions and temptations.

Yet beneath the light-hearted veneer, a crucial message emerges. The trials we endure, the desires we chase, and the quest for happiness can sometimes lead us astray. Epictetus,

REFLECTING AFTER THE MIND MARATHON

via his teachings, encourages us to pause, reflect, and claim full responsibility for our lives. He enlightens us that the *Theory of Happiness* is not about controlling our external environment, but rather about mastering our own thoughts, responses, and attitudes.

As you integrate lessons from Epictetus into your life, remember to approach them with a light heart. Despite the inevitability of life's absurdities, we hold the power to transcend them. Embrace Stoic teachings, armouring them with resilience and an unshakeable commitment to personal growth.

And now, your personal journey awaits. Let Epictetus' words resonate within you and manifest in your everyday experiences. Discover the transformational potential they hold. May the wisdom of Epictetus continue to light your way, reminding you to ponder life's complexities and appreciate the miraculous adventure of being human.

In the spirit of Epictetus's teachings, remember: despite the world's chaos, you hold the key to inner peace. So, meet adversity with steadfast resolve, navigate challenges with determination, and live with a heart brimming with gratitude.

Farewell, and may your journey be brightened by the profound Stoic wisdom of Epictetus!

Ben van de Beld